W9-AHG-061

DATE DUE

Public Opinion and Criminal Justice

Public Opinion and Criminal Justice

Edited by

Jane L. Wood and Theresa A. Gannon

WILLAN
PUBLISHING

Published by

Willan Publishing
Culmcott House
Mill Street, Uffculme
Cullompton, Devon
EX15 3AT, UK
Tel: +44(0)1884 840337
Fax: +44(0)1884 840251
e-mail: info@willanpublishing.co.uk
website: www.willanpublishing.co.uk

Published simultaneously in the USA and Canada by

Willan Publishing
c/o ISBS, 920 NE 58th Ave, Suite 300
Portland, Oregon 97213-3786, USA
Tel: +001(0)503 287 3093
Fax: +001(0)503 280 8832
e-mail: info@isbs.com
website: www.isbs.com

First published 2009

ISBN   978-1-84392-400-5 paperback
       978-1-84392-401-2 hardback

British Library Cataloguing-in-Publication Data

A catalogue record for this book is available from the British Library.

FSC
Mixed Sources
Product group from well-managed
forests and other controlled sources
Cert no. SGS-COC-2482
www.fsc.org
© 1996 Forest Stewardship Council

Project managed by Deer Park Productions, Tavistock, Devon
Typeset by GCS, Leighton Buzzard, Bedfordshire
Printed and bound by T.J. International Ltd, Padstow, Cornwall

Contents

Part 2 Public Opinion: Victims and Offenders

List of abbreviations

ACPO	Association of Chief Police Officers
AMHCA	American Mental Health Counselors Association
APS	Attitudes to Punishment Scale
ATP	attitudes towards prisoners
ATS	attitudes towards sex offenders
BCS	British Crime Survey
BSPQ	Belson Social Philosophy Questionnaire
C-CABS	Consensus-Conflict Attitudes and Beliefs Scale
CJS	criminal justice system
CPS	Crown Prosecution Service
DP	deliberative poll
ECA	Epidemiologic Catchment Area Study
ELM	elaboration likelihood model
HMIC	Her Majesty's Inspectorate of Constabulary
HSM	heuristic-systematic model
IAAOC	International Association of Addictions and Offender Counselors
IAT	implicit association test
JBS	Juror Bias Scale
NC	need for cognition
NCS	National Comorbidity Study
NFA	no further action
NIMBY	'not in my back yard'
NOTA	National Organisation for the Treatment of Abusers
OCD	obsessive compulsive disorder
PIO	public information officer

RMA   rape myth acceptance
SEU   Social Exclusion Unit
TAC   Treatment Advocacy Center
VCS   Victim Concern Scale
VPS   Victim Personal Statement

Notes on contributors

Brandon K. Applegate is Associate Professor of Criminal Justice at the University of Central Florida. His primary areas of research interest include punishment and rehabilitation policy, juvenile justice, jail operations and populations, offenders' perceptions of their sentences and public views of correctional policies. He has served as Secretary of the Academy of Criminal Justice Sciences and as President of the Southern Criminal Justice Association.

Kristie R. Blevins is an Assistant Professor in the Department of Criminal Justice at the University of North Carolina at Charlotte. Her research interests include corrections, the occupational reactions of criminal justice employees and public opinion about criminal justice issues. Her work can be found in the *Journal of Offender Rehabilitation, Criminal Justice Policy Review, American Journal of Criminal Justice, Deviant Behavior* and *International Journal of Police Science and Management*. She has also co-authored several book chapters and co-edited *Taking Stock: The Status of Criminological Theory* and *Transformative Justice: Critical and Peacemaking Themes Influenced by Richard Quinney*.

Douglas P. Boer has been Director of Clinical Psychology at the University of Waikato in Hamilton, New Zealand since January 2006. He is an Associate Editor of the e-journal *Sex Offender Treatment* and the New Zealand editor of the journal *Sexual Abuse in Australia and New Zealand: An Interdisciplinary Journal*. Prior to 2006, Doug was employed by the Correctional Service of Canada (CSC) for 15 years in a variety of contexts including sex offender therapist, institutional psychologist, sex offender programme director, and senior and regional psychologist. While working for the CSC, he also published a number of articles and structured clinical guideline manuals for use with offenders, most notably the *Sexual Violence Risk* – 20 with a number of co-authors from Simon Fraser University. Doug continues to publish and present in the area of risk assessment and management of offenders, although his favourite academic activity is teaching and presenting workshops. Doug has also held a number of Adjunct Professorships in Canada (Simon Fraser University, University of British Columbia) and is currently an Adjunct Professor of Disability Studies at the Royal Melbourne Institute of Technology (RMIT) University.

Gerd Bohner is Professor of Social Psychology at Bielefeld University, Department of Psychology, Bielefeld, Germany. He has research interests in social cognition, attitudes and persuasion, including applications to intergroup relations, sexual violence and consumer psychology. He is chief editor of the journal *Social Psychology* and serves as consulting editor for several international journals. Recent publications include G. Bohner, H.-P. Erb and F. Siebler (2008) 'Information processing approaches to persuasion: integrating assumptions from the dual- and single-processing perspectives', in W. D. Crano and R. Prislin (eds), *Attitudes and Attitude Change*. New York: Psychology Press.

Sarah Brown is a Senior Lecturer in Psychology at Coventry University, where she has been a member of the Psychology Department since 1999. She is a Chartered Forensic Psychologist and the University's Forensic Psychology and Law Applied Research Group Leader. In addition, Sarah is the Course Director for the MSc Forensic Psychology, the Editor of the *Journal of Sexual Aggression* and the Division of Forensic Psychology representative in the British Psychology Society's Research Board and Press Committee. Sarah's research interests cover a range of forensic psychology issues including sexual grooming, risk assessment, jury decision-making and attitudes towards sex offenders and their punishment and treatment. Sarah is the author of the book *Sex Offender Treatment Programmes* published by Willan in 2005.

Patrick W. Corrigan has been Professor and Associate Dean for Research, Institute of Psychology at the Illinois Institute of Technology since 2005. He came to the IIT after more than a dozen years at the University of Chicago where he directed the Center for Psychiatric Rehabilitation. Professor Corrigan is also chief of the Joint Research Programs in Psychiatric Rehabilitation. The Programs are research and training efforts dedicated to the needs of people with psychiatric disability and their families. Professor Corrigan has also been principal investigator of federally funded studies on rehabilitation, team leadership, consumer-operated services and supported employment, and seven years ago became principal investigator of the Chicago Consortium for Stigma Research (CCSR), the only NIMH-funded research centre examining the stigma of mental illness. Professor Corrigan's currently funded research on stigma includes a study on self-stigma, a nationally representative survey on affirmative action and a cross-cultural examination of the stigma of employers in Hong Kong, Beijing and Chicago. Professor Corrigan is a prolific researcher having authored ten books and more than 250 papers.

Leam A. Craig is a Consultant Forensic Psychologist and a Partner in Forensic Psychology Practice Ltd. His current practice includes direct services to forensic NHS Adult Mental Health Trusts and consultancy to prison and probation services. He acts as an expert witness to civil and criminal courts in the assessment of sexual and violent offenders. He has published numerous research articles and chapters in a range of research and professional journals. He has recently completed a book co-authored with Professors Kevin Browne and Anthony Beech entitled *Assessing Risk in Sex Offenders: A Practitioners Guide* (published by J. Wiley, 2008) and an edited book entitled *Assessment and Treatment of Sexual Offenders: A Handbook* (published by J. Wiley, 2009). He is an Honorary Senior Research Fellow at the Centre for Forensic and Family Psychology, University of Birmingham.

Francis T. Cullen is Distinguished Research Professor of Criminal Justice and Sociology at the University of Cincinnati. His works include *Reaffirming Rehabilitation, Combating Corporate Crime, Corporate Crime Under Attack, Rethinking Crime and Deviance Theory, Taking Stock: The Status of Criminological Theory, Criminological Theory: Context and Consequences* and *Criminological Theory: Past to Present – Essential Readings*. His current research focuses on the impact of social support on crime, the measurement of sexual victimisation, public opinion about crime control and rehabilitation as a correctional policy. He is a Past President of both the American Society of Criminology and the Academy of Criminal Justice Sciences.

Bonnie S. Fisher is a Professor in the Division of Criminal Justice at the University of Cincinnati and a senior research fellow at the Criminal Justice Research Center. She edited Campus Crime: *Legal, Social and Political Perspectives,* 2nd edition and *Violence at Work: Causes, Patterns, and Prevention.* She is currently coediting the *Encyclopedia of Victimology and Crime Prevention* with Professor Steven Lab. Her current research includes examining the extent and nature of repeat sexual victimization and alcohol-and-drug-enabled sexual assault among college women, assessing the efficacy of the protective action – sexual victimization nexus, and examining public opinion about crime control.

Theresa A. Gannon is Senior Lecturer and Director of the MSc in Forensic Psychology at the University of Kent. Theresa is also the developer and lead facilitator for sexual offender treatment at the Trevor Gibbens Unit, Kent. Her research interests include sexual offender rehabilitation, sexual offenders' cognition and attitudes toward offender rehabilitation and reintegration into society.

Elizabeth Gilchrist is a Chartered Forensic Psychologist and Professor in Forensic Psychology at the Glasgow Caledonian University. Professor Gilchrist's expertise is in the area of domestic violence, with particular focus on risk assessment and the impact of victimisation, criminal justice decision-making and fear of crime. She has both clinical and research experience, and provides expert evidence to courts in the area of domestic violence, particularly in relation to child protection matters. She led the national study, funded by the Home Office, to explore criminogenic need in domestic violent offenders, and has presented nationally and internationally as well as written on risk, domestic violence and other related areas over many years. Professor Gilchrist has been involved in training postgraduate forensic psychologists since 1996 and is a member of various forensic and professional committees within the British Psychological Society. Professor Gilchrist is also a member of the Research Advisory Group for the RMA, a recognised training provider for the RMA and a part-time psychologist member of the Parole Board for England and Wales.

Jacqueline M. Gray is a Senior Lecturer in Forensic Psychology at Middlesex University. Her research interests include the impact of rape supportive attitudes in the trial process and public understanding of law and the criminal justice system. Dr Gray also has interests in the impact of terrorism on the public, how the public interprets policy responses to terrorism and factors influencing this interpretation.

Jennifer A. Pealer is the Assistant Commissioner of Research and Program Development for the Kansas Juvenile Justice Authority. She received her BA and MA from East Tennessee State University and her PhD from the University of Cincinnati. She has served as a consultant to many correctional programmes throughout the United States by providing training and technical assistance in offender risk/need instruments and evidence-based practices in risk reduction. Her research areas include public opinion, assessing risk/need/ responsivity characteristics of offenders, programme evaluation and effective correctional practices in risk reduction.

Natalie Reynolds has completed a Bachelor's Honours and Master's degree at the University of Waikato majoring in Psychology. Since March 2007, she has been working for the Probation Service in New Zealand following the completion of her Master's degree in February 2007. Natalie's thesis topic focused on the subject of perception and attention; however, she has since moved on to concentrate on criminal behaviour and risk assessment. A particular interest of hers is the diagnosis and assessment of psychopathy.

Shannon A. Santana is an Assistant Professor in the Department of Sociology and Criminal Justice at the University of North Carolina Wilmington. Her research interests include violence against women, the effectiveness of self-protective behaviours in violent victimisations, workplace violence and public attitudes towards crime and criminal justice. Her work has appeared in *Violence and Victims*, the *Justice System Journal* and the *Security Journal*. In addition, she has also co-authored chapters in several books including 'Campus Crime: Legal, Social and Policy Issues', 'Violence at Work: Causes, Patterns, and Prevention' and 'Changing Attitudes to Punishment: Public Opinion, Crime and Justice'.

Angela Scholes is currently based at the University of Surrey, where she is conducting research into political assassinations. She has previously worked at the Home Office looking at intensive probation schemes for young offenders. Other work includes research on attitudes towards jury service. Her main interests are terrorism and homicide, along with other areas of forensic psychology.

G. Tendayi Viki is a Senior Lecturer in Forensic Psychology at the University of Kent. He is interested in and has been researching various topics within organisational psychology, social psychology and forensic psychology. These include intra- and intergroup dynamics, social-cognitive processes, attitudes to crime and punishment, the social consequences of infrahumanisation, policing ethnic minorities and merger and acquisitions.

James D. Unnever is Associate Professor of Criminology at the University of South Florida-Sarasota. His works have appeared in journals such as *Criminology*, the *Journal of Research in Crime and Delinquency*, *Justice Quarterly* and *Social Forces*. His current research includes the development of a theory of individual differences in punitiveness, how racial intolerance encourages support for the death penalty cross-nationally, racial differences in public opinion about crime and justice, and criminologists' historical neglect of racial discrimination as a source of offending.

Michaela Wänke is a full Professor of Social and Economic Psychology at the University of Basel in Switzerland. Her research interests are mainly in social cognition and consumer psychology, in particular the formation of attitudinal judgments. In addition to many publications in journals she is together with Gerd Bohner co-author of a textbook on attitudes and attitude change.

Jessica L. Walton received her Bachelor's degree from Loyola University, New Orleans. She is currently a doctoral student in clinical psychology specialising in rehabilitation at the Illinois Institute of Technology in Chicago. She is currently employed as a job coach for the Rehabilitation Institute of Chicago.

Margaret Wilson is a Chartered Forensic Psychologist and currently works at the University of Surrey where she is course director for the Masters programme. She has a wide range of interests in forensic psychology but is particularly interested in the social psychology of offence behaviour.

Jane Wood is a Lecturer in Forensic Psychology in the Department of Psychology at the University of Kent. Her research interests include prisoner group formation and gang-related activity, bullying in prisons and schools, resettlement and rehabilitation of ex-offenders and the role of emotion in perceptions and judgments of offenders.

Preface

Too often reports of what the public thinks reflect assumptions rather than hard facts. The simplicity of media headlines claiming that the public thinks this or that do little justice to the public because they fail to capture the complexity of what people really think. Nowhere is this effect more apparent than in the arena of criminal justice. Our interest in compiling this book developed from concerns that *assumptions* of what people think have more influence over criminal justice policies than people's real thoughts. Of course, capturing a potentially open-ended phenomenon such as the public's opinion of criminal justice is not a straightforward task: people can and do change their minds. However, there are consistencies in people's attitudes and opinions regarding justice. The purpose of this book is to identify such consistencies and the factors that feed into the formation of public opinion and its subsequent impact on the justice process. We take the view that research offers valuable insight into public opinion by revealing the broad and specific aspects of what people think and why they think it. The book offers a comprehensive examination of public opinion that will be useful to policymakers, researchers and students. It also provides evidence that challenges enduring assumptions and confronts the myths that infect our understanding of what people think about the criminal justice system.

The book is divided into two parts. Part 1 reviews existing research into the formation and function of public opinion. In Chapter 1, Gerd Bohner and Michaela Wänke introduce key concepts in the social psychology of how people form their attitudes. The chapter provides an evaluation of what attitudes are and why they are important and reviews research evidence of the genetic, social and contextual influences in attitude formation. The consequences of attitude formation are also discussed in relation to the attitude–behaviour link and the chapter considers when and how attitudes predict behaviour. Finally, the research on attitude change is reviewed (e.g. dual-processing models) and the chapter concludes by highlighting how the above research and theoretical concepts may be utilised to study public attitudes to crime and punishment. In Chapter 2 Jane Wood focuses on *why* public opinion is important to the criminal justice system. This chapter explains the interdependence between members of the public and the criminal justice system since the public relies on the system to arrest and punish offenders, while the system depends on the public to report crimes and participate in court as witnesses and jurors. The chapter begins by examining how perceptions of public opinion influence decisions regarding criminal justice policies and procedures. The chapter then examines the debate regarding whether public opinion deserves a role in the development of criminal justice policies and considers the consequences for government and the justice system when public support is not forthcoming. It concludes by examining the issue of how to adequately inform the public so that they can develop more informed opinions of criminal justice issues.

Jackie Gray examines evidence explaining which members of the public are likely to hold which opinions regarding the justice system in Chapter 3. Factors such as conservatism, religiosity, just world beliefs and the philosophical belief in free will have all been thought to feed opinion formation. This chapter argues that although these individual differences need to be taken into consideration when evaluating public opinion, the research does not offer us a definitive picture of what shapes public opinion. The chapter concludes with a discussion of how perceptions that the media impacts public opinion persist, despite little empirical support for such a position. In Chapter 4, Francis Cullen and his colleagues examine public opinion of capital punishment. It is sometimes assumed that public opinion in the UK favours a return to the use of capital punishment. This chapter uses recent research and data drawn from a national survey in the USA to demonstrate that even in countries that employ capital punishment public opinion is not necessarily in favour of the death penalty. Close scrutiny of the evidence shows considerable uncertainty about the use of the death penalty. Research also reveals that strong support for capital punishment exists mainly among white

Americans harbouring racial animus. Furthermore, an examination of opinion polls cross-culturally suggests that the key factor why the United States retains capital punishment is not the nature of public attitudes but the symbolic use of the death penalty by political elites. The chapter concludes that an accurate understanding of public opinion will enrich future policy discussions about the continued use of capital punishment in the United States. Tendayi Viki and Gerd Bohner present us in Chapter 5 with a critical evaluation of the research methodology used to assess public opinion of the criminal justice system. For example, politicians may estimate public opinion by relying on opinion polls that have little validity (e.g. BBC or Channel Four polls) and tend to ask very broad questions. The chapter argues that a more useful approach is to ask about specific aspects of the criminal justice system since members of the public may hold different views regarding different aspects, e.g. rehabilitation, conditional release, prison sentencing and the police and policing. Similarly, people may hold different views concerning different types of crime and so broad questions may lead to confusing findings that fail to capture the essence of people's thoughts. The chapter concludes by discussing potential methodologies that could offer us more accurate insight into public opinion.

Where the first part of the book provides a more generic view of public opinion, Part 2 looks at specific aspects of public opinion, i.e. victims' opinions and opinions regarding victims and specific types of offenders. In Chapter 6, Margaret Wilson and Angela Scholes consider public opinion of the criminal justice system from the crime victims' perspective by considering how victims' perceptions of the justice system affect decisions to report victimisation. It focuses specifically on rape victims and their expectations of how the justice system is likely to treat them. It reports research showing that negative views result in victims not coming forward to report rape. It goes on to discuss the implications of such views in terms of the adequate functioning of the justice system. The chapter closes with a discussion of how the under-reporting of rape may send a message to potential offenders and affect one of the main aims of the criminal justice system – general deterrence. Looking at a similar issue from a different viewpoint, Elizabeth Gilchrist examines public opinion of victims in Chapter 7. In particular, are the public and the police always sympathetic towards the victims of crimes? Or are there some circumstances which reduce the likelihood of such sympathy? The chapter examines, in particular, the crimes of rape and domestic violence and identifies a host of empirical factors that predict negative attitudes towards such victims.

Particular emphasis is placed upon how these negative attitudes may affect the prosecution of offenders, and even entail further negative experiences for victims such as arrest or further physical abuse from a domestically violent partner. In Chapter 8, Natalie Reynolds, Leam Craig and Douglas Boer examine public opinion regarding prisoners and ex-prisoners and public readiness to accept ex-prisoners back into society. This chapter presents a review of the research and examines the psychometric scales used to assess public attitudes towards offenders. The characteristics of members of the public who are likely to have more positive views of offenders are also discussed as are the possible ways in which positive perceptions of offenders could be encouraged and how negative attitudes may be altered. Finally, this chapter concludes with a discussion of the potential obstacles that ex-prisoners face in the outside world when they must obtain employment, accommodation and relationships.

Chapter 9 continues the theme of public opinion of offenders with Sarah Brown describing the common myths and stereotypes that surround sexual offenders and their rehabilitation and evaluating research which has helped to dispel such myths. The chapter moves on to critically review the current empirical research investigating attitudes towards sexual offenders by comparing and contrasting the reactions to sexual offenders of prison officers, police officers, mainstream prisoners and sexual offender therapists. This chapter also describes some recent research which illustrates that public opinion tends to support prison-based rather than community-based treatment and considers the NIMBY (not in my back yard) issue, i.e. the public stance opposing community treatment in their 'back yard' because they fear crimes being committed in their neighbourhood and a decrease in property values. Empirical evidence in support of the NIMBY is examined and suggestions for increasing the public's support for sexual offenders to make the tricky shift from prison to the outside world are made. Finally, the negative effects associated with public hostility towards sexual offenders are discussed and promising methods of changing such attitudes are presented. In Chapter 10, Patrick Corrigan and Jessica Walton describe the common myths and stereotypes that surround mentally and personality disordered offenders and the complex relationship that exists between mental illness and violent crime. A particular focus of this chapter is on the attitudes of the police when dealing with such offenders. Could the attitudes that justice officials hold result in mentally unwell offenders being referred to the criminal justice system as opposed to hospital? How do attitudes impact upon appropriate versus inappropriate placements of these offenders? Following this, the public's attitudes towards mentally unwell and personality disordered offenders are evaluated by looking at recent empirical research. The chapter concludes by considering how public opinion influences decisions made regarding the treatment of mentally disordered and personality disordered offenders.

To link diverse fields of research such as people's attitudes and opinions to criminal justice issues and policies is an immense task and we cannot overstate the effort that goes into collating and evaluating the complex evidence associated with public opinion of criminal justice. As such we owe many thanks to all the authors in this volume for taking the time out of demanding schedules to prepare chapters that are high in quality and yet accessible to readers of all levels. Many thanks also go to the people who have supported us with words, deeds and cups of tea! Special thanks go to Steve, Sam, Lydia, Becca and Bobs for their love, friendship and support. We would also like to thank Mariamne Rose and Charlotte Simms from the University of Kent for their unwavering support with proofreading.

Jane Wood and Theresa Gannon

To my mum, Doreen, for her belief – J.L.W.

For Jim, my confidant – T.A.G.

Part 1

Public Opinion: Its Formation and Function

Chapter 1

The psychology of attitudes and persuasion

Gerd Bohner and Michaela Wänke

Introduction

Evaluating people and things is one of the most basic mental processes (Tesser and Martin 1996). Attitudes, or summary evaluations of an object, are formed quickly, are communicated daily and influence people's thoughts, feelings and actions. For these reasons, attitudes have long been a key concept in social and applied psychology (Allport 1935; Bohner and Wänke 2002; Eagly and Chaiken 1998, Wood and Viki 2004). As important as the study of attitudes is the study of persuasion, the processes by which attitudes change. Because attitudes influence thought and action, knowing how to change attitudes is of vital importance for changing unwanted behaviour and strengthening desirable behaviour. Crime might be reduced if we could change attitudes that encourage criminal acts (e.g. hate crimes, pollution); court proceedings might become fairer if we could tackle attitudes that lead to unfair treatment of certain defendants; and secondary victimisation might be avoided if we could root out attitudes that contribute to blaming victims of violence (Bohner 1998).

In this chapter, we first discuss conceptual issues in attitude research. We then present a selective review of work on the formation and change of attitudes, with particular emphasis on recent integrative models of persuasion (for attitude measurement, see Viki and Bohner, this volume).

Conceptual issues in attitude research

Definition of attitude

We define attitude as a summary evaluation of an object of thought (Bohner and Wänke 2002). Central to this definition are the mental process of evaluation and the presence of an attitude object. An attitude object may be anything a person perceives or holds in mind. Attitude objects may be concrete (e.g. anchovy pizza) or abstract (e.g. justice), may be inanimate things (e.g. firearms), persons (e.g. Gordon Brown), groups (e.g. lawyers, homosexuals), or behaviours (e.g. littering, tax evasion, shoplifting).

Regarding the nature of the summary evaluation, researchers disagree as to whether an evaluation has to be enduring to qualify as an attitude. Some define attitudes as dispositions which are stored in long-term memory and retrieved when needed (e.g. Allport 1935; Eagly and Chaiken 1993, 2007; Petty *et al.* 1994). This approach has been called the 'file-drawer model' (Wilson and Hodges 1992) because it portrays attitudes as mental files which individuals consult when evaluating an object (for recent theories adopting this view, see Cohen and Reed 2006; Petty 2006). Contextual variation in the evaluation of a given object would thus be due either to people's unwillingness to report their 'true' attitude, or to their inability to retrieve an existing attitude from memory.

A competing view proposes that attitudes are temporary constructions which are formed when needed, based on information that is accessible in the given situation (e.g. Schwarz 2007; Tourangeau and Rasinski 1988; for reviews, see Schwarz and Bohner 2001; Wilson and Hodges 1992). Contextual variation in evaluative judgments would thus point to a change of the attitude itself. This approach has been called the 'attitudes-as-constructions model'.

We prefer the attitudes-as-constructions model for reasons of parsimony and comprehensiveness. The model is more parsimonious because it does not claim as necessary an enduring disposition – although it does allow for the possibility that a previous evaluation is remembered and used, forming part of the attitude construction process. It is more comprehensive because it can explain contextual flexibility of attitudes as well as stability over time and contexts without treating evaluations that are recalled from memory any differently from other pieces of information used in attitude construction. If evaluative judgments remain stable, this is because the evaluative aspects of the material retrieved in order to construct an attitude themselves remain stable (for discussion, see Schwarz 2007; Schwarz and Bohner 2001).

Components and processes involved in attitude formation and expression

Both the experiences that lead to a certain attitude and the attitude's expressions are often divided into three components: beliefs about the attitude object make up the *cognitive* component; emotions and feelings elicited by the attitude object form the *affective* component; and (intended) actions directed at the attitude object form the *behavioural* component (Breckler 1984; Rosenberg and Hovland 1960). A person's negative attitude toward the police, for example, may thus entail: (1) the expectation that police officers are corrupt (negative belief); (2) fear of police violence (negative emotion); and (3) the intention to avoid police patrols in the street (negative behaviour).

The process of constructing an attitude judgment can be either effortful and controlled or spontaneous and automatic. When asked about their evaluation of a particular entity, people may consciously and deliberately construct an *explicit attitude* from relevant information that is accessible from memory or given in the situation (Schwarz and Bohner 2001; Wilson and Hodges 1992). It has also been shown, however, that the mere presence of an attitude object may elicit an automatic evaluative response, without any conscious thought or recollection taking place (Bargh 1997; Bargh *et al.* 1992). Importantly, such automatic attitudes may influence seemingly unrelated judgments or behaviours, and such influence may happen outside of a person's awareness. For example, people evaluate letters of the alphabet that are part of their own name more positively than other letters, without being aware of the name–letter connection (Nuttin 1985; for a review, see Koole and Pelham 2003). Deliberately retrieved or construed attitudes are often referred to as *explicit* attitudes whereas automatically activated attitudes – of which one may or may not be consciously aware – are often referred to as *implicit* attitudes. Implicit and explicit attitudes may sometimes differ in valence, for example a jury member may spontaneously feel negative towards the defendant but may deliberately take extenuating circumstances into account and thereby arrive at a more positive attitude.

At the level of measurement, we distinguish between directly asking respondents about their evaluation of an attitude object and indirect indicators of attitudes (e.g. the time respondents take in categorising or recognising objects). Analogous to the terminology introduced above, direct measures are also referred to as explicit measures and indirect measures as implicit measures (but see De Houwer 2006, for a more refined distinction). Indirect measures are useful for assessing aspects of attitudes that respondents may be either unwilling or unable to express when asked explicitly for an evaluation (see Fazio and Olson 2003; Viki and Bohner, this volume).

Attitude functions

Various taxonomies of attitude function have been proposed to describe the needs that attitudes may serve (e.g. Katz 1960; Shavitt 1989; Smith *et al.* 1956). Drawing on this research, we propose two main types of attitude function: (1) knowledge functions and (2) symbolic functions (see Bohner and Wänke 2002: Chapter 1).

To some extent, all attitudes serve a knowledge function. They help us in 'sizing up' objects and events in our environment, and an easily accessible attitude saves us the effort of figuring out anew how to behave each time we encounter an object (Smith *et al.* 1956: 41). Attitudes can thus regulate approach and avoidance, helping people to attain positive outcomes and to avoid negative outcomes. For example, a person's attitude toward the rehabilitation of offenders may be based on the attitude object's benefits (e.g. overall reduction of crime, implementing humanity and fairness) and costs (e.g. risk of reoffending, alienating victims of crime). It may guide behaviour that maximises the benefits and minimises the costs (e.g. supporting rehabilitation policies, but only for non-violent crimes).

Symbolic functions of attitudes comprise the aspects of value-expression, social identification and self-esteem maintenance. Some attitudes are central to a person's self-concept; Prentice and Carlsmith (2000) have likened such attitudes to valued possessions. By expressing them, the person can affirm his or her core values. Also, attitudes can establish a person's identification with particular reference groups. For example, we may define ourselves as members of the social group of environmentalists by holding and expressing 'environmentalist' attitudes. Finally, attitudes can serve the goal of self-esteem maintenance (Shavitt 1989) in at least two ways. Firstly, negative attitudes toward outgroups help to distance the individual from the threat that these groups are perceived to pose (Katz 1960; Smith *et al.* 1956). Secondly, positive attitudes toward liked objects and groups enable the individual to 'bask in reflected glory' (e.g. by wearing the colours of one's favourite sports team; Cialdini *et al.* 1976).

Evaluations of the same object may entail different functions for different people; attitude functions have thus been described as aspects of personality (Smith *et al.* 1956). According to the matching hypothesis, attempts at changing an attitude should be most effective if they tackle the attitude's functional basis (e.g. Katz *et al.* 1956; Petty and Wegener 1998b; for a review, see Maio and Olson 2000). Note, however, that an attitude may serve various functions simultaneously, and the impact of a particular function may depend on which aspect of the attitude object is temporarily most salient (Shavitt 1989).

Cognitive representations of attitudes and of related knowledge

Cognitive representations of attitudinal knowledge may be studied in relation to (1) a single attitude's representation in memory (intra-attitudinal structure) and (2) the mental relations between attitudes toward different objects (inter-attitudinal structure; Bohner and Wänke 2002: chapter 3; Eagly and Chaiken 1993, 1998).

Intra-attitudinal structure
Considerations of intra-attitudinal structure need to address how the attitude object, its associated summary evaluation and the link between the two are mentally represented (Fazio 2007). Going beyond these minimal requirements, researchers of attitude structure have addressed the memory contents that serve as inputs to the construction of attitudes, such as feelings and beliefs about the attitude object. They have also studied to what extent individual components of such an extended attitude representation (e.g. beliefs and evaluations) are consistent with each other.

An attitude may be represented along a bipolar continuum, functioning like a cognitive *schema* in information processing. Thus information 'fitting' the attitude schema is often processed more efficiently than information not fitting the schema. In a study by Judd and Kulik (1980), students read belief statements concerning several issues (e.g. 'The Equal Rights Amendment should be supported by all who believe that discrimination is wrong') and indicated how much they agreed with each statement; response times were measured, and free recall for the statements was assessed later. Results showed that more extremely evaluated statements were processed faster and recalled better than less extreme statements. Thus information may fit an attitude schema to the extent that it is located near the poles of a bipolar continuum.

But not all attitudes are likely to be represented as bipolar. Pratkanis (1989) showed that bipolar representations are most common for controversial social issues, whereas *unipolar structures* are usually found for less disputed topics like music and sports. For these unipolar issues, people mainly possess knowledge congruent with their own position and find it difficult to encode information opposing their attitudes.

Another question of intra-attitudinal structure is how attitudes are integrated from more elementary cognitions about the attitude object. Some researchers (e.g. Fishbein 1967), have described an attitude as the sum of 'expectancy × value' products:

$$A_o = \sum_{i=1}^{n} b_i e_i$$

In this equation, A_o is the attitude toward object O, b_i denotes the belief or expectancy that the object possesses a certain attribute I, and e_i stands for the evaluation of that attribute. The equation comprises only *salient* attributes – those that a person considers relevant and attends to. The model can be illustrated by calculating a person's attitude toward jury service on the basis of his or her individual beliefs and evaluations (see Table 1.1). Composite attitude scores that result from summing belief–evaluation products usually correlate highly with direct self-report measures of attitude (e.g. Fishbein and Coombs 1974).

An important structural issue is *intra-attitudinal consistency*. People may evaluate an attitude object both favourably and unfavourably at the same time. Our example in Table 1.1 shows how a moderately positive attitude can result from integrating beliefs with clearly positive and negative evaluation components. This coexistence of favourable and unfavourable beliefs is called *attitudinal ambivalence* (e.g. Kaplan 1972). A typical example is attitudes toward drinking alcohol. People may evaluate favourably the taste of a pint of beer and the social aspects of going out for a drink, but at the same time they may be repelled by the prospect of a hangover or of being fined for drunk driving. Generally, research has shown that more internally consistent attitudes are more stable over time and more predictive of behaviour (Rosenberg 1960; Chaiken *et al.* 1995).

Some structural aspects of attitudes that contribute to their resistance against persuasion, their persistence over time and their consistency with behaviour have been subsumed under the label of *attitude strength* (for a review, see Petty and Krosnick 1995). Strong

Table 1.1   Attitude as the sum of belief × evaluation products

Beliefs about the attitude object 'serving as a juror'	Belief (expectancy)	Evaluation	Belief × Evaluation product
Allows me to play a vital part in the legal system	+2	+3	+6
Is an interesting experience	+1	+2	+2
Will raise my social prestige	+2	+2	+4
Is time-consuming	+3	−1	−3
May be emotionally disturbing	+1	−3	−3
Attitude (sum of belief × evaluation products):			+6

Note: This hypothetical person believes that serving as a juror probably (b_1 = +2) allows her to play a vital part in the legal system, which she evaluates very positively (e_1 = +3). Further, she thinks that jury service perhaps (b_2 = +1) is an interesting experience (e_2 = +2), etc. Given that the five beliefs listed in the table are salient, her overall attitude toward serving in a jury would be moderately positive.

attitudes are more resistant to persuasion, change less over time and are more relevant to behaviour. The construct of attitude strength is multidimensional (e.g. Krosnick *et al.* 1993; Prislin 1996) and comprises aspects such as *non-ambivalence* of relevant beliefs (Thompson *et al.* 1995) or high *consistency* among attitude components (Chaiken *et al.* 1995). Other aspects reflect the strength of the evaluative response itself, for example its *extremity* (Abelson 1995) or *accessibility* (i.e. the ease with which an attitude comes to mind; Fazio 1995).

Inter-attitudinal structure

The question of how attitudes toward different objects are linked in people's minds has been analysed mainly in two ways. One approach highlighted the hierarchical aspect of thematic cognitive structures, or *ideologies*, in which attitudes are embedded. From this viewpoint, an attitude toward a novel social issue may be derived from more general values a person holds in that area (see Kinder and Sears 1985).

The other approach, Heider's (1946, 1958) balance theory, has been more influential in social psychology. Like other *cognitive consistency theories* (see Abelson *et al.* 1968), balance theory proposes that people strive for consistency among their cognitions. Of particular interest to Heider was how attitudes toward issues and attitudes toward people are related in a perceiver's mind. Assume that Pam loves her partner Oliver and detests breaking the law; she knows, however, that Oliver is planning to cheat on their joint income tax declaration. These three cognitions form a *triad* involving the perceiver (*P*, e.g. Pam), another person (*O*, e.g. Oliver) and some non-person object (*X*, e.g. cheating on the tax declaration). These elements may be linked by positive or negative relations which may reflect feelings (e.g. 'Pam loves Oliver') or proximity (e.g. 'Pam and Oliver are married'). The elements in a triad are said to be in a balanced (i.e. stable) state if multiplying the signs of all three relations yields a positive sign. For all possible balanced and imbalanced triads, see Figure 1.1.

As Figure 1.1 shows, if Pam perceives that Oliver, whom she loves (a positive *P–O* relation), is planning to cheat (a positive *O-X* relation), which Pam detests (a negative *P–X* relation), one relation would be negative and two positive (triad f)). Thus imbalance would exist; Pam should experience discomfort and be motivated to change her cognitive structure toward balance. She could do so by changing the *P–X* relation (i.e. herself adopting a more positive attitude toward cheating: 'Well, nobody is completely honest when it comes to declaring their income'), changing the *P–O* relation (i.e. feeling less affection for Oliver) or changing the *O–X* relation (i.e. persuading Oliver that cheating would be wrong). Each of these courses of action would result in a balanced state (*a*), (*d*) or (*b*)).

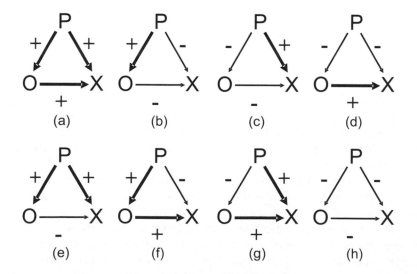

Figure 1.1 Balanced and imbalanced cognitive triads.

Research has shown that people rate balanced triads to be more pleasant than imbalanced triads (e.g. Jordan 1953; Zajonc 1968). But this was mainly true for those balanced triads in which *P* likes *O* and agrees with *O* in the evaluation of *X* (triads (a) and (b) in Figure 1.1). In addition to balance, then, attraction (sign of the *P–O* relation) and agreement (match of the *P–X* and *O–X* relations) also predict the pleasantness of triads (see Eagly and Chaiken 1993: 133–44). Balance theory has been used to explain the fact that similarity of attitudes often leads to interpersonal liking (e.g. Newcomb 1961; Cialdini *et al.* 1995). Also, people can better encode and learn information that represents balanced (vs. imbalanced) states (Zajonc and Burnstein 1965). Balanced patterns often appear most strongly when attitudes are assessed via implicit measures (Greenwald *et al.* 2002).

Attitude dynamics: formation and change

Although some theorists have studied genetic influences on attitudes (see Tesser and Martin 1996), research on attitude dynamics has mainly been concerned with the formation and change of attitudes through individual experiences. We address here the areas of attitude learning and persuasion, starting with processes that entail low levels of awareness and effort, then moving on to more effortful, conscious message processing, and finally presenting integrative 'continuum models' of persuasion that cover a spectrum of processing effort from low to high.

Attitude formation by learning without awareness

There are at least two ways in which attitudes may be acquired effortlessly and even outside of a person's awareness. One is called the mere exposure effect, the other evaluative conditioning.

Mere exposure

Liking increases with exposure, even in the absence of any gathering of information about the attitude object. An experiment by Saegert *et al.* (1973) manipulated how often students had to pass each other when they moved between experimental cubicles for different tasks. Although the students did not communicate, they later reported greater liking for those other participants whom they had passed more often. Because simple exposure to objects is sufficient to increase their evaluation, this effect is known as the *mere exposure effect* (Zajonc 1968). It has been demonstrated in hundreds of studies with a wide range of stimulus materials (e.g. nonsense words, geometric forms, photographs – for a review, see Bornstein 1989). Moreover, Bornstein's meta-analysis showed that the effect is strongest under conditions that render effortful, conscious processing unlikely or even impossible, such as short exposure times (including subliminal exposure). This rules out explanations of the mere exposure effect claiming that it is based on positive affect being elicited by the conscious recognition of familiar stimuli. Accordingly, Zajonc (1980) argued that 'preferences need no inferences', meaning that a stimulus may directly elicit an attitude without any cognitive mediation. In the light of current knowledge, absence of awareness certainly should not be equated with absence of cognition (see Banaji *et al.* 2001; Bargh 1997). A current explanation of the mere exposure effect holds that people experience facilitated encoding or greater 'perceptual fluency' when perceiving an object for a repeated time (Bornstein and D'Agostino 1994). They may then attribute the pleasant experience that accompanies facilitated processing to the object itself, hence evaluate it more positively (Reber *et al.* 1998). In line with this explanation, it has been shown that mere exposure effects disappear if people are led to attribute the positive experience of perceptual fluency to an irrelevant cause (Winkielman *et al.* 2003).

Evaluative conditioning

Starting from early assumptions that attitudes are learned dispositions (Allport 1935; Doob 1947), researchers tried to explain attitude change as a result of *conditioning*. *Evaluative conditioning* refers to a change in the liking of stimuli that is due to the fact that stimuli were paired in a certain manner (De Houwer, in press). For example, research participants' evaluation of political slogans increased if these slogans were repeatedly presented during a free lunch, whereas evaluations decreased if the slogans were repeatedly presented while participants were required to inhale putrid odours (Razran 1940). Similarly, neutral pictures of human faces were liked better after being paired with liked than with disliked pictures of human faces (e.g. Levey and Martin 1975), and products presented in the context of pleasant music were preferred to products presented with unpleasant music (Gorn 1982). Different processes may be responsible for evaluative conditioning. Whereas some involve a conscious propositional knowledge about contingencies between stimuli as a basis for their evaluation of those stimuli, others may involve an automatically formed association, which may occur outside of awareness (for a review, see De Houwer, in press). Evidence for an effortlessly acquired conditioning effect comes from studies in which the paired stimuli were presented so briefly that they could not be detected consciously (e.g. De Houwer *et al.* 1997; Dijksterhuis 2004).

Low-effort persuasion

From attitude formation without awareness we move to the effects of conscious information processing on attitudes. From an attitudes-as-constructions perspective, the formation and change of attitudes are not conceptually distinct; we therefore conceive of persuasion research as studying a subset of the conditions that give rise to the construction of an attitude judgment (see Schwarz and Bohner 2001), usually in response to a message about the attitude object. We begin with selected examples of low-effort persuasion.

Impact of subjective experiences

As we have seen in the section on mere exposure, an important factor in attitude formation is the *experienced ease* with which information can be processed. This is true also in relation to judging the evidential quality of persuasive messages (Howard 1997) or generating arguments by oneself (Wänke *et al.* 1996; Wänke *et al.* 1997). Information that can easily be generated and processed is likely to be judged as valid or important. In one experiment (Howard 1997), students listened to radio adverts whose wording was varied; depending on experimental condition, some of the adverts' arguments were presented either in the form of familiar idiomatic phrases (e.g. 'Don't put all your eggs in one basket') or in more literal form ('Don't risk everything on a single venture'). Under conditions of low-effort processing (e.g. when participants were distracted), the familiar phrases were clearly more persuasive than the standard phrases. This finding indicates that greater ease of processing can enhance persuasion.

While the effect just described is due to the ease with which externally presented arguments can be processed, ease of processing can affect persuasion even when no external evidence is presented at all. Wänke and her colleagues (1997) exposed students to a print advert that merely suggested generating either one reason or ten reasons for choosing a BMW over a Mercedes (e.g. 'There are many reasons to choose a BMW – can you name ten?"). Students who saw the one-reason advert anticipated that generating the one requested reason would be easy and judged BMW more favourably than Mercedes;

conversely, students who saw the ten-reasons advert anticipated that generating ten reasons would be difficult and consequently judged BMW *less* favourably than Mercedes. Importantly, it did not matter whether participants actually generated any reasons at all; just the anticipated experience of ease versus difficulty was sufficient in reversing the advert's persuasive effect.

Heuristic processing

Although making attitude judgments based on one's internal experiences can be understood as an example of heuristic processing (Chen and Chaiken 1999), persuasion researchers have usually highlighted heuristics that pertain to external cues (Chaiken 1987). Heuristics are simple decision rules like 'Experts' statements are valid', 'I agree with people I like', or 'The majority is usually right.' Applying these rules leads people to agree with experts, likeable communicators and majorities more than with non-experts, dislikeable communicators and minorities. To do so, they must (a) perceive a relevant heuristic cue and (b) retrieve an applicable heuristic from memory (Chaiken *et al.* 1989). As with evaluative conditioning and the use of subjective experiences, a person does not have to be aware that he or she is applying a heuristic in generating an attitude judgment. Heuristic influences on attitudes are strongest if an individual has little motivation or ability to engage in more extensive forms of processing; they provide convenient shortcuts to a judgment with minimal cognitive effort (see Bohner *et al.* 1995).

High-effort persuasion

The learning of message content and persuasion

None of the processes discussed above involve any detailed consideration of the content of a persuasive message. The processing of message content was first emphasised by researchers at Yale University in their message-learning approach to persuasion (e.g. Hovland *et al.* 1953). They proposed that the learning and recall of message content, which would be facilitated by incentives to adopt the advocated position, mediates attitude change. Their research was organised around elements of the persuasion setting that may affect message learning, guided by the question 'Who says what in which channel to whom with what effect?' (Smith *et al.* 1946). Accordingly, the classes of independent variables studied were the message *source* ('who?', e.g. a person high or low in trustworthiness), the *message* ('what?', e.g. message content and structure), *recipient characteristics* ('to whom?', e.g. self-esteem, intelligence) and the communication *channel* (e.g. spoken vs. written). The mediating processes studied by the Yale researchers included *attention* to the message, *comprehension* of its content, *rehearsal* of arguments and *acceptance* of the message position (see McGuire 1985). The main dependent variables studied ('with what effect?') were changes in *beliefs*, *attitudes* and *behaviour*.

Through its attempt to delineate the important elements of persuasion and to examine a host of important phenomena, the message-learning approach significantly influenced later generations of persuasion research (for a review, see Petty and Cacioppo 1981: chapter 3). However, the message-learning approach never reached the status of a unified theory; instead, it generated ad hoc explanations for a variety of effects which could not be meaningfully integrated. Furthermore, its central assumption that *reception* of a message would mediate persuasion was not supported. Message reception was assumed to be reflected in the recall of message content; therefore, attitude change was predicted to correlate highly with message recall. Empirically, however, no consistent correlation between memory for message content and persuasion was found (see Eagly and Chaiken 1993: chapter 6). As a consequence, researchers turned their attention to more active thought processes as mediators of attitude change.

Active thought
Early research by King and Janis (1956) into the role of active thought addressed *role playing* as a persuasion technique. In their study, some participants actively improvised a speech based on arguments they had read before; other participants simply read the arguments either aloud or silently to themselves. The results showed that attitude change was largest for the active improvisation group. Later, McGuire and Papageorgis (1962) demonstrated that *forewarning* recipients of a message's persuasive intent may help them to resist persuasion by stimulating the generation of counter-arguments. Finally, work by Tesser (1978) revealed that merely thinking about an attitude object in the absence of a persuasive message can lead to more extreme attitudes. This supposedly happens because people use their prior attitudes as a cognitive schema, which makes evaluatively consistent attributes of an object more salient and thus leads to more polarised representations.

The cognitive response approach
The insight that active thought processes play an important role in attitude change culminated in the formulation of the *cognitive response*

approach to persuasion (Greenwald 1968; Petty *et al.* 1981). Its main assumptions are these:

1 Recipients of a persuasive message actively relate its content to their existing knowledge about and attitude toward the message topic, thereby generating new thoughts or *cognitive responses*.
2 These cognitive responses mediate attitude change.
3 The amount and direction of attitude change are a function of the cognitive responses' favourability in relation to the message position.
4 The greater the proportion of favourable responses and the smaller the proportion of unfavourable responses elicited by a message, the more recipients' attitudes change in the direction advocated.

To assess the mediating role of cognitive responses, researchers introduced the thought-listing technique (Cacioppo *et al.* 1981; Greenwald 1968). This method asks research participants to list any thoughts they had while listening to or reading a persuasive message. The listed thoughts may later be content-analysed and coded according to their favourability (see Petty and Cacioppo 1986a: 38–40). For example, respondents who have listened to a message advocating increased funding of the National Probation Service may list thoughts like these: 'Having more probation officers will help to prevent serious crime' (a favourable thought); 'Taxes are too high already' (an unfavourable thought); 'What will I have for lunch today?' (an irrelevant, neutral thought).

In order to predict a variable's effect on persuasion, it is important to know how this variable will affect cognitive responding. Any variable that increases the likelihood of unfavourable thoughts (e.g. forewarning of persuasive intent) should decrease persuasion, whereas any variable that increases the likelihood of favourable thoughts should increase persuasion. Furthermore, if a recipient's message-related thoughts are likely to be mainly favourable (e.g. a devout catholic listening to a sermon held by the Pope), then any factor reducing the overall amount of message processing (e.g. distraction) should decrease persuasion; but if a recipient's message-related thoughts are likely to be mainly unfavourable, then reducing the overall amount of message processing should increase persuasion. Empirical evidence generally supports the cognitive response approach, showing that the valence of cognitive responses to a message is a good predictor of attitude change, especially under conditions of extensive processing (see next section).

Continuum models of persuasion

Assumptions of the cognitive response approach and of older theories regarding low-effort processing have been incorporated and further developed in more recent theories that we may call *continuum models of persuasion*. This is because they cover the whole range of processing effort along a continuum running from low to high.

Dual-processing models

The most influential continuum models since the 1980s have been the elaboration likelihood model (ELM; Petty and Cacioppo 1986a, 1986b; Petty and Wegener 1999) and the heuristic-systematic model (HSM; Bohner *et al.* 1995; Chaiken *et al.* 1989; Chen and Chaiken 1999), which are often dubbed dual-processing models of persuasion. Each model distinguishes two prototypical modes of persuasion that lie near the end points of the processing continuum.

In the ELM, these modes are called the *central route*, which involves effortful scrutiny of message arguments and other relevant information, and the *peripheral route*, which includes a variety of low-effort mechanisms such as mere exposure, evaluative conditioning and the use of heuristics. The two routes are conceived as antagonistic: the higher the effect of central route processing, then the lower should be the effect of peripheral route processing on persuasion outcomes (Petty and Cacioppo 1986a, 1986b; Petty and Wegener 1998a). The HSM features an effortful *systematic* mode and an effortless *heuristic* mode of processing (Bohner *et al.* 1995; Chaiken *et al.* 1989; Chen and Chaiken 1999). Systematic processing is defined – much like central-route processing – as a comprehensive and analytic mode in which an individual scrutinises and uses all potentially relevant information in forming a judgment. *Heuristic processing* is defined more narrowly and more specifically than the ELM's peripheral route. It entails the application of *heuristics*, simple rules of inference like 'consensus implies correctness' or 'experts' statements are valid' (see section on heuristic processing above).

Because people have limited time and resources, they cannot elaborate or process systematically the details of every persuasive message they encounter – peripheral route or heuristic processing should thus be the more common mode of processing. Whether more extensive processing occurs, according to both the ELM and the HSM, is a function of two broad factors: motivation and cognitive capacity. In ELM terminology, these factors determine the *elaboration likelihood* of a given persuasive message. The higher this likelihood, the greater should be the impact of central-route processing, mediated through the favourability of the recipient's cognitive responses, and the lower should be the impact of peripheral mechanisms on attitude change.

A useful innovation that Petty and his colleagues introduced in order to study influences of other (motivational or capacity-related) variables on the degree of processing is the *systematic variation of argument quality*. Strong and weak arguments are selected by pilot-testing a pool of arguments to establish the kind of thoughts they evoke when scrutinised. Arguments are defined as strong if central-route processing produces mainly favourable thoughts, and arguments are defined as weak if central-route processing produces mainly unfavourable thoughts (see Petty and Cacioppo 1986a: chapter 2). By introducing argument quality as an experimental factor, ELM-based research successfully re-examined the effects of persuasion variables that had produced seemingly inconsistent findings in previous studies. Many variables that affect either motivation or capacity to process, such as personal involvement or distraction, sometimes had led to increased persuasion, sometimes to decreased persuasion, and sometimes had had no effect (for discussion, see Petty and Cacioppo 1981). But once argument quality is taken into account, meaningful predictions are possible: any factor that increases message processing should increase persuasion if arguments are strong but decrease persuasion if arguments are weak. To illustrate this principle, let us look at a key study on the effects of personal involvement.

Petty *et al.* (1981) asked undergraduate students to listen to a message advocating the introduction of comprehensive examinations in their major area of study as a requirement for graduation. Three experimental factors were varied in a $2 \times 2 \times 2$ factorial design: personal involvement, source expertise and argument strength. To vary involvement, the students were informed that the new examination policy would be introduced either in the following year and thus affect them personally (high involvement) or ten years later (low involvement). To vary source expertise, the message source was said to be either 'the Carnegie Commission on Higher Education' (expert source) or a local high-school class (inexpert source). Finally, the proposal was backed with arguments that were either based on hearsay (weak arguments) or on extensive research evidence (strong arguments). After listening to the message, participants reported their attitude toward comprehensive exams on several items that were later combined to form a standardised attitude index. Petty and his colleagues predicted that students for whom involvement was high would show central-route processing and thus report more positive attitudes after listening to strong rather than weak arguments. Students for whom involvement was low, on the other hand, were predicted to form an attitude via the peripheral route and thus to agree more with an expert source than with an inexpert source. As can be seen in Figure 1.2, the results supported both predictions.

(a) Attitude by involvement and argument quality

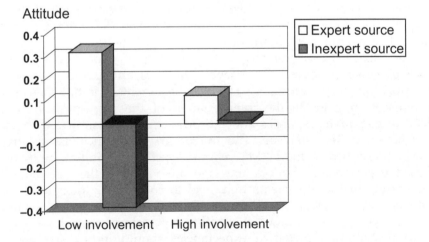

(b) Attitude by involvement and source expertise

Figure 1.2 The effect of personal involvement on attitude: (a) interaction of involvement and argument quality; (b) interaction of involvement and source expertise (adapted from Petty *et al.* 1981).

Using similar designs, researchers have shown that other motivational or capacity-related variables also reliably affect the degree of message processing. These include temporary variables like *distraction* (e.g. Petty *et al.* 1976) or recipients' *mood* (e.g. Bless *et al.* 1990) as well as chronic individual differences like the *need for cognition* (NC; Caccioppo and Petty 1982). Individuals high in NC generally enjoy effortful thinking, whereas individuals low in NC generally try to avoid expending much cognitive effort. High-NC (vs. low-NC) individuals have been found to show more central-route processing of messages but to be less susceptible to the impact of peripheral cues (e.g. Keller *et al.* 2000; for a review, see Caccioppo *et al.* 1996).

Whereas these results are compatible with both dual-processing models, the HSM goes beyond the ELM in specifying ways in which its two processing modes may jointly influence persuasion at high levels of motivation and capacity. This *interplay of processing modes* can happen either independently or in an interactive fashion, and its conditions have been described in four co-occurrence hypotheses (Bohner *et al.* 1995). According to the *additivity hypothesis*, heuristic and systematic processing exert independent main effects on attitude judgments if the results of each process do not contradict each other – for example, if a likable communicator presents convincing arguments. Often, however, systematic processing generates a greater amount of relevant information, such that any added effect of heuristic processing is negligible (*attenuation hypothesis*). Each of these hypotheses received ample support (e.g. Bohner *et al.* 1998; Chaiken and Maheswaran 1994; Maheswaran and Chaiken 1991).

The HSM's *bias hypothesis* refers to an interaction between the two processing modes. If message content is ambiguous or mixed (comprising both strong and weak arguments), initial heuristic inferences may guide the interpretation of the message and thus lead to cognitive responses and attitudes that are assimilated to the valence of a heuristic cue. The mirror image of such assimilative bias is described in the HSM's *contrast hypothesis*: if initial, heuristic-based expectancies about a message are violated, then systematic processing of the arguments may lead to contrasting interpretations (Bohner *et al.* 1995). Specifically, the disconfirmation of positive expectancies should induce a negative processing bias, whereas the disconfirmation of negative expectancies should induce a positive processing bias. Evidence for both the bias and the contrast hypothesis comes from a study by Bohner *et al.* (2002). They showed that initial information about high or low source expertise may evoke clear expectations that the message will be strong or weak, respectively. If message content was mixed, these expectations led to more positive cognitive responses and attitudes when the message allegedly came from an expert rather than from a non-expert, supporting the HSM's bias hypothesis. If, however, message content blatantly contradicted the heuristic-based expectations, evidence for the HSM's contrast hypothesis was found. For example, a message ascribed to a famous expert that contained weak arguments led to much more negative cognitive responses (see Figure 1.3) and attitudes than did the same message ascribed to a non-expert. Other heuristic cues also may produce assimilative or contrasting biases in systematic processing, as was demonstrated for high vs. low consensus (Bohner, Dykema-Engblade, Tindale and Meisenhelder 2008; 2008; Erb *et al.* 1998) and source credibility (Chaiken and Maheswaran 1994).

Dual-processing models have shaped the field of persuasion research for two decades. The ELM provides a comprehensive framework and includes effortful processing as well as a diversity of low-effort processes. The HSM provides a more limited conceptualisation of low-effort processing, but at the same time comprises more specific and detailed predictions regarding the interplay of its processing modes. Both models were generally supported in empirical tests and

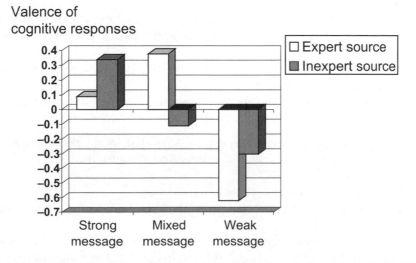

Figure 1.3 Interplay of processing modes in the heuristic-systematic model. Biased processing in line with presumed source expertise is evident in the mixed-message conditions, whereas contrast from presumed source expertise is evident in both the strong and weak argument conditions (based on data reported in Bohner *et al.* 2002).

stimulated a vast amount of research on persuasion and other areas of social judgment. Recently, however, the dual-processing models have been challenged by an alternative one-process theory.

Unimodel of persuasion

With their unimodel of persuasion, Kruglanski and Thompson (1999) proposed a more radical view of cognitive effort in persuasion being located on a continuum. They argue that the dual-processing distinction simply represents *types of information* (i.e. message arguments vs. source cues) – as did the Yale programme with its 'who says what …' slogan – rather than truly different *processes*. According to the unimodel, persuasion can be reduced to a single process of syllogistic reasoning about persuasive 'evidence' (for older approaches that conceived of attitudinal processing as quasi-logical, see McGuire 1960, 1981; Wyer 1970; Wyer and Hartwick 1980). Both heuristic cues and message arguments serve as evidence, which forms the minor premise of a syllogism. The major premise is part of the recipient's knowledge, which is retrieved from memory, and the conclusion would be an attitudinal belief. Consider the following syllogisms:

Variant A:
> *Minor premise*: Dr Bloggs, an expert, says that long prison sentences are an effective deterrent of crime and should thus be imposed more often.
> *Major premise*: Anything that is an effective deterrent of crime should be implemented.
> *Conclusion*: Long prison sentences should be imposed more often.

Variant B:
> *Minor premise*: Dr Bloggs, an expert, says that long prison sentences are an effective deterrent of crime and should thus be imposed more often.
> *Major premise*: Experts' statements are valid.
> *Conclusion*: Long prison sentences should be imposed more often.

The only difference between these two variants lies in the major premise, or the particular piece of knowledge that the recipient uses to draw an attitudinal inference. In variant A, this is specific knowledge related to an argument, whereas in variant B it is a heuristic related to a source cue.

Importantly, Kruglanski and Thompson (1999) propose that the psychological process is exactly the same in both cases. They do acknowledge that processing effort varies in quantity with motivation and ability, but they deny any theoretically useful qualitative distinction between two processing modes. Thus under conditions of low motivation or ability any information that is relatively easy to process would be processed preferentially, no matter if it is an argument or a cue, whereas under high motivation and ability processing would be more exhaustive (cf. Bohner and Siebler 1999). Parameters that determine how easy or difficult it is to process a given piece of information are its length, complexity and position in the information sequence (i.e. whether it is presented early or late).

As we have shown above, much empirical support for the dual-processing models comes from demonstrations that source cues interact with motivation and capacity factors in exactly the opposite way to message arguments (e.g. Petty *et al.* 1981; see Figure 1.2). A closer look at Petty *et al.*'s (1981) procedures, however, reveals that information about source expertise was presented to participants earlier and was considerably shorter and less complex than the message arguments. It is therefore possible that cue information in this research had greater persuasive impact under low (vs. high) motivation only because it was less complex and appeared earlier in the processing sequence. To test this alternative interpretation more systematically, Pierro *et al.* (2005) reviewed 19 major dual-processing publications that reported the manipulation of both cue and message argument information. Independent raters found that in all of these studies the cue information was easier to process than the message information, and for a vast majority the cue was shorter and appeared earlier in the processing sequence than the message arguments. It is thus possible that the seemingly overwhelming support for dual-processing models is due to their confounding of type of information (cues versus message arguments) with informational length, complexity and ordinal position.

In a series of studies, Kruglanski and Thompson (1999) tested the notion that controlling for processing difficulty may eliminate the differences in the persuasive effects of cues and arguments. One experiment (Study 1) showed, for example, that long and complex cue information about the source's expertise had a greater impact on attitudes under high (vs. low) issue-involvement – just as long and complex message arguments had done in prior persuasion research. In another experiment (Study 4), Kruglanski and Thompson varied both the quality and ordinal position of message arguments favouring comprehensive exams. Brief arguments that were either strong or weak were presented early, and lengthy arguments that also were either strong or weak were presented later. They found that strong (vs. weak) initial brief arguments elicited greater agreement if recipients' personal involvement was low rather than high. Conversely, strong (vs. weak) subsequent and lengthy arguments elicited greater agreement if personal involvement was high rather than low. These and related results (Pierro *et al.* 2005) show that qualitatively disparate types of information do not need to be processed in qualitatively distinct modes. Rather, cues and arguments function as equivalent pieces of evidence once we control for their length, complexity and ordinal position.

The unimodel provides an interesting and parsimonious alternative to the dual-processing models. It also shares many assumptions with these models – most notably their concept of a continuum of processing effort and the emphasis on motivation and capacity factors determining the amount of processing recipients expend to process persuasive information. This is why we subsumed all three models under the heading 'continuum models'. One fruitful way of combining insights from the unimodel with the notion of an interplay of processing modes (as in the HSM) is by formulating more general hypotheses about how information presented early may affect the processing of information presented later. Three of the HSM's co-occurrence hypotheses, the attenuation, bias and contrast hypotheses, are *asymmetrical*: for example, heuristic cues are assumed to be capable of biasing the subsequent processing of message arguments, but not vice versa (e.g. Chaiken *et al.* 1999). The unimodel removes this constraint by showing that the cue versus argument distinction is irrelevant. It thus warrants the question of whether and how any information type presented early might affect the processing of any information type presented later in the persuasion sequence, supposing that the recipient invests sufficient effort in processing the later-appearing information. In other words, it is useful to examine how assumptions about the interplay of pieces of evidence similar to the HSM's attenuation, additivity, bias and contrast hypotheses could be integrated and expanded within the broader unimodel perspective (for an extended discussion, see Bohner, Erb and Siebler 2008). This line of research may prove particularly useful in applied settings, because often the processing sequence is under complete control of the communicator, who can decide which evidence to present first and which to present later (think, for example, of a prosecutor in the courtroom). Taken together, the continuum models thus have considerable generative potential for empirical research on attitude formation and change in basic and applied areas.

Summary

In this chapter we discussed conceptual issues in attitude research and reviewed theories of attitude formation and change. Attitudes are summary evaluations of objects, comprising affective, cognitive and behavioural components and serving important functions for the individual. Attitudes develop and change through a variety of cognitive processes that may be unconscious or conscious and more or less effortful. Attitudes may form without awareness as people are repeatedly exposed to the attitude object or learn to associate it with pleasant or unpleasant contexts. More deliberate low-effort processing may entail people's reliance on their subjective experiences or on simple heuristics. Effortful persuasion may be achieved through the learning of extensive message content, but is mediated particularly by the thoughts that people actively generate in response to message content. Integrating previous approaches, continuum models (ELM, HSM and unimodel) portray attitude change as the result of processing a variety of pieces of evidence, whose impact and interplay depend on the recipient's motivation and cognitive capacity.

Author note

We would like to thank Friederike Eyssel and G. Tendayi Viki for their helpful comments on a previous draft.

References

Abelson, R.P. (1995) 'Attitude extremity', in R.E. Petty and J.A. Krosnick (eds), *Attitude Strength: Antecedents and Consequences*. Mahwah, NJ: Erlbaum, pp. 25–41.

Abelson, R.P., Aronson, E., McGuire, W.J., Newcomb, T.M., Rosenberg, M.J. and Tannenbaum, P.H. (eds) (1968) *Theories of Cognitive Consistency: A Sourcebook*. Chicago: Rand-McNally.

Allport, G.W. (1935) 'Attitudes', in C. Murchison (ed.), *Handbook of Social Psychology*. Worcester, MA: Clark University Press, pp. 798–844.

Banaji, M.R., Lemm, K.M. and Carpenter, S.J. (2001) 'The social unconscious', in A. Tesser and N. Schwarz (eds), *Blackwell Handbook of Social Psychology*, Vol.1: *Intraindividual Processes*. Oxford: Blackwell, pp. 134–58.

Bargh, J.A. (1997) 'The automaticity of everyday life', in R.S. Wyer and T.K. Srull (eds), *Advances in Social Cognition*. Mahwah, NJ: Erlbaum, Vol. 10, pp. 1–61.

Bargh, J.A., Chaiken, S., Govender, R. and Pratto, F. (1992) 'The generality of the automatic attitude activation effect', *Journal of Personality and Social Psychology*, 62: 893–912.

Bless, H., Bohner, G., Schwarz, N. and Strack, F. (1990) 'Mood and persuasion: a cognitive response analysis', *Personality and Social Psychology Bulletin*, 16: 331–45.

Bohner, G. (1998) *Vergewaltigungsmythen [Rape Myths]*. Landau: Verlag Empirische Pädagogik.

Bohner, G. and Siebler, F. (1999) 'Paradigms, processes, parsimony, and predictive power: arguments for a generic dual-process model', *Psychological Inquiry*, 10: 113–18.

Bohner, G. and Wänke, M. (2002) *Attitudes and Attitude Change*, Hove: Psychology Press.

Bohner, G., Dykema-Engblade, A., Tindale, R.S. and Meisenhelder, H. (2008) 'Framing of majority and minority source information in persuasion: when and how "consensus implies correctness"', *Social Psychology*, 39: 108–16.

Bohner, G., Erb, H.-P. and Siebler, F. (2008) 'Information processing approaches to persuasion: integrating assumptions from the dual- and single-processing perspectives', in W.B. Crano and R. Prislin(eds), *Attitudes and Attitude Change*. New York: Psychology Press, pp. 161–88.

Bohner, G., Frank, E. and Erb, H.-P. (1998) 'Heuristic processing of distinctiveness information in minority and majority influence', *European Journal of Social Psychology*, 28: 855–60.

Bohner, G., Moskowitz, G.B. and Chaiken, S. (1995) 'The interplay of heuristic and systematic processing of social information', *European Review of Social Psychology*, 6: 33–68.

Bohner, G., Ruder, M. and Erb, H.-P. (2002) 'When expertise backfires: contrast and assimilation effects in persuasion', *British Journal of Social Psychology*, 41: 495–519.

Bornstein, R.F. (1989) 'Exposure and affect: overview and meta-analysis of research, 1968–1987', *Psychological Bulletin*, 106: 265–89.

Bornstein, R.F. and D'Agostino, P.R. (1994) 'The attribution and discounting of perceptual fluency: preliminary tests of a perceptual fluency/attribution model of the mere exposure effect', *Social Cognition*, 12: 103–28.

Breckler, S.J. (1984) 'Empirical validation of affect, behavior, and cognition as distinct components of attitude', *Journal of Personality and Social Psychology*, 47, 1191–205.

Cacioppo, J.T. and Petty, R.E. (1982) 'The need for cognition', *Journal of Personality and Social Psychology*, 42: 116–31.

Cacioppo, J.T., Harkins, S.G. and Petty, R.E. (1981) 'The nature of attitudes and cognitive responses and their relationships to behavior', in R. Petty, T. Ostrom and T. Brock (eds), *Cognitive Responses in Persuasion*. Hillsdale, NJ: Erlbaum, pp. 31–54.

Cacioppo, J.T., Petty, R.E., Feinstein, J.A. and Jarvis, W.B.G. (1996) 'Dispositional differences in cognitive motivation: the life and times of individuals varying in need for cognition', *Psychological Bulletin*, 119: 197–253.

Chaiken, S. (1987) 'The heuristic model of persuasion', in M.P. Zanna, J.M. Olson and C.P. Herman (eds), *Social Influence: The Ontario Symposium*. Hillsdale, NJ: Erlbaum, Vol. 5, pp. 3–39.

Chaiken, S. and Maheswaran, D. (1994) 'Heuristic processing can bias systematic processing: effects of source credibility, argument ambiguity, and task importance on attitude judgment', *Journal of Personality and Social Psychology*, 66: 460–73.

Chaiken, S., Duckworth, K.L. and Darke, P. (1999) 'When parsimony fails', *Psychological Inquiry*, 10: 118–23.

Chaiken, S., Liberman, A. and Eagly, A.H. (1989) 'Heuristic and systematic information processing within and beyond the persuasion context', in J.S. Uleman and J.A. Bargh (eds), *Unintended Thought*. New York: Guilford, pp. 212–52.

Chaiken, S., Pomerantz, E.M. and Giner-Sorolla, R. (1995) 'Structural consistency and attitude strength', in R.E. Petty and J.A. Krosnick (eds), *Attitude Strength: Antecedents and Consequences*. Mahwah, NJ: Erlbaum, pp. 387–412.

Chen, S. and Chaiken, S. (1999) 'The heuristic-systematic model in its broader context', in S. Chaiken and Y. Trope (eds), *Dual-Process Theories in Social Psychology*. New York: Guilford, pp. 73–96.

Cialdini, R.B., Borden, R.J., Thorne, A., Walker, M.R., Freeman, S. and Sloan, L.R. (1976) 'Basking in reflected glory: three (football) field studies', *Journal of Personality and Social Psychology*, 34: 366–75.

Cialdini, R.B., Trost, M.R. and Newsom, J.T. (1995) 'Preference for consistency: the development of a valid measure and the discovery of surprising behavioral implications', *Journal of Personality and Social Psychology*, 69: 318–28.

Cohen, J. and Reed, A. II (2006) 'A multiple pathway anchoring and adjustment (MPAA) model of attitude generation and recruitment', *Journal of Consumer Research*, 33: 1–15.

De Houwer, J. (2006) 'What are implicit measures and why are we using them', in R.W. Wiers and A.W. Stacy (eds), *Handbook of Implicit Cognition and Addiction*. Thousand Oaks, CA: Sage, pp. 11–28.

De Houwer, J. (in press) 'Conditioning as a source of liking: there is nothing simple about it', in M. Wänke (ed.), *Frontiers in Social Psychology: The Psychology of Consumer Behavior*. Hove: Psychology Press.

De Houwer, J., Hendrickx, H. and Baeyens, F. (1997) 'Evaluative learning with subliminally presented stimuli', *Consciousness and Cognition*, 6: 87–107.

Dijksterhuis, A. (2004) 'I like myself but I don't know why: enhancing implicit self-esteem by subliminal evaluative conditioning', *Journal of Personality and Social Psychology*, 86: 345–55.

Doob, L.W. (1947) 'The behavior of attitudes', *Psychological Review*, 54: 135–56.

Eagly, A.H. and Chaiken, S. (1993) 'The Psychology of Attitudes. Fort Worth, TX: Harcourt Brace Jovanovich.

Eagly, A.H. and Chaiken, S. (1998) 'Attitude structure and function', in D. Gilbert, S.T. Fiske and G. Lindzey (eds), Handbook of Social Psychology, 4th edn. New York: McGraw-Hill, Vol. 1, pp. 269–322.

Eagly, A.H. and Chaiken, S. (2007) 'The advantages of an inclusive definition of attitude', Social Cognition, 25: 582–602.

Erb, H.-P., Bohner, G., Schmälzle, K. and Rank, S. (1998) 'Beyond conflict and discrepancy: cognitive bias in minority and majority influence', Personality and Social Psychology Bulletin, 24: 620–33.

Fazio, R.H. (1995) 'Attitudes as object-evaluation associations: determinants, consequences, and correlates of attitude accessibility', in R.E. Petty and J.A. Krosnick (eds), Attitude Strength: Antecedents and Consequences. Mahwah, NJ: Erlbaum, pp. 247–82.

Fazio, R.H. (2007) 'Attitudes as object-evaluation associations of varying strength', Social Cognition, 25 (5): 603–37.

Fazio, R.H. and Olson, M.A. (2003) 'Implicit measures in social cognition research: their meaning and use', Annual Review of Psychology, 54: 297–327.

Fishbein, M. (1967) 'A consideration of beliefs, and their role in attitude measurement', in M. Fishbein (ed.), Readings in Attitude Theory and Measurement. New York: Wiley, pp. 257–66.

Fishbein, M. and Coombs, F.S. (1974) 'Basis for decision: an attitudinal analysis of voting behavior', Journal of Applied Social Psychology, 4: 95–124.

Gorn, G.J. (1982) 'The effects of music in advertising on choice behavior: a classical conditioning approach', Journal of Marketing, 46: 94–101.

Greenwald, A.G. (1968) 'Cognitive learning, cognitive response to persuasion, and attitude change', in A. Greenwald, T. Brock and T. Ostrom (eds), Psychological Foundations of Attitudes. New York: Academic Press, pp. 148–70.

Greenwald, A.G., Banaji, M.R., Rudman, L.A., Farnham, S.D., Nosek, B.A. and Mellott, D.S. (2002) 'A unified theory of implicit attitudes, stereotypes, self-esteem, and self-concept', Psychological Review, 109: 3–25.

Heider, F. (1946) 'Attitudes and cognitive organization', Journal of Psychology, 21: 107–12.

Heider, F. (1958) The Psychology of Interpersonal Relations. New York: Wiley.

Hovland, C.I., Janis, I.L. and Kelley, H.H. (1953) Communication and Persuasion. New Haven, CT: Yale University Press.

Howard, D.J. (1997) 'Familiar phrases as peripheral persuasion cues', Journal of Experimental Social Psychology, 33: 231–43.

Jordan, N. (1953) 'Behavioral forces that are a function of attitudes and of cognitive organization', Human Relations, 6: 273–87.

Judd, C.M. and Kulik, J.A. (1980) 'Schematic effects of social attitudes on information processing and recall', Journal of Personality and Social Psychology, 38: 569–78.

Kaplan, K.J. (1972) 'On the ambivalence-indifference problem in attitude theory and measurement: a suggested modification of the semantic differential technique', *Psychological Bulletin*, 77: 361–72.

Katz, D. (1960) 'The functional approach to the study of attitudes', *Public Opinion Quarterly*, 24: 163–204.

Katz, D., Sarnoff, I. and McClintock, C. (1956) 'Ego-defense and attitude change', *Human Relations*, 9: 27–46.

Keller, J., Bohner, G. and Erb, H.-P. (2000) 'Intuitive und heuristische Verarbeitung – verschiedene Prozesse? Präsentation einer deutschen Fassung des "Rational-Experiential Inventory" sowie neuer Selbstberichtskalen zur Heuristiknutzung [Intuitive and heuristic judgment – different processes? Presentation of a German version of the Rational-Experiential Inventory and of new self-report scales of heuristic use],' *Zeitschrift für Sozialpsychologie*, 31: 87–101.

Kinder, D.R. and Sears, D.O. (1985) 'Public opinion and political action', in G. Lindzey and E. Aronson (eds), *Handbook of Social Psychology*, 3rd edn. New York: Random House, Vol. 2, pp. 659–741.

King, B.T. and Janis, I.L. (1956) 'Comparison of the effectiveness of improvised versus non-improvised role-playing in producing opinion change', *Human Relations*, 9: 177–86.

Koole, S. and Pelham, B.W. (2003) 'On the nature of implicit self-esteem: the case of the name letter effect', in M.P. Zanna, J.M. Olson, S.J. Spencer and S. Fein (eds), *Motivated Social Perception: The Ontario Symposium*. Mahwah, NJ: Lawrence Erlbaum Associates, Vol. 9, pp. 93–116.

Krosnick, J.A., Boninger, D.S., Chuang, Y.C., Berent, M.K. and Carnot, C.G. (1993) 'Attitude strength: one construct or many related constructs?', *Journal of Personality and Social Psychology*, 65: 1132–51.

Kruglanski, A.W. and Thompson, E.P. (1999) 'Persuasion by a single route: a view from the unimodel', *Psychological Inquiry*, 10: 83–109.

Levey, A.B. and Martin, I. (1975) 'Classical conditioning of human "evaluative" responses', *Behaviour Research and Therapy*, 13: 221–6.

Maheswaran, D. and Chaiken, S. (1991) 'Promoting systematic processing in low motivation settings: the effect of incongruent information on processing and judgment', *Journal of Personality and Social Psychology*, 61: 13–25.

Maio, G.R. and Olson, J.M. (2000) 'Emergent themes and potential approaches to attitude function: the function-structure model of attitudes', in G.R. Maio and J.M. Olson (eds), *Why We Evaluate: Functions of Attitudes*. Mahwah, NJ: Erlbaum, pp. 417–42.

McGuire, W.J. (1960) 'A syllogistic analysis of cognitive relationships', in M.J. Rosenberg, C.I. Hovland, W.J. McGuire, R.P. Abelson and J.W. Brehm (eds), *Attitude Organization and Change: An Analysis of Consistency among Attitude Components*. New Haven, CT: Yale University Press, pp. 65–111.

McGuire, W.J. (1981) 'The probabilogical model of cognitive structure and attitude change', in R. Petty, T. Ostrom and T. Brock (eds), *Cognitive Responses in Persuasion*. Hillsdale, NJ: Erlbaum.

McGuire, W.J. (1985) 'Attitudes and attitude change', in G. Lindzey and E. Aronson (eds), *Handbook of Social Psychology*, 3rd edn. New York: Random House, Vol. 2, pp. 233–346.

McGuire, W.J. and Papageorgis, D. (1962) 'Effectiveness of forewarning in developing resistance to persuasion', *Public Opinion Quarterly*, 26: 24–34.

Newcomb, T.M. (1961) *The Acquaintance Process*. New York: Holt, Rinehart & Winston.

Nuttin, J.M. (1985) 'Narcissism beyond Gestalt and awareness: the name letter effect', *European Journal of Social Psychology*, 15: 353–61.

Petty, R.E. (2006) 'A metacognitive model of attitudes', *Journal of Consumer Research*, 33: 22–4.

Petty, R.E. and Cacioppo, J.T. (1981) *Attitudes and Persuasion: Classic and Contemporary Approaches*. Dubuque, IA: Brown.

Petty, R.E. and Cacioppo, J.T. (1986a) *Communication and Persuasion: Central and Peripheral Routes to Attitude Change*. New York: Springer.

Petty, R.E. and Cacioppo, J.T. (1986b) 'The elaboration likelihood model of persuasion', *Advances in Experimental Social Psychology*, 19: 124–203.

Petty, R.E. and Krosnick, J.A. (eds) (1995) *Attitude Strength: Antecedents and Consequences*. Mahwah, NJ: Erlbaum.

Petty, R.E. and Wegener, D.T. (1998a) 'Attitude change: multiple roles for persuasion variables', in D. Gilbert, S.T. Fiske and G. Lindzey (eds), *Handbook of Social Psychology*, 4th edn. New York: McGraw-Hill, Vol. 1, pp. 323–90.

Petty, R.E. and Wegener, D.T. (1998b) 'Matching versus mismatching attitude functions: implications for scrutiny of persuasive messages', *Personality and Social Psychology Bulletin*, 24: 227–40.

Petty, R.E. and Wegener, D.T. (1999) 'The elaboration likelihood model: current status and controversies', in S. Chaiken and Y. Trope (eds), *Dual Process Theories in Social Psychology*. New York: Guilford, pp. 41–72.

Petty, R.E., Cacioppo, J.T. and Goldman, R. (1981) 'Personal involvement as a determinant of argument-based persuasion', *Journal of Personality and Social Psychology*, 41: 847–55.

Petty, R.E., Ostrom, T.M. and Brock, T.C. (eds) (1981) *Cognitive Responses in Persuasion*. Hillsdale, NJ: Erlbaum.

Petty, R.E., Priester, J.R. and Wegener, D.T. (1994) 'Cognitive processes in attitude change', in R.S. Wyer, Jr and T.K. Srull (eds), *Handbook of Social Cognition*, 2nd edn, Vol. 2: *Applications*. Hillsdale, NJ: Erlbaum, pp. 69–142.

Petty, R.E., Wells, G.L. and Brock, T.C. (1976) 'Distraction can enhance or reduce yielding to propaganda: thought disruption versus effort justification', *Journal of Personality and Social Psychology*, 34: 874–84.

Pierro, A., Mannetti, L., Erb, H.-P., Spiegel, S. and Kruglanski, A.W. (2005) 'Informational length and order of presentation as determinants of persuasion', *Journal of Experimental Social Psychology*, 41: 458–69.

Pratkanis, A.R. (1989) 'The cognitive representation of attitudes', in A.R. Pratkanis, S.J. Breckler and A.G. Greenwald (eds), *Attitude Structure and Function*. Hillsdale, NJ: Erlbaum, pp. 71–98.

Prentice, D.A. and Carlsmith, K.M. (2000) 'Opinions and personality: on the psychological functions of attitudes and other valued possessions', in G.R. Maio and J.M. Olson (eds), *Why We Evaluate: Functions of Attitudes*. Mahwah, NJ: Erlbaum, pp. 223–48.

Prislin, R. (1996) 'Attitude stability and attitude strength: one is enough to make it stable', *European Journal of Social Psychology*, 26: 447–77.

Razran, G.H.S. (1940) 'Conditioned response changes in rating and appraising sociopolitical slogans', *Psychological Bulletin*, 37: 481.

Reber, R., Winkielman, P. and Schwarz, N. (1998) 'Effects of perceptual fluency on affective judgments', *Psychological Science*, 9, 45–8.

Rosenberg, M.J. (1960) 'An analysis of affective-cognitive consistency', in M.J. Rosenberg, C.I. Hovland, W.J. McGuire, R.P. Abelson and J.W. Brehm (eds), *Attitude Organization and Change*. New Haven, CT: Yale University Press, pp. 15–64.

Rosenberg, M.J. and Hovland, C.I. (1960) 'Cognitive, affective, and behavioral components of attitudes', in M.J. Rosenberg, C.I. Hovland, W.J. McGuire, R.P. Abelson and J.W. Brehm (eds), *Attitude Organization and Change*. New Haven, CT: Yale University Press, pp. 1–14.

Saegert, S.C., Swap, W.C. and Zajonc, R.B. (1973) 'Exposure, context, and interpersonal attraction', *Journal of Personality and Social Psychology*, 25: 234–42.

Schwarz, N. (2007) 'Attitude construction: evaluation in context', *Social Cognition*, 25: 638–56.

Schwarz, N. and Bohner, G. (2001) 'The construction of attitudes', in A. Tesser and N. Schwarz (eds), *Blackwell Handbook of Social Psychology*, Vol. 1: *Intraindividual Processes*. Oxford: Blackwell, pp. 436–57.

Shavitt, S. (1989) 'Operationalizing functional theories of attitude', in A.R. Pratkanis, S.J. Breckler and A.G. Greenwald (eds), *Attitude Structure and Function*. Hillsdale, NJ: Erlbaum, pp. 311–37.

Smith, B.L., Lasswell, H.D. and Casey, R.D. (1946) *Propaganda, Communication, and Public Opinion*. Princeton, NJ: Princeton University Press.

Smith, M.B., Bruner, J.S. and White, R.W. (1956) *Opinions and Personality*. New York: Wiley.

Tesser, A. (1978) 'Self-generated attitude change', in L. Berkowitz (ed.), *Advances in Experimental Social Psychology*. New York: Academic Press, Vol. 11, pp. 289–38.

Tesser, A. and Martin, L.L. (1996) 'The psychology of evaluation', in E.T. Higgins and A.W. Kruglanski (eds), *Social Psychology: Handbook of Basic Principles*. New York: Guilford, pp. 400–32.

Thompson, M.M., Zanna, M.P. and Griffin, D.W. (1995) 'Let's not be indifferent about (attitudinal) ambivalence', in R.E. Petty and J.A. Krosnick (eds),

Attitude Strength: Antecedents and Consequences. Mahwah, NJ: Erlbaum, pp. 361–86.

Tourangeau, R. and Rasinski, K.A. (1988) 'Cognitive processes underlying context effects in attitude measurement', *Psychological Bulletin*, 103: 299–314.

Wänke, M., Bless, H. and Biller, B. (1996) 'Subjective experience versus content of information in the construction of attitude judgments', *Personality and Social Psychology Bulletin*, 22: 1105–13.

Wänke, M., Bohner, G. and Jurkowitsch, A. (1997) 'There are many reasons to drive a BMW: does imagined ease of argument generation influence attitudes?', *Journal of Consumer Research*, 24: 170–7.

Wilson, T.D. and Hodges, S.D. (1992) 'Attitudes as temporary constructions', in L.L. Martin and A. Tesser (eds), *The Construction of Social Judgments*. Hillsdale, NJ: Erlbaum, pp. 37–65.

Winkielman, P., Schwarz, N., Fazandeiro, T. and Reber, R. (2003) 'The hedonic marking of perceptual fluency: implications for evaluative judgment', in J. Musch and K.C. Klauer (eds), *The Psychology of Evaluation*. Mahwah, NJ: Lawrence Erlbaum Associates, pp. 189–218.

Wood, J. and Viki, G.T. (2004) 'Public perceptions of crime and punishment', in J. Adler (ed.), *Forensic Psychology: Debates, Concepts and Practice*. Cullompton: Willan, pp. 16–36.

Wyer, R.S. Jr (1970) 'Quantitative prediction of belief and opinion change: a further test of a subjective probability model', *Journal of Personality and Social Psychology*, 166: 559–70.

Wyer, R.S. Jr and Hartwick, J. (1980) 'The role of information retrieval and conditional inference processes in belief formation and change', *Advances in Experimental Social Psychology*, 13: 241–84.

Zajonc, R.B. (1968) 'Attitudinal effects of mere exposure', *Journal of Personality and Social Psychology Monograph Supplement*, 9 (No. 2, Pt 2): 1–27.

Zajonc, R.B. (1980) 'Feeling and thinking: preferences need no inferences', *American Psychologist*, 35: 151–75.

Zajonc, R.B. and Burnstein, E. (1965) 'Structural balance, reciprocity, and positivity as sources of cognitive bias', *Journal of Personality*, 33: 570–83.

Chapter 2

Why public opinion of the criminal justice system is important

Jane Wood

Why public opinion is important

Allusions to public opinion and its influence in a democratic society are common. Media assumptions of what the public wants in a whole host of areas permeate our daily reading. But the question that few seem to give any consideration to is: why is public opinion important? The answer lies at the heart of our democratic structure: we elect officials to represent us and, as such, we expect them to bear our opinions in mind as they structure policies that guide the way we live. Of course there will be areas that the public take less interest in and areas that interest the public more. The purpose of this chapter is to outline the influence that public opinion seems to have on some of the key areas in the justice system. It also examines the effects of ignoring public opinion, whether public opinion has a justified place in the formation of political policies and whether public opinion adequately summarises people's thoughts on criminal justice issues.

In a democracy the public has a central function in the administration of justice and it is crucial to the criminal justice system that the public fulfils this function, otherwise specific parts of the justice system would be unable to operate. For instance, the reporting of crime, providing evidence to the police and attending court as jury members or as witnesses all stem from public cooperation with the justice system. Since the public has this vital role in the administration of justice any lack of confidence they may have in the system could undermine or seriously disrupt the justice process. Consequently, to prevent the public from losing faith in the system it is necessary that there is at least some congruence between public opinion and criminal justice arrangements and procedures (Morgan 2002).

Few could argue that the public do not hold opinions about the criminal justice system. Indeed, public opinion on criminal justice issues seems to be subject to almost incessant 'temperature taking' by various factions of the media, researchers and government officials, all of whom are intent on pinning down our views on broad and specific criminal justice issues. As Green (1996) notes, '... public opinion should be the ultimate basis of the law' (p. 116) and 'The citizen's voice in the running of the country, and confidence that it will be heard, are what give governments and the state their legitimacy and authority' (Faulkner 2006: 63). If the criminal justice system has moral credibility then the people it governs will respect it and abide by its laws (Robinson and Darley 1998). If people become dissatisfied with the criminal justice system they may refuse to comply with its laws and resort to vigilante justice (Flanagan *et al.* 1985).

The centrality of public opinion in governance is apparent by the way public opinion penetrates policies. Public opinion regarding a political policy sets the 'boundaries of political permission' (Yankelovich 1991), that is the limits or borders within which the public will support or tolerate a policy. In the USA public opinion has apparently driven a multitude of domestic policies such as term limits, tax cuts and a patients Bill of Rights (Doble 2002). In the USA justice system public opinion instigated laws such as Megan's law, 'three strikes' laws, the Brady Bill and the assault weapon ban (Doble 2002). In the UK the Labour government has placed an emphasis on 'evidence-based' policy formation and uses focus groups, the People's Panel, citizens' juries and opinion surveys to gauge public opinion before forming new policies. As a result, in both the UK and USA significant policy changes have been attributed to the influence of public opinion. Public opinion also seems to have influenced the more operational side of the criminal justice system

The importance of public opinion in constructing criminal justice policies

Policing

In the UK there exists an ideal of 'policing by consent' (Carter 2002). This holds that the police can only achieve their goals if they have the support and cooperation of the public. However, the relationship between the police and the public is more reciprocal than the above statement suggests. The police service provides services to the public that they cannot obtain elsewhere and so the quality of policing is critical to a public that relies on its efficiency (Lipsey 1980). It also follows that the public's opinion of the service that stands at the interface of society and the criminal justice system will be strong and potentially influential.

In the USA the police service needs the support of taxpayers in order to be granted budget requests. The public's confidence in the police is considered the cornerstone for public cooperation and the basis for police legitimacy (Rosenbaum *et al*. 2005). A communications/public relations sector of the police service was created following the public outcry against police tactics used to manage urban and civil rights protests during the 1960s (Motschall and Cao 2002). During the 1990s the Los Angeles riots following the death of Rodney King led the then Police Chief Willian Liquori to state:

> Extensive media and citizen attention to recent events in the country has shone a spotlight on all of us. We must protect our cities, our departments and our employees against the erosion of citizen confidence and negative publicity. (cited in Motschall and Cao, p. 155)

Since then the public relations side of policing has expanded and increasing numbers of civilian personnel with journalism/communications backgrounds have been employed as public information officers (PIOs). The PIO's job is to inform members of the media and the public on the progress/advent of agency operations, events and activities. PIOs also assess public opinion which is then used to inform the formation of internal police policies.

Although police services in the UK are not budget-dependent on the public in the same way as they are in the USA, public perceptions of police performance play an important role in police functioning. Between 2000 and 2003 public confidence in the police deteriorated (e.g. Hough 2003) despite a fall in crime rates (Simmons 2002). This lack of confidence was attributed to the public's fear of crime (Thorpe and Wood 2004). Public perceptions of the UK as a high-crime society conflicted with statistics which suggested a decrease in crime and created a 'reassurance gap' between actual crime levels and public opinion. The Association of Chief Police Officers (ACPO) called for reassurance strategies to change this culture of fear of crime (ACPO 2001) and reassurance was embedded in subsequent policies regarding police services (e.g. the Police Reform Act 2002, the National Policing Plan 2002, the National Reassurance Policing Programme 2003). The 2004 White Paper *Building Communities, Beating Crime* outlined measures intended to create a closer bond between the police and the public to provide the public with the reassurance they needed (and, of course to enhance the public's opinion of the police service). In the White Paper the public are considered *consumers* of police services and factors one might associate with consumerism thread throughout the document. For instance, customer services were to be included in all police forces, police performance would be assessed according to the public's priorities and views about police services and local communities would be given the right to trigger action by relevant agencies to deal with acute or persistent problems of crime and anti-social behaviour.

That the government should reform the police service on the basis of the public's *fear* of crime rather than *actual* crime levels seems to show that governing bodies do attend to public opinion – even if that opinion is formed according to perceptions and not hard facts. The rationale for acting on the public's *perception* of crime is provided in the *Open All Hours* report (Povey 2001) which maintains that if the public feels reassured they will have more confidence in the police and be more likely to provide intelligence, act as witnesses and engage with courts. In turn, this would lead to a reduction in crime and thus reassure the public even more. While this is intuitively sensible, some warn that despite its apparent good intentions, reassurance policing, with its focus on public concerns, may run into conflict with Home Office targets for policing (Herrington and Millie 2006). In such cases governmental priorities for policing end up being given more precedence than the overall goal of improving neighbourhood security. In this way, despite its worthy aims, reassurance policing runs the risk of being seen more as ' ... a public relations exercise than a way to significantly contribute to the fight against crime and disorder' (Herrington and Millie 2006: 156). As a result, it seems that public opinion may be influential in policing but only if it does not conflict with government objectives.

Sentencing and sentencing policy

In theory sentencing decisions are influenced only by officially approved considerations, whether embodied in stature, practice direction case law or circular. In real life most sentencers admit to having some regard to what they believe to be public opinion.

(Walker 1985: 64)

The report of the Sentencing Review in England and Wales (Home Office 2001a) acknowledges that the confidence of the public needs to be considered when sentencing offenders. Also in 2001, the government commissioned two reports on the penal system both of which addressed the issue of public confidence in the criminal justice system. The Halliday Report (Home Office 2001a) concluded that if people are expected to uphold the law and not take it into their own hands then they must feel confident that justice is being achieved in sentencing. Halliday sees public confidence, together with a reduction in offending, as an important aim in sentencing. In other words, Halliday sees public opinion as something that should be taken into consideration in sentencing practice. However, for Halliday, consideration of public opinion in sentencing is desirable but not *essential* and he cautions against sentencers being '... driven before the wind' of apparent public mood, regardless of the principles that need to govern sentencing' (p. ii). Although Halliday's report presents sound reasons why public opinion is important in sentencing it also acknowledges that the public is badly under-informed about sentencing practices since they tend to underestimate the severity of sentences and believe them to be more lenient than they actually are. To address this lack of knowledge Halliday proposed that more systematic efforts were needed to explain sentencing practices to the public.

In the second report (Home Office 2001b: The Auld Report), Auld, like Halliday, acknowledges the importance of public confidence in the criminal justice system but unlike Halliday who proposed that public opinion should be *considered* in sentencing, Auld recommends that it should be *ignored* on the basis that public opinion is not knowledgeable or consistent enough to warrant a role in sentencing. Like Halliday, Auld maintains that the public should be better informed but only of their own ignorance since he states that '... if public ignorance stands in the way of public confidence, take steps adequately to demonstrate to the public that it is so' (p. 106).

Even though the public seems to be under- or ill-informed it seems that public opinion still manages to influence sentencing. Evidence from Australia suggests that public opinion believes that community protection is paramount and this has led to community protection being embedded in various sentencing acts and laws (Tomaino 1997). The Australian government maintained it was attuned to the heartfelt concerns of public opinion and this gave it a mandate to get tough on crime (Fox 1987). In Canada it has been suggested that judges impose more punitive sentences if they believe that this is what the public wants (Ouimet and Coyle 1991). Although sentencers, just like Halliday and Auld, are aware that public opinion is often formed with little knowledge and may be based on misperceptions, they continue to take public opinion into account. As Walker (1985) observes:

> ... few sentencers regard the public as competent to dictate the choice of sentence; but a substantial number of sentencers and policy-makers regard it as important that sentencers should not strain public tolerance. (pp. 72–3)

So, for example, if sentencers think that public tolerance would be strained by a sentence at the lower end of the sentencing tariff they may be inclined to hand down a harsher sentence. If, however, the sentencer believes that public tolerance is not an issue then he or she may feel free to hand down a sentence at the lower end of the tariff.

In the UK both Labour and Conservative governments have favoured mandatory sentences of imprisonment for those offences that seem to evoke strong feelings among members of the public (Faulkner 2006). The murder of two-year-old James Bulger in 1993 by the ten-year-olds Robert Thompson and Jon Venables resulted in the two boys being treated by the media (both tabloid and broadsheet) with the '... kind of outbreak of moral condemnation that is usually reserved for the enemy in times of war' (King 1995: 172). Public outrage was so strong that the vehicle transporting Venables and Thompson to court was attacked as people called for the offenders to be imprisoned for the rest of their lives, or worse (Fionda 1998: p.86). In the midst of the media's demonisation of children and the public's apparent view that children needed tougher measures to keep them under control, the Conservative government introduced Secure Training Orders for children aged 12–14 leading to a rise in the incarcerated population of young offenders by 30 per cent between 1993 and 1997. Other measures introduced to assuage the 'moral panic' associated with child offenders included zero tolerance, boot camps, curfews, electronic monitoring, mandatory minimum sentences, the naming and shaming of young offenders, an increase in the sentencing powers of the Youth Court and an erosion of the right to silence (Mugani 2001). The 1997 White Paper, *No More Excuses* spelt out how the new Labour government intended to hold children accountable for their actions and in 1998 *doli incapax* was abolished. *Doli incapax* was the presumption that children aged 10–13 could not be held criminally responsible unless the prosecution showed that the defendant(s) fully understood that their behaviour was wrong (as happened in the Bulger case). The abolition of *doli incapax* meant that children from the age of 10 were deemed to fully understand the difference between right and wrong unless the defence could show that they did not, i.e. the child had severe learning difficulties etc. In 2001 the Criminal Justice and Police Bill added to this backlash against young offenders when it gave courts the power to remand children who repeatedly committed medium level offences (e.g. assault, theft and criminal damage) to secure accommodation.

These policies and law amendments imply that public outrage/ concerns are influential in shaping political mandates. The idea that public opinion has been the cornerstone for the criminal justice policies noted above is supported by statistics that show that there had been little or no increase in criminal activity by young people for the ten years preceding the introduction of the harsher tougher penalties (Ahmed, n.d.). If there was little change in youth crime it remains that the increase in punitive policies was probably due to the influence of public opinion coupled with an effort by politicians to appear to be tough on crime to avoid being perceived by the public as weak and being voted out of power (Ahmed, n.d.). That politicians are intent on currying public opinion is evidenced by the fact that they will support public opinion even if it is inaccurate. For example, statistics at the time of the James Bulger case showed a decrease in crime rates yet, in an effort to 'play to the public gallery', Tony Blair, the then Shadow Home Secretary (1993), stated in the popular press that if people believed crime was rising, then, regardless of official statistics, it *was* rising (see Green 2006).

Ignoring public opinion: political consequences

Although the above seems to spell out the political sensitivity to public opinion and the facilitating role that public opinion can play in policy formation, there are exceptions. As noted above, in a democracy the government functions within the 'boundaries of political permission' (Yankelovich 1991). If a government forms policies outside these boundaries of permission it may see the public renounce the policy (Doble 2002) and run into 'confrontation politics' (Moran 2001). Radical policy changes that are introduced without building public support also run the risk of provoking such 'confrontation politics' between public and government.

In 1991 the Conservative government formulated the poll tax in the space of three months (Moran 2001). When the proposed changes were sent out for public consultation the warnings of imminent disaster were ignored by the government who appeared to dismiss the importance of compromise with public opinion (McConnell 2000). The result of the government ignoring public opinion led to a 'climate of objection' and the largest campaign of civil disobedience in the UK in the twentieth century (Cowley 1995). As public dissent increased, the UK witnessed some of the worst riots since the Second World War and this combination of political protest together with people's perceptions of unfairness and the substantial increases in average tax rates undermined people's willingness to pay the tax. Non-payment rose to well above 50 per cent in some areas, which, in concert with acts of civil disobedience, resulted in government promises to abandon the tax (Besley *et al.* 1997). The poll tax protests are also thought to have been so influential that they became an important, if not the main, reason Margaret Thatcher was forced to resign as Prime Minister (e.g. Cowley 1995). Understandably, those who stood for leadership of the Conservative Party following her departure all promised to abolish the tax (Besley *et al.* 1997).

That the public's objections to the poll tax succeeded in changing policy where other expressions of public opinion such as the anti-Iraq war protests did not is odd. One explanation could be the number and type of counteractive measures available for the public to take against government policy. For instance, during the poll tax protests people of all ages resisted the tax by refusing to pay it. The subsequent imprisonment of elderly erstwhile law-abiding members of the public for non-payment of the tax may have stimulated public opinion further and prompted even more resistance, i.e. more people refusing to pay. In other protests, such as the Iraq war demonstrations, although the number of people who took to the streets was high (in excess of half a million), other courses of action such as financial withdrawal were not feasible weapons of persuasion. Here it seems that although public opinion is *deemed* to be important and, as one politician put it, 'This country is ruled by consent and we forget that at our peril' (Cowley 1995: 110), if people have only one course of action, i.e. protestation, open to them, politicians may not always pay attention to public opinion. If, on the other hand, people have additional options for protesting (e.g. refusing payment) that can be used to impede a policy's successful implementation, then the influence of public opinion on policy may be more profound.

Another compelling feature of confrontation politics seems to be which members of the public express an opinion. Socially and economically dominant groups have the power to affect the criminal justice system in their own interests while socially and economically marginalised groups are more likely to be adversely affected by the system (e.g. Liska 1987). So, we may expect that when the middle classes protest, more attention will be paid to their views. Also, pensioners who express their objections to their members of parliament (MPs) may make more of an impression *because* they are pensioners (Cowley 1995). During the poll tax protests a lot of pensioners attended their MP surgeries to state their objections to, and difficulties with, the tax. That pensioners would protest in this way seemed to impact on MPs leading them to make comments such as, 'What was worrying were the amount of old and vulnerable people coming along with their bills who palpably couldn't afford them. That was really distressing' (Cowley 1995: 106). Moreover, many members of the public who protested about the poll tax often did so armed with political/financial arguments that explained *why* they objected to the tax. An informed public offering sound arguments as to why the tax was unfair, together with the impact of street-based protests, instigated the abolition of the poll tax (Cowley 1995). This suggests that although public opinion is important in policy formation/change, which members of the public protest, how they do so and why they object are important factors that possibly determine whether public opinion has any impact on the formation/amendment of government policies.

One of the problems inherent in examining the role of public opinion in policy formation is identifying a causal relationship. In an instance such as the poll tax protests the influence of public opinion on policy change seems to be reasonably clear. However, such instances are rare. It is generally assumed that policies are formed in response to public preferences because the threat of electoral sanction hangs over governments (Hobolt and Klemmemsen 2005) and a large body of research examining democratic politics does indicate a general congruence between public opinion and policy behaviour (e.g. Franklin and Wlezien 1997; Stimson *et al.* 1995). However, some authors contend that public opinion is not formed independent of political influence but results from a politically manipulative process (e.g. Brooks 1990). Such opinions are, nonetheless, in a minority: the majority of authors maintain that public opinion forms first and government policy is formed to be congruent with public views. Nevertheless, even if public opinion is a consequence of an autonomous decision-making process and does influence policies, it is very difficult to establish this empirically. A correspondence between public opinion and government policy may equally result from: public opinion influencing policy; policy influencing public opinion; a reciprocal process between public opinion and policy; or even some unidentified factor that influences both policy and opinion that leads to a spurious relationship between the two (Hobolt and Klemmemsen 2005). As yet, no empirical methodology has been completely successful in addressing these problems. Consequently definitive documentation of the influence of public opinion on policy remains elusive.

Is listening to public opinion justified?

Since, as noted earlier in this chapter, the public are generally under – or ill – informed about the functioning of the criminal justice system, is the government justified in taking public opinion into account when forming policies? Some argue that politicians are quite justified in ignoring public opinion since politicians cannot be expected to take public opinion into account if the public pays little attention to what politicians do (Franklin and Wlezien 1997). However, crime is capable of generating public passion in a way that is unheard of in other areas (Warr 1995) and the public pays more attention to policy areas that are salient and important to them. This heightened attention is then used to form opinions that shape party support and voting behaviour (e.g. Abramovitz 1994). When an issue is salient and important, people are also more likely to pay closer attention to the related actions of politicians and the media will respond by concentrating reports on areas that reflect this level of interest (Brody 1991). However, media reports rarely disclose all the relevant facts (Green 1996). For example, when forming opinions regarding appropriate sentencing the public needs to know the facts of a case as it was presented in court and not as they were presented later in television reports or interviews (Green 1996). Green's argument is that the public's opinion is a vital component of criminal justice policy but the public needs to develop an opinion based on *all* the facts of a case and not just the snippets that are summarised at a later date. Rarely are all the facts disclosed or, indeed, reported accurately and all too often the cases that are brought to the public's attention are atypical, which is *why* they are deemed worthy of reporting (Green 1996). As Green (1996) observes:

... the conclusions about sentencing reached by the average member of the public are drawn from inaccurate or inadequate reports of a small and unrepresentative sample of sentencing cases. (p. 116)

Observations such as these fuel arguments such as that proposed by Auld (Home Office, 2001b – see above) who maintains that the level of public ignorance rightly gives judges and politicians a free hand to make policies that they consider fair and efficient. In addition to public ignorance it needs to be considered that public opinion, whether developed from an informed or ill-informed perspective, is apt to change. This means that if governments take public opinion into account, policies could be formed according to erratic trends. For example, the doctrine of less eligibility dictates that during times of high unemployment, members of the public expect prison conditions to be more austere than the conditions endured by the poorest members of society, whereas in times of economic prosperity the public tends to be more sympathetic towards offenders (Sparks 2000). So, if governments form policies according to a vacillating public's opinion they run the risk of appearing to be indecisive, which in turn may undermine public confidence that the country has an effective leadership. If, however, public opinion was to be set aside and policies were to be formed by politicians and judges alone, then the government would avoid being seen as ineffective. Nevertheless, elected politicians also run the risk of being voted out if they appear to ignore the opinion of their constituents (Green 2006).

Some authors argue that even if the public is not closely conversant with the facts of many public policy arrangements this does not give justice officials carte blanche to form policies or make policy changes which are likely to affect most people (Morgan 2002). Yankelovich (1991) points out that experts are small in number and although they may not deliberately mislead the public, they exclude public contribution by using inaccessible jargon and tend to dismiss the views of ordinary people who do not command their level of expert knowledge. As such, Yankelovich (1991) maintains that these experts effectively impose their personal values on other people because they '... fail to distinguish their own value judgements from their technical expertise' (p. 4). If these experts go too far and commandeer the public's role in governance, then we will have ' ... the formal trappings of democracy without the substance, and everyone will suffer' (p. 4). On the other hand, we cannot afford for the public to dominate governance because this will result in demagoguery (Yankelovich 1991).

Yankelovich (1991) insists that what we need is a balance of power and influence where public and experts coexist in sympathy and support of one another. However, currently, governments all too frequently rely on 'top-of-the-head' opinion polls to gauge public opinion. As Green (2006) notes, politicians tend to make use of 'inadequate assessments of public opinion for political ends ...' and '... respond to the filtered public sentiments offered by the media – the most commanding substitute for the real thing available.' (p. 141). The government effectively fails to acknowledge the limits of public knowledge and fails to introduce strategies that will help improve public knowledge (Roberts and Hough 2002). This can be achieved but it needs to be fostered in a culture where the public is encouraged to contribute to its own governance and where experts do not resist this happening (Yankelovich 1991).

Yankelovich (1991) considers the issue of public opinion to be even deeper than the mere gleaning of 'top-of-the-head' thoughts garnered in opinion polls. Yankelovich makes the distinction between public opinion and public judgment. Public judgment is a specific form of public opinion that shows people have given an issue more thought, have weighed up the alternatives and have taken a wider variety of factors into account than the opinions measured by opinion polls.

Green (2006) advocates that using deliberative polls (DPs) governments would obtain more considered public views based on public judgment rather than public opinion. DPs were introduced in the UK during the 1990s and involve interviews and questionnaire administration to members of the public on any relevant issue, e.g. crime and punishment, a period of deliberation and subsequent interviews some time later (see Hough and Park 2002). Green (2006) argues that DPs should become part of the consultation process that inform White Paper development. Indeed, the efforts by the current Labour government to employ focus groups etc. (see above) to inform policy seems to support this view. DPs would be expensive but not as expensive as policy u-turns often are (Green 2006). DPs could be conducted as part of the annual British Crime Survey and when a serious issue such as juvenile crime (such as followed the Bulger case) arises. Although Green (2006) acknowledges that some of the points regarding the implementation of DPs are possibly idealistic, DPs also have a democratic utility since '... the importance of public consultation and of building public confidence is recognized by many as self-evident' (Green 2006: 150) and the value of conducting DPs lies in their ability to provide politicians with more accurate and more considered public opinions. These they can then use or discard when formulating policies, but at least they will know them to be an accurate assessment of public opinion and not ill-informed, ill-conceived, top-of-the-head opinions.

Conclusions

Public opinion undoubtedly has some role to play in the development of criminal justice policies. What we cannot know for certain is the magnitude of that role. Certainly successive governments seem to have taken public opinion at least into consideration when forming justice policies relating to policing and sentencing. The exact relationship between policy formation and public opinion remains a matter for speculation as to whether public opinion informs policy or policy informs opinion. What we do know is if a policy transcends the boundaries of political permission public opinion can result in swift retribution that undermines the policy and even calls the legitimacy of a government into question. Yet the notion that the public is ill-informed permeates public opinion debates and provides some with the ammunition to argue that public opinion should be dismissed in favour of expert opinions. However, to replace public opinion with expert opinions alone would potentially undermine our democracy and invite public wrath. It seems that public opinion and public consultation are increasingly important features of policy formation. Consequently, whether we use deliberative polls or some other derivative to assess public opinion, it is clear that governments, even if they disregard those opinions, should be presented with people's considered views and not some off-the-cuff opinion formed with little thought. Public opinion lies at the heart of a democratic culture and as such its role is crucial in permitting and censuring the actions that governments take on our behalf.

References

Abramowitz, A.I. (1994) 'Issue evolution reconsidered: racial attitudes and partisanship in the U.S. electorate', *American Journal of Political Science*, 38: 1–24.

ACPO (2001) *Reassurance – Civility First: A Proposal for Police Reform*. London: Association of Chief Police Officers of England, Wales and N. Ireland.

Ahmed, D. (n.d.) *The Abolition of the Presumption of Doli Incapax*. Retrieved 25 April 2008 from: http://elsalondon.org/export/sites/ELSA/upload_gallery/4DoliIncapaxAhmed.pdf.

Besley, T., Preston, I. and Ridge, M. (1997) 'Fiscal anarchy in the UK: modelling poll tax noncompliance', *Journal of Public Economics*, 64: 137–52.

Brody, R.A. (1991) *Assessing the President: The Media, Elite Opinion, and Public Support*. Stanford, CA: Stanford University Press.

Brooks, J.E. (1990) 'The opinion–policy nexus in Germany', *Public Opinion Quarterly*, 54 (4): 508–29.

Carter, D.L. (2002) *The Police and the Community*, 7th edn. Englewood Cliffs, NJ: Prentice Hall.

Cowley, P. (1995) 'Parliament and the poll tax: a case study in parliamentary pressure', *Journal of Legislative Studies*, 1 (1): 94–114.

Doble, J. (2002) 'Attitudes to punishment in the US – punitive and liberal opinions', in J.V. Roberts and M. Hough (eds), *Changing Attitudes to Punishment: Public Opinion, Crime and Justice*. Cullompton: Willan, pp. 148–62.

Faulkner, D. (eds) (2006) *Crime, State and Citizen: A Field Full of Folk*. Winchester: Waterside Press.

Fionda, J. (1998) 'Case commentary: R v Secretary of State for the Home Department ex parte Venables and Thompson: the age of innocence? The concept of childhood in the punishment of young offenders', *Child and Family Quarterly*, 10 (1): 77–87.

Flanagan, T.J., McGarrell, E.F. and Brown, E.J. (1985) 'Public perceptions of the criminal courts: the role of demographic and related attitudinal variables', *Journal of Research in Crime and Delinquency*, 22 (1): 66–82.

Fox, R.G. (1987) 'Controlling sentencers', *Australian and New Zealand Journal of Criminology*, 20 (4): 218–46.

Franklin, M.N. and Wlezien, C. (1997) 'The responsive public: issue salience, policy change, and preferences for European Unification', *Journal of Theoretical Politics*, 9: 347–63.

Green, D.A. (2006) 'Public opinion versus public judgement about crime: correcting the "Comedy of Errors"', *British Journal of Criminology*, 46: 131–54.

Green, G. (1996) 'The concept of uniformity in sentencing', *Australian Law Journal*, 70: 112–14.

Herrington, V. and Millie, A. (2006) 'Applying reassurance policing: is it "business as usual"?', *Policing and Society*, 16 (2): 146–63.

Hobolt, S.B. and Klemmemsen, R. (2005) 'Responsive government? Public opinion and government policy preferences in Britain and Denmark', *Political Studies*, 53: 379–402.

Home Office (2001a) *Making Punishments Work. Report of a Review of the Sentencing Framework for England and Wales*. The Halliday Report. London: Home Office.

Home Office (2001b) *Review of the Criminal Courts of England and Wales* (The Auld Report). London: HMSO.

Hough, M. (2003) 'Modernisation and public opinion: some criminal justice paradoxes', *Contemporary Politics*, 9: 143–55.

Hough, M. and Park, A. (2002) 'How malleable are attitudes to crime and punishment? Findings from a British deliberative poll', in J.V. Roberts and M. Hough (eds), *Changing Attitudes to Punishment: Public Opinion, Crime and Justice*. Cullompton: Willan, pp. 163–83.

King, M. (1995) 'The James Bulger murder trial: moral dilemmas and social solutions', *International Journal of Children's Rights*, 3: 167–87.

Lipsey, M. (1980) *Street Level Bureaucracy*. New York: Russell Sage Foundation.

Liska, A. (1987) 'A critical examination of macro perspectives', *Annual Reviews of Sociology*, 13: 67–88.

McConnell, A. (2000) 'Local taxation, policy information and policy change: a reply to Peter John', *British Journal of Politics and International Relations*, 2 (1): 81–8.

Moran, M. (2001) 'Not steering but drowning: policy catastrophes and the regulatory state', *Political Quarterly*, 72 (4): 414–27.

Morgan, R. (2002) 'Privileging public attitudes to sentencing?', in J.V. Roberts and M. Hough (eds), *Changing Attitudes to Punishment: Public Opinion, Crime and Justice*. Cullompton: Willan, pp. 215–28.

Motschall, M. and Cao, L. (2002) 'An analysis of the public relations role of the Police Public Information Officer', *Police Quarterly*, 5 (2): 152–80.

Mugani, E. (2001) *Serves You Right! Playing Populist Politics with Children Who Kill*. London: Children's Legal Centre, p.10. (Case reference: *T v. UK* [2000] 2 All ER 1024.)

Ouimet, M. and Coyle, E.J. (1991) 'Fear of crime and sentencing punitiveness: comparing the general public and court practitioners', *Canadian Journal of Criminology*, 33 (2): 149–62.

Povey, K. (2001) *Open All Hours: A Thematic Inspection Report on the Role of Police Visibility and Accessibility in Public Reassurance*. London: Her Majesty's Inspectorate of Constabulary (HMIC).

Roberts, J.V. and Hough, M. (2002) *Changing Attitudes to Punishment: Public Opinion, Crime and Justice*. Cullompton: Willan.

Robinson, P.H. and Darley, J.M. (1998) 'Objectivist versus subjectivist views of criminality: a study in the role of social science in criminal law theory', *Oxford Journal of Legal Studies*, 18: 409–47.

Rosenbaum, D.P., Schuck, A.M., Costello, S.K., Hawkins, D.F. and Ring, M.K. (2005) 'Attitudes toward the police: the effects of direct and vicarious experience', *Police Quarterly*, 8 (3): 343–65.

Simmons, J. (2002) *Crime in England and Wales 2001/2002*. London: Home Office Research, Development and Statistics Directorate.

Sparks, R. (2000) 'The media and penal politics, review essay', *Punishment and Society*, 2 (1): 98–105.

Stimson, J.A., MacKuen, M.B. and Erikson, R.S. (1995) 'Dynamic representation', *American Journal of Political Science*, 89: 543–65.

Thorpe, K. and Wood, M. (2004) 'Antisocial behaviour', in S. Nicholas and A. Walker (eds), *Crime in England and Wales 2002/2003: Supplementary*

Volume 2: Crime and Disorder and the Criminal Justice System – Public Attitudes and Perceptions, Home Office Statistical Bulletin 02/04. London: Home Office.

Tomaino, J. (1997) 'Guess who's coming to dinner? A preliminary model for the satisfaction of public opinion as a legitimate aim in sentencing', *Crime, Law and Social Change*, 27: 109–19.

Walker, N. (1985) *Sentencing: Theory, Law and Practice*. London: Butterworths.

Warr, M. (1995) 'The polls – poll trends', *Public Opinion Quarterly*, 59: 296–310.

Yankelovich, D. (1991) *Coming to Public Judgement: Making Democracy Work in a Complex World*. Syracuse, NY: Syracuse University Press.

Chapter 3

What shapes public opinion of the criminal justice system?

Jacqueline M. Gray

It is not uncommon to see newspaper headlines protesting about the way in which a particular offender has been either punished too leniently or too harshly, or that victims have been 'failed by the system'. Indeed, the treatment of people by the police, courts, probation and prison systems are topics that seem to be of enduring interest to the general public. In the current climate of concern over perceived increases in crime, disorder and incivilities, whether accurate or not, the public clearly have their individual opinions regarding the criminal justice system (CJS). While it is of interest to determine what the public attitude actually is towards the CJS, this chapter is not directly concerned with what that opinion is, but rather with what contributes to the formation of public opinion.

A brief consideration of the literature regarding public opinions of the CJS will be given to provide a basis for the subsequent discussion of where these opinions come from. This will be followed by a consideration of the various sources of information on which the public are likely to base their opinions, such as personal or vicarious experience, educational campaigns and the media. The discussion then moves on to address a number of individual factors such as prejudice, authoritarianism and socio-economic factors that may also be influential.

Knowledge and public opinion of the criminal justice system

A substantial body of research has been carried out around the world to identify public opinion of the criminal justice system, and one of the most common measures of opinion is perceived leniency of sentencing. On first view of this literature it seems that the findings from various countries including Holland, Canada and the USA indicate that the public generally sees the CJS as being too lenient, particularly in terms of sentencing of offenders (Doob and Roberts 1988; St Amand and Zamble 2001; Sprott and Doob 1997; Wemmers 1999). A similar finding is seen throughout a series of studies in the UK based on the British Crime Survey, where it has been consistently found that around 80 per cent of respondents consider that the CJS is too lenient (Chapman *et al.* 2002; Hough and Roberts 1998; Mattinson and Mirrlees-Black 2000; Mirrlees-Black 2001). These findings are also evident from qualitative research, in which a fairly general belief in the leniency of the CJS is evident (Hough 1996; Johnson *et al.* 2005). However, despite this very common finding it is evident that this global assessment of attitude to the CJS does not tell us the full story.

While many people say that they believe the CJS to be too lenient, there is evidence that this is due to a lack of knowledge and understanding of how the system actually operates and treats offenders (Hough and Roberts 2004). This is illustrated by a number of studies that have shown that when given a description of a crime and asked to recommend a sentence the sentences suggested by the public are not substantially different from those given by the courts, despite the overall evaluation of the CJS as too lenient (e.g. Zamble and Kalm 1990). It has also been noted in a Canadian study that the public underestimate the severity of the sentences that are handed down by the courts (St Amand and Zamble 2001).

While leniency in sentencing is a common measure of public opinion others are also used, including measures of satisfaction with individual parts of the CJS, crime rates, appropriate treatment of victims and offenders, and perceptions of justice. It has been suggested that the public has varying degrees of familiarity with different aspects of the CJS, and that this may influence their perceptions. Indeed, taking a cross-cultural perspective, Hough and Roberts (2004) have shown that the police are generally the most favourably rated part of the CJS, whereas the courts tend to be least favourably judged. The authors argue that this reflects greater public knowledge about the role of the police, which is confirmed by Johnson *et al.* (2005). Multiple research studies have demonstrated that the public have inaccurate perceptions of the CJS. Some of the more commonly found misperceptions in the UK include: beliefs that crime is rising; overestimates in the rate of violent crime; ignorance regarding sentencing; and underestimation of the use of prison for serious offenders (Chapman *et al.* 2002; Hough and Roberts 1998; Mattinson and Mirrlees-Black 2000). Thus, it is likely that this erroneous knowledge of the practice of the CJS plays a formative role in evaluations of the CJS and is hence influential on public opinion. Given this inaccuracy, it is therefore important to investigate how the public obtains knowledge regarding the CJS.

Where does public knowledge of the CJS come from?

Whatever the public, as a whole, believes about the CJS, as individuals they acquire their knowledge whether right or wrong and the associated attitudes in a variety of ways. These essentially fall into two categories, being either direct or indirect experiences, and for the many people who have both it is likely that these interact in the formation of individual opinions.

The public may obtain personal experience of the CJS in various ways. They may have direct experiences such as being a victim of crime, a witness, a volunteer in organisations such as Victim Support or a prison, a lay contributor through jury service, or indeed as an offender or a professional working within the CJS. Individuals may also acquire their information indirectly, perhaps through being a vicarious victim of crime, knowing others who have been involved in the CJS and hearing their experiences, and also through 'common knowledge'. It is likely that a large proportion of this common knowledge is now disseminated through the media, which as well as providing information can be influential in the formation of public opinion. Mirrlees-Black (2001) provides evidence of the prevalence of direct CJS experience, with 59 per cent of the British Crime Survey 2000 respondents having ever been victims of crime, 12 per cent ever been arrested, 10 per cent having ever appeared in court and 34 per cent having ever had other contact with the courts such as being a witness or juror. This victimisation figure therefore differs from the usual British Crime Survey rate which reflects victimisation in the last year. The following discussion will focus on the effects of being a victim, juror and witness, as these are the experiences that seem to affect the greatest proportion of the public.

It would seem logical to predict that being a victim of crime, and hence having dealings with various aspects of the CJS, would influence an individual's knowledge and attitude towards the CJS. Personal experience of the manner in which a victim is dealt with by the police and courts, the identification or otherwise of the offender, whether or not a conviction is obtained and any ultimate sentence are factors that would be expected to influence an individual's opinion. However, the research evidence regarding the influence of these factors makes it evident that the relationship is complex, and that specific types of crime and victim need to be considered rather than taking a generalised view (Sprott and Doob 1997).

There is some evidence that the experience of being a victim of crime may be influential upon attitudes. Sprott and Doob (1997) identified a relationship between the punitiveness of crime victims and the nature of their victimisation, with those who had been victims of crimes such as assault and sexual assault being somewhat less punitive than non-victims, whereas those who were victims of robbery or burglary were somewhat more punitive than non-victims. It is of course possible that such differences are related to systematic differences in the way in which different types of crime are handled by the various aspects of the CJS, other support that is available or taken up, or some effect of the type of victimisation. Without more information it is not possible to draw clear inferences, but, for example, it may be that victims of assault are more likely to be concerned with their own recovery and well-being and are hence less focused on punishment. However, this relationship is not clear, with Hough *et al.* (1988) finding no significant difference between victims and non-victims in their level of punitiveness. It is likely that there are a number of factors that may interact to influence punitiveness, and it seems that this is an area where more work is needed to tease apart this relationship.

The importance of experience of the CJS, rather than simply the experience of being a victim, in shaping public attitudes has been identified, in particular in the concept of secondary victimisation. The actions of the police and the courts and other parts of the CJS can have the effect of further victimising those who come to them as victims through unsympathetic, careless or indeed hostile treatment. Much of the research into secondary victimisation has focused on crimes such as rape and domestic violence, where victims are particularly likely to have negative experiences of the CJS (e.g. Campbell 2005; Ullman and Townsend 2007). However, interactions between the CJS and victims of other types of crime, such as crimes of violence (Orth 2002), can also lead to secondary victimisation. There seems to be some inconsistency between these findings and those of Sprott and Doob (1997), as victims of sexual assault are likely to have poor experiences of the CJS yet have reported less punitiveness. This may be because satisfaction with the CJS and punitiveness are two separate constructs, or it may be further evidence for the need for a more detailed understanding of how public attitudes around the CJS are related.

As noted above, victims of sexual crimes are especially likely to have negative experiences of the various stages of the CJS, with there being ample evidence of hostile and embarrassing questioning both by the police and the courts (Lees 2002; Temkin 2002). The rate of victims reporting rape to the police in England and Wales is estimated at around only 15–20 per cent, based on British Crime Survey responses (Myhill and Allen 2002; Walby and Allen 2004; see also Wilson and Scholes, this volume). Victims frequently cite fear of not being believed and of the intimidating investigative and trial processes as reasons for not reporting or for withdrawing their complaint (Feist *et al.* 2007; Kelly *et al.* 2005). Of the few who do report their victimisation in the UK, only 5.3 per cent of cases, as measured in 2004/5, result in a conviction (Home Office 2005). Lees (2002) provides a detailed study of rape victims' experiences of the CJS, from which it is evident that for many the system does not provide justice, leaving them feeling hurt and dissatisfied and believing that justice has not been done as they have not seen their attacker convicted. It is therefore likely that such individuals will not hold a particularly favourable view of the CJS.

While experiencing secondary victimisation can be seen to negatively impact on victims' attitudes to the CJS, the beneficial effects of good procedures in the CJS can be seen in research conducted in the Netherlands, reported by Wemmers (1999). It was found that victims who were kept informed of the progress of their case were more satisfied with police performance, more supportive of the police and more in agreement with sentencing practices. Similar findings are also reported in the UK, where victims who were kept well informed of the progress of their case by police were particularly likely to be satisfied (Allen *et al.* 2006). Allen *et al.* also note that victims who have face-to-face contact with the police are more likely to report being satisfied than are those who do not.

As well as affecting general attitudes towards the CJS and 'customer satisfaction', it can therefore be seen that the treatment of victims of crime can also influence the decisions they make regarding reporting the crime and later engagement with the system. For example, rape victims who are aware that other victims of rape have experienced scepticism or hostile attitudes from police, courts and others in the CJS may decide that they will not report their victimisation to avoid the potential further victimisation by the CJS. The potential impact of victims' experiences of the CJS is therefore hard to estimate, as it may also affect other people to whom they describe their experiences, with potential further influence if the likelihood of a negative experience with the CJS becomes a subject of common knowledge.

Experience of being a juror or witness at a trial may also be a source of knowledge regarding the CJS, and may hence impact on the opinions of those involved. While in England and Wales, as well as many other jurisdictions, it is prohibited to ask jurors about their discussions and deliberations in a particular case, Matthews et al. (2004) conducted a study to assess jurors' satisfaction with their experience, as well as their perceptions, understanding and confidence in the court system. They found that most of the jurors reported an increased understanding of the criminal trial and were more positive regarding the jury system after their service than they were before, and that they considered the court personnel to be professional and helpful. Interestingly positive reports of the competence and performance of judges was higher after jury service. This is a potentially important point for efforts to improve public opinion of the CJS, given that other studies have reported a high level of public scepticism of judges and the feeling that they are out of touch (Hough and Roberts 1998; Mattinson and Mirrlees-Black 2000). Matthews et al. also note that confidence in the jury system was associated with a number of factors reflecting the proper functioning of the trial system, such as jury diversity, adherence to due process and the process being considered to be fair. Factors that were found to associate with reduced confidence were poorly prepared cases, poor quality evidence and the hearing of cases that they considered to be minor.

The Home Office has also commissioned studies to assess the satisfaction of witnesses who participate in criminal trials. Whitehead (2001) and Angle et al. (2003) both report that over 75 per cent of the witnesses in their studies were satisfied with their experience. Angle et al. report that dissatisfaction was associated with the feeling that they were taken for granted or intimidated by the process or the environment. Those witnesses who felt that they were able to say everything they wanted to and were treated courteously by both prosecution and defence counsels were more likely to report being satisfied. Whitehead also found that satisfaction was related among other things to the amount of information witnesses received, court facilities and waiting times. It was also found that victim witnesses were less satisfied with the process than were other witnesses, which may relate to the concerns of secondary victimisation as discussed above. Thus it seems that experience as a witness and the way in which they are treated during their involvement in a case may well influence witnesses' opinion of the courts.

It can be seen that individual members of the public may have interactions with various aspects of the CJS, and that these may inform their knowledge of the system and also affect their opinions. However, the operation of the CJS as a whole may have a more general influence upon public opinion. Indeed it has been argued in the Court of Appeal that it is the duty of the courts to lead public opinion rather than reflect it, and that the sentences handed down by the courts should influence public perceptions and disapproval of crimes (Walker and Marsh 1988). However, Walker and Marsh did not find support for this hypothesis, even when the sentences were made very clear to participants. In relation to real-life knowledge of particular cases there was some awareness of sentences handed down among a substantial minority of participants, although these were mostly of high-profile, serious cases rather than the routine cases that form the vast majority of trials. Thus whatever knowledge there was among the public of sentencing practice this is unlikely to be representative of the situation in routine cases, and furthermore these findings indicate that the decisions of the courts may have little general effect on public perception and disapproval of crime. However, this does not preclude the possibility that ongoing publicity regarding the CJS may influence opinions other than the disapproval of particular crimes and have a cumulative effect on public opinion of the CJS.

The literature reviewed above has examined various areas of experience that the public may have of the CJS. However, a separate but related concept is knowledge of the CJS. While it would be anticipated that those with experience of the CJS would have more knowledge this is not necessarily the case, and there may be people with good knowledge but little direct experience of the CJS. It has been argued that lack of knowledge regarding the CJS may be a significant factor in accounting for why the public are dissatisfied and generally have a view of the CJS being too lenient (e.g. Chapman *et al.* 2002). Therefore, if the level of knowledge is improved, one might reasonably conclude that public attitudes to the CJS should become more positive. A number of studies have been conducted to investigate the impact on public attitudes of providing information.

Chapman *et al.* (2002) report findings from a sub-sample of the 2000 British Crime Survey who received information about the CJS through a booklet, a seminar run by experts or a video of a seminar. It was found that information in any format led to significantly increased knowledge scores. There was also some evidence that this increased knowledge was associated with a number of changes in attitudes and beliefs, such as a reduction in the belief that sentencing was too lenient, increased confidence that the CJS brings offenders to justice, and increased support for sentences other than prison, although support for imprisonment also rose. A subsequent study (Salisbury 2004) compared the responses of participants who had been provided an information booklet about the CJS to those who had not. Approximately 25 per cent of the participants said that the booklet had changed their views and had made them more aware. There was also evidence that the booklet was associated with some increased knowledge and confidence regarding the CJS over and above that experienced by those who did not receive the booklet.

These UK-based studies do suggest that providing information to the public may be helpful in improving public attitudes to the CJS. However, they relied upon quite focused interventions that were part of the British Crime Survey, which may therefore have generally raised participants' awareness and hence engagement with the information. The difficulty in getting information to the general public is highlighted by Kuttschreuter and Weigman (1998) in an evaluation of a multimedia campaign in the Netherlands. The campaign included local newspapers and radio, together with a 'Crime Prevention Van' provided by the police, all aimed at giving accurate information regarding crime and crime prevention. There was limited awareness of the campaign, although there was a small positive influence on attitudes, among all people including those aware and those unaware of the campaign. A campaign of this type may influence people's attitudes, even if they are not consciously aware of it if there are more signs of the CJS doing its job. However, problems with the implementation of the intervention meant that it was not clear whether it was the information or the increased police presence and contact that led to the changes.

These studies suggest that attempts to improve the knowledge of the general public regarding criminal justice matters and to improve their opinion of the CJS have met with some success. However, they have employed fairly brief and one-off interventions which still leave the question of whether a deeper, specialist understanding of the CJS can be associated with more positive attitudes. Evidence suggests that having contact with the CJS and generally having an interest in matters related to criminal justice as well as a higher level of education is associated with a better knowledge of the CJS (Chapman *et al.* 2002). In China, where the public receive ongoing education regarding the law, public legal education has been found to influence inmates' perceptions of the fairness of their punishment (Zhang *et al.* 1999). However, this level of education is still short of that obtained by specialists such as those working in the CJS or who are formally educated in related topics.

It would seem reasonable to expect that people studying subjects such as law, criminology or forensic psychology should have a better knowledge of the CJS than the general public. Therefore if knowledge is associated with confidence then these people with greater knowledge should also report higher levels of confidence. Riley (2006) in an unpublished study identified that both police and students taking law-related postgraduate degrees demonstrated a higher level of knowledge of criminal justice issues than did members of the general public. However, the relationship between knowledge and confidence was less clear-cut. Considered overall those with more knowledge reported more confidence in the CJS as a whole, but the postgraduate students showed a significantly lower level of confidence that the CJS meets the needs of the accused. It therefore seems that it is not just quantity of knowledge that is important in influencing attitudes to the CJS, but that it is also necessary to consider the way in which the knowledge is obtained, as courses such as criminology and forensic psychology tend to take a critical stance to the operation of the CJS. By way of contrast the police have a high degree of familiarity with the law and the legal system, but their training has a different emphasis from that of the postgraduate students in this study. If steps are to be taken to improve attitudes to the CJS, this study indicates that it is necessary to consider not just the knowledge provided but the manner of engagement with it. Furthermore – and perhaps more significantly – this raises the question of what type of attitude shift is desirable to the government and the CJS. In other words, is the ultimate goal an unquestioning positive shift in attitudes or is it a better informed public who are better able to evaluate and engage with the CJS, even if their immediate attitude is no more positive?

While Riley (2006) found significant differences in knowledge and confidence in the CJS between those with specialist knowledge and the general public in the UK, in the USA Lambert and Clarke (2004) found some, but in their words not 'striking', differences in the level of knowledge of the death penalty and other CJS issues between students majoring in criminal justice and those majoring in other subjects. This difference between the two studies may be reflecting the differences between postgraduate and undergraduate level studies, or may reflect differences in approach to the teaching of this topic between the UK and the USA. Research also suggests that there may be some areas in which public opinion and that of specialists may be quite similar, with both public and legal professionals in the USA showing a pattern of becoming less supportive of the use of the death penalty if they are presented with the option of a life sentence without the possibility of parole (McGarrell and Sandys 1996; Whitehead 1998).

The media

The late twentieth and early twenty-first centuries have seen a massive increase in the opportunities for the media to influence and inform public opinion on a range of subjects, including the CJS. The public has access to news through newspapers, radio, television and the Internet, as well as the myriad of other sources of information such as documentaries, dramas and 'real-life' shows such as those in which footage is taken from real police chases and raids. Indeed, as argued by Walker and Marsh (1988), the media is the only realistic way in which most people find out about issues such as sentencing, as most people would not hear about a sentence by word of mouth and only a relatively few people attend trials.

The media provides the public with a vicarious experience of the CJS, but one which is focused and selected in such a way as to meet the needs of the media. As Howitt (1998) points out, the media focuses on sensational crimes such as those of a sexual or violent nature, rather than the more mundane property crimes which affect many more people. As well as being selective in what cases to report, the media also only provides brief information, which rarely reflects the complexity of the decision-making in the cases, meaning that the public do not get to understand the logic behind decisions that may seem to them to be wrong (Doob and Roberts 1988; see also Wood, this volume). The potential impact of this process of selection and politicisation of criminal justice in the media can be seen when it is considered that around 75 per cent of people responding to the 2000 British Crime Survey reported obtaining their information regarding the CJS from television and radio, 50 per cent from documentaries, local and tabloid newspapers, and 33 per cent from broadsheet newspapers (Mirrlees-Black 2001). These respondents also considered that their sources of information were either fairly or very accurate. Earlier research conducted in Canada and the UK has also shown the importance of the media, with a vast majority of respondents stating that this was their primary source of information about the CJS (Doob and Roberts 1988; Hough *et al.* 1988).

While there is debate as to whether the media guides or reflects public opinion, it is likely that the selection processes that guide what is presented by the media to the public will influence how the public perceive crime and the criminal justice system. As described by Howitt (1998) the media constructs an image of crime with an emphasis on dramatic events which are sensationalised and personalised. As well as telling the public about crime, or at least certain types of crime, the media also tells the public what to think about it. The influence of the media can be seen in the responses of 8 per cent of the participants in a Home Office study (Salisbury 2004) who reported that they did not find the Home Office-produced information booklet that they were given believable as the statistics provided were different from those presented by the media. This may reflect a distrust, at least among some members of the public, of politicians and hence government statistics, and therefore they consider the media to be more likely to provide an unbiased picture of crime.

The under-representation of the more mundane and routine crimes and the over-representation of the sensational yet statistically rarer crimes (Ericson *et al.* 1991; Graber 1980) means that the public receive a distorted picture of the patterns of crime. While the public may be selective in what they choose to pay attention to and their views do not necessarily simply reflect what they encounter in the media (Graber 1980), this unrepresentative picture is likely to make certain aspects of crime and the CJS more easily brought to mind. When forming an opinion regarding the CJS, individual members of the public are unlikely to have a complete set of relevant and accurate data available to them. They are therefore likely to rely upon the information that is most available to them, and rely upon heuristic processing which simplifies decision-making and opinion formation based upon the limited information provided by the media (Tversky and Kahneman 1974, 1982; see also Bohner and Wänke, this volume, for an in-depth discussion regarding attitude formation).

While there is not clear agreement regarding the mechanisms by which the media may influence public opinion (Howitt 1998) there is evidence that it does have an effect. Goidel *et al.* (2006) found that increased television viewing, of both news and 'reality' crime shows, was associated with misperceptions regarding juvenile crime and justice in a state in the US. Although this study considers the impact of television viewing on the understanding of juvenile justice rather than on attitudes to the juvenile justice system, it does demonstrate that there is an association that would be relevant to the information on which members of the public could base their opinions. Thus the nature of the media to which members of the public are exposed, in terms of its accuracy, representativeness and the degree of sensationalism, may influence public opinion as this is the information that is most likely to be available as a basis for their views.

Individual differences and attitude to the CJS

The research discussed above provides a general picture of public dissatisfaction with the CJS, although this seems frequently to be based on a poor knowledge of what actually happens, particularly in the courts. As well as the various means by which the public obtain their knowledge of the CJS and any biasing effects that may have, an individual's opinions will also be influenced by a range of individual difference factors. Kaukinen and Colavecchia (1999) highlight the necessity to consider this complex area in more detail by focusing on specific attitudes and the views of particular social groups. However, positive attitudes to one area of the CJS may well be part of a constellation of more positive attitudes to the CJS, as shown by Jansson et al. (2007) who identified that confidence in the police was associated with confidence that the CJS brought offenders to justice, believing that prisons do a good job, not believing that the crime rate is rising and perceiving a low level of anti-social behaviour in their local area.

There is some evidence to support the association between attitudes to the CJS and the demographic factors of age and gender. Hough et al. (1988) found that men in older and younger age groups were more punitive than were women, although there was no gender difference in the middle-aged group. They also found that in general older people held more punitive views than did their younger counterparts. While punitiveness is not directly an opinion regarding the CJS, as stated earlier in this chapter the public seem to generally believe that the CJS is insufficiently punitive and hence punitiveness is likely to relate to attitudes to the CJS. Similar findings are also reported by Mirrlees-Black (2001), who identified that men expressed less confidence in the CJS than did women, that the middle-aged were less confident than were the young and the old, and that the most educated and those with professional or managerial job roles were least confident.

Kaukinen and Colavecchia (1999) found that their Canadian respondents saw the CJS as protecting the rights of the accused, but nearly half considered that the courts did not provide enough help to victims. The significant predictors of belief in the ability of the courts to help victims of crime were age, income, education and gender, with older, educated males living in urban areas being more likely to consider that the courts do not provide help to victims. As well as these demographic characteristics a number of attitudinal and experiential factors were also predictors of the belief that the courts do not provide enough help to victims. These included having been a victim of property crime, previous contact with the courts, seeing crime as increasing and believing that the police do a bad job. Fear of becoming a victim of crime and believing that the police were doing a bad job were also predictors of belief in the courts protecting the rights of the accused. Of particular note was the finding that those of higher income were more likely to see the courts as protecting the rights of the accused but not of victims, whereas those of lower income were more likely to believe that the rights of the accused were not protected by the courts. This may reflect a range of beliefs about the types of people who are likely to be either victims or offenders, with these higher-income participants probably perceiving the courts as not protecting the rights of people like them.

The relationship between social class rather than income and attitude to the CJS is less clear in the literature, which is likely to be due to difficulties in operationalising this variable, and also to its interrelationship with other variables such as education, income and area of residence. However, it has been found that those living in areas of disadvantage had a high degree of dissatisfaction with the police and reported greater cynicism regarding the law, over and above that which could be accounted for by local crime rates and demographic composition (Sampson and Bartusch 1998). It seems likely that this is associated with perceived discrimination and prejudice by the police and the wider CJS, which is discussed in greater depth below. These findings are therefore consistent with those of Kaukinen and Colavecchia (1999) regarding the relationship between income and perceptions of the protection of the rights of the accused.

Research suggests that members of social groups that have traditionally experienced prejudice and discrimination are likely to perceive the CJS as discriminatory. Hagan and Albonetti (1982) identified the influential roles of both race and social socio-economic group in the perception of injustice in the CJS. Black American participants have been found to be more likely to perceive the CJS as discriminatory (Hagan and Albonetti 1982), and to be less likely to support punitive actions such as capital punishment and the police use of force (e.g. Halim and Stiles 2001; Unnever and Cullen 2007) than were their white counterparts. Similarly the unemployed perceived a greater degree of injustice than did those in employment. Wortley (1996) also identified that black participants were more likely than those from other groups in Canada to perceive the CJS as discriminatory.

In the UK, there is also evidence that race is associated with attitudes to the CJS. Mirrlees-Black (2001) identified that black and Asian participants in the 2000 British Crime Survey were less likely to hold the view that the British CJS was too lenient in its sentencing of offenders. Black participants were also less likely to consider that the CJS respected the rights of those accused of crime. However, in some other aspects of the CJS, such as being effective in bringing offenders to justice, efficiency in handling cases and meeting victims' needs, ethnic minorities reported a greater level of confidence. Recent findings in the UK have shown that white and mixed-race respondents were less likely than other ethnic groups to perceive both local police and the police in general as doing a good job (Jansson et al. 2007). There were also racial differences in attitudes to various other aspects of the CJS, such as white respondents being less confident than other ethnic groups that the CJS met the needs of victims or dealt effectively with young people accused of crime. In contrast, black respondents were less confident than other groups that the CJS respected the rights of the accused and treated witnesses well (Jansson et al. 2007).

As well as ethnicity, Jansson et al. (2007) also identified that Muslims and Hindus were more likely than Christians or Buddhists to believe that local police and the police in general do a good job. Muslims and Hindus were also found to be more confident in the CJS on five of the seven measures of performance included in the British Crime Survey. These were: being effective in reducing crime, bringing offenders to justice, meeting the needs of victims, effectiveness in dealing with young people accused of crime and dealing with cases promptly. However, it was also noted that confidence in the CJS bringing those accused of crime to justice was most strongly predicted by age, area of residence and perceptions of anti-social behaviour and sentence severity, rather than religion.

As well as the views of members of various ethnic groups about the CJS it is also of relevance to consider the effects of race in terms of the relationship between racial prejudice and attitudes to the CJS. A number of US-based studies have found that white Americans' racial prejudice against African Americans is associated with support for more punitive sanctions against criminals (e.g. Barkan and Cohn 1994; Peffley and Hurwitz 2002; Soss et al. 2003). Racial discrimination has also been found to be related to support for the death penalty, with white, racially prejudiced students being more likely to recommend the use of the death penalty for a black defendant than for a white defendant (Dovidio et al. 1997: see also Cullen et al., this volume). As well as support for punitive sanctions, racial prejudice has also been found to be associated with support for increased spending on crime reduction measures (Barkan and Cohn 2005). The authors of these US studies make it clear that they are based upon the premise that many white Americans associate crime, particularly violent crime, with African Americans. While this may not be the case to such an extent in the UK these findings do suggest that racial prejudice could be a factor in determining public attitudes to the CJS.

The factors discussed above consider individual differences identified through various group memberships, such as race and social class. However, it also seems likely that people's attitudes to the CJS would be influenced by certain psychological characteristics, such as personality and general attitudinal orientation towards issues such as liberalism/conservatism, dogmatism and authoritarianism (Hough et al. 1988). In assessing correlates with punitiveness Hough et al. identified that a measure of attitudes to discipline at school, work and in the army was associated, as would be predicted, with punitiveness. In the multivariate analysis this was found to be the most significant predictor. They also identified that those who reported being more concerned about the possibility of being burgled or walking alone at night in their area, used as measures of fear of crime, held more punitive views toward offenders.

Punitiveness has also been found to be predicted by right-wing authoritarianism and social dominance orientation (Capps 2002). Consistent findings are also reported by Sidanius et al. (2006) who identified that those high in social dominance orientation were more supportive of harsh penalties for offenders, and that this relationship was mediated by participants' beliefs in the deterrent and retributive nature of such punishments.

Hessing et al. (2003) focused on attitudes to the death penalty in the Netherlands and the factors predicting support in a country which is largely not supportive of this form of punishment. They identified that those who supported harsh treatment of offenders, who supported granting extensive powers to criminal justice authorities, who felt that the government was not effective in the fight against crime and who were concerned about the extent of crime were more likely to support the use of the death penalty. They also found more support among those who did not vote or who voted for extreme parties at either end of the political spectrum, the younger and the least well educated. It thus seems possible that attitude to punishment, and hence to some extent the CJS, may be supported by a generally orienting set of beliefs including those towards authority, social beliefs and style of thinking about oneself in society.

So, what does shape public opinion of the CJS?

It seems likely that most people will have some opinions regarding the CJS, however clear or otherwise these may be. They may reflect concerns over whether the various aspects of the system, such as the police, courts, judiciary or prison, are doing an effective job, whether the CJS is effective in reducing crime, or whether the system is fair to both the accused and victims of crime. It can be seen that such opinions may reflect very specific issues like support for the use of the death penalty, or may reflect much broader concepts such as whether any particular system is perceived to distribute justice fairly. However, overall evaluations are often given in terms of satisfaction with the various parts of the system and the perceived leniency of sentencing offenders. This complexity means that it is difficult to establish what 'public opinion' actually is, as it can be multifaceted, and this is reflected in the variety of measures that are used in research around this topic (see Chapter 5, this volume, for a discussion of methodology).

Fortunately, in considering the factors that shape public opinion it has not been necessary to get too involved in trying to determine exactly what the public thinks of the CJS, although many of the studies reviewed in this chapter do also speak to this subject. Clearly, for an individual to have an opinion on any topic they must have some knowledge on which to base their evaluation. However, this knowledge may vary in its accuracy, and individuals may believe the knowledge that they have to greater or lesser extents. For example, someone may have an opinion that offenders are sentenced too leniently, but be aware that this opinion is based upon vague and potentially inaccurate knowledge. On the other hand someone else with the same opinion may hold very firmly to the belief that their knowledge is accurate.

It is evident that the public generally has a fairly poor knowledge of the CJS, and this has been found internationally and over time. It has also been reasoned that at least some of the negative evaluations of the CJS are due to this poor knowledge. Studies have shown that when given case information the public select sentences at a similar level to the judiciary, despite believing judges' sentences to be too lenient. It is therefore often concluded that increasing public knowledge of sentencing would mean that they would be more likely to realise that the sentences that are given are in line with what they would want to see, and hence not be evaluated as being too lenient.

Studies in the UK and elsewhere have shown some success in increasing public knowledge of the CJS for measures such as information booklets and seminars. These have also been associated with increases in confidence in the CJS and more positive attitudes to other aspects of the system. It therefore seems that improving knowledge of the CJS is an effective approach to improving attitudes. However, increased knowledge does not universally lead to a more positive attitude to the CJS, as the depth and manner in which knowledge is acquired, as well as the extent of critical engagement with the subject, may also impact on the resulting attitude. Thus the question arises of whether uncritical, positive appraisal of the CJS is the goal, or whether the aim should be a well informed and engaged public who may as a result identify hitherto ignored flaws in the CJS.

While efforts have been made to identify effective means of improving public knowledge, most members of the public do not receive information booklets or attend classes to gain an in-depth understanding of the CJS. For the majority of the public their learning about the CJS is going to be more implicit, either through direct or vicarious experience. Direct experience of the system may come through having been a victim, an offender or a witness, or acting in a professional or voluntary role within the system. Much of the literature available on this aspect focuses on the consequences of being a victim, and it seems that while this may have some small impact upon attitudes to the system, the effects are not consistent, and it is not these experiences per se that seem to be influential, but rather it is other factors such as the way the CJS treats the individual that have a greater effect.

The impact of the CJS on victims' attitudes to the CJS is demonstrated with stark clarity in the case of victims of rape, who frequently have to face the prospect of their complaint not being believed to be genuine, an intrusive physical examination and being questioned in long, embarrassing detail about the assault and other areas of their lives both by the police and in court. Victims of rape often report fear of what they will have to face as a reason for not reporting their victimisation or for withdrawing from the case part way through. These victims are therefore disengaging from the system, and even when they do report the case to the police the low conviction rate means that many feel that justice has not been done. The problem of secondary victimisation, as mentioned earlier, by the CJS is well established, and is an issue that needs to be addressed if the system itself is not to have a negative impact on public opinion of the CJS.

Involvement in the CJS as either a witness or a juror also provides members of the public with first-hand experience of the CJS. Research has shown that both of these groups are largely satisfied with their experiences. It is evident that the way in which the system is seen to operate by these members of the public can impact upon their perceptions and satisfaction with the system. Inefficiency, rudeness, delays and a variety of other factors may have a negative impact on perceptions of the CJS, and conversely good experiences can have a positive impact. For example, those serving as jurors have been found to be particularly satisfied with the performance of judges, which contrasts with other studies which have found very negative public assessments of judges. It therefore seems that seeing the efficient and appropriate handling of a case may influence opinions in a positive manner, and this may indicate a way forward for other areas of the CJS that wish to increase public support.

While some people may obtain some of their views of the CJS through direct experience there are substantial numbers who only obtain their information and knowledge indirectly. For these people there may be some who are informed by people they know about their experiences, but for most people, including those with direct experience, the media is an important source of information. Much research points to the media as a key source of information about the CJS, and also that many people consider it to be a reliable source of information. Indeed it seems that the public may trust the information in the media more than they do information provided by official sources, perhaps reflecting a lack of trust in the reliability of information ultimately provided on behalf of politicians.

It has been seen that the media provides the public with a selective and politicised account of crime and criminal justice. Stories are selected for their sensational or unusual nature, with an over-representation of stories about crimes of a sexual or violent nature and an under-representation of the more mundane but far more common crimes. Even if the public are selective in what they choose to pay attention to or in what they choose to believe, this means that the baseline information on which any attitudes are formed is distorted and does not represent the reality of the CJS. Thus when considering their opinion of the CJS the information that will be most available will consist of a high proportion of serious crimes, cases where offenders have been sentenced particularly leniently or harshly, wrongful convictions, or where some other perceived injustice or error has been made. Thus the run of the mill cases that are handled without incident will not be part of the general publics' consciousness and there is likely to be a widespread perception of an inefficient and flawed system.

In addition to the information that the public receives about the CJS their evaluations will also depend upon their individual characteristics and attitudes. There are numerous studies that have studied various attitudes related to the CJS and attempted to relate these to a range of demographic variables. While the findings of these studies are not always consistent, there have been a number of associations that have been identified such as age, gender, education, income, social class and ethnicity. However, these relationships are complex, and it seems likely that many of these are interrelated and are also associated with other relevant variables.

Of perhaps greater interest than pure demographic characteristics are the relationships between attitudes to the CJS and other psychological characteristics. In the USA it has been argued that criminality, and particularly violent offending, is frequently presented in politics and the media as being predominantly committed by African Americans. Therefore it has been predicted that attitudes to the CJS, especially those relating to support for punitive punishments and similar concerns, would be predicted by racial prejudice, and this has been found in numerous research studies. While the portrayal of offenders in the UK may not, arguably, be as racially biased as is the case in the USA, there do seem to be common stereotypes regarding the types of people who are offenders. Therefore stereotyping and prejudice could have similar patterns of association with attitudes to the CJS in the UK, an area that appears to be in need of further research.

While there is a substantial amount of research examining the role of prejudice in attitudes related to the CJS, other attitudes have also been found to be associated. These include punitiveness, authoritarianism, liberalism/conservatism, dogmatism and social dominance orientation. It also seems likely that there is a variety of other beliefs that may be related to attitudes to the CJS, as an individual's view of the CJS is likely to be influenced by a wide range of beliefs about government, compliance with authority, society and one's position therein.

Conclusions

It seems that there is a range of factors that are implicated in the formation of public attitudes to the CJS. While methodological issues such as the choice of variables studied and wording of questionnaire items make comparisons between studies difficult, it has been seen that these include personal characteristics, attitudes and experiences, as well as the important role of the media. The relationship between these variables is unlikely to be simple, and studies into this area can of necessity only consider a few of these factors at a time. However, research has identified a number of possible means by which attitudes to the CJS may be improved. However, this is of course predicated upon the assumption that the CJS performs well enough that it deserves the public to hold a better opinion, and it is clear that in some aspects there is still work to be done.

References

Allen, J., Edmonds, S., Patterson, A. and Smith, D. (2006) *Policing and the Criminal Justice System – Public Confidence and Perceptions: Findings from the 2004/05 British Crime Survey*, Home Office Online Report 07/06. London: Home Office.

Angle, H., Malam, S. and Carey, C. (2003) *Witness Satisfaction: Findings from the Witness Satisfaction Survey 2002*, Home Office Online Report 19/03. London: Home Office Research Development and Statistics Directorate.

Barkan, S.E. and Cohn, S.F. (1994) 'Racial prejudice and support for the death penalty by Whites', *Journal of Research in Crime and Delinquency*, 31: 202–9.

Barkan, S.E. and Cohn, S.F. (2005) 'Why whites favor spending more money to fight crime: the role of racial prejudice', *Social Problems*, 52: 300–14.

Campbell, R. (2005) 'What really happened? A validation study of rape survivors' help-seeking experiences with the legal and medical systems', *Violence and Victims*, 20: 55–68.

Capps, J.S. (2002) 'Explaining punitiveness: right-wing authoritarianism and social dominance', *North American Journal of Psychology*, 4: 263–78.

Chapman, B., Mirrlees-Black, C. and Brawn, C. (2002) *Improving Public Attitudes to the Criminal Justice System: The Impact of Information*, Home Office Research Study 245. Home Office: London Research Development and Statistics Directorate.

Doob, A.N. and Roberts, J. (1988) 'Public punitiveness and public knowledge of the facts: some Canadian surveys', in N. Walker and M. Hough (eds), *Public Attitudes to Sentencing: Surveys From Five Countries*. Aldershot: Gower.

Dovidio, J.F., Smith, J.K., Donnella, A.G. and Gaertner, S.L. (1997) 'Racial attitudes and the death penalty', *Journal of Applied Social Psychology*, 27: 1468–87.

Ericson, R.V., Baranek, P.M. and Chan, J.B.L. (1991) *Representing Order: Crime, Law and Justice in the News Media*. Milton Keynes: Open University.

Feist, A., Ashe, J., Lawrence, J., McPhee, D. and Wilson, R. (2007) *Investigating and Detecting Recorded Offences of Rape*, Home Office Online Report 18/07. London: Home Office Research Development and Statistics Directorate.

Goidel, R.K., Freeman, C.M. and Procopio, S.T. (2006) 'The impact of television viewing on perceptions of juvenile crime', *Journal of Broadcasting and Electronic Media*, 50: 119–39.

Graber, D.A. (1980) *Crime News and the Public*. New York: Praeger.

Hagan, J. and Albonetti, C. (1982) 'Race, class and the perception of criminal injustice in America', *American Journal of Sociology*, 88: 329–55.

Halim, S. and Stiles, B.L. (2001) 'Differential support for police use of force, the death penalty, and perceived harshness of the courts: effects of race, gender, and region', *Criminal Justice and Behavior*, 28: 3–23.

Hessing, D.J., Keijser, J.W. de and Elffers, H. (2003) 'Explaining capital punishment support in an abolitionist country: the case of the Netherlands', *Law and Human Behavior*, 27: 605–22.

Home Office (2005) *Criminal Statistics, England and Wales 2004*, Home Office Statistical Bulletin May 19, 2005. London: Home Office Research Development and Statistics Directorate.

Hough, M. (1996) 'People talking about punishment', *Howard Journal*, 35: 191–214.

Hough, M. and Roberts, J. (1998) *Attitudes to Punishment: Findings from the British Crime Survey*, Home Office Research Study 179. London: Home Office Research Development and Statistics Directorate.

Hough, M. and Roberts, J.V. (2004) *Confidence in Justice: An International Review*, Findings 243. London: Home Office Research Development and Statistics Directorate.

Hough, M., Lewis, H. and Walker, N. (1988) 'Factors associated with "punitiveness" in England and Wales', in N. Walker and M. Hough (eds), *Public Attitudes to Sentencing: Surveys From Five Countries*. Aldershot: Gower.

Howitt, D. (1998) *Crime, the Media and the Law*. Chichester: John Wiley & Sons.

Jansson, K., Budd, S., Lovbakke, J., Moley, S. and Thorpe, K. (2007) *Attitudes, Perceptions and Risks of Crime: Supplementary Volume 1 to Crime in England and Wales 2006/7*, Home Office Statistical Bulletin 19/07. London: Home Office Research Development and Statistics Directorate.

Johnson, A., Wake, R. and Hill, R. (2005) *Confidence in the Criminal Justice System: Explaining Area Variation in Public Confidence*, Findings 251. London: Home Office Research Development and Statistics Directorate.

Kaukinen, C. and Colavecchia, S. (1999) 'Public perceptions of the courts: an examination of attitudes toward the treatment of victims and accused', *Canadian Journal of Criminology*, 41: 365–84.

Kelly, L., Lovett, J. and Regan, L. (2005) *A Gap or a Chasm? Attrition in Reported Rape Cases*, Home Office Research Study 293. London: Home Office Research and Statistics Directorate.

Kuttschreuter, M. and Wiegman, O. (1998) 'Crime prevention and the attitude toward the criminal justice system: the effects of a multimedia campaign', *Journal of Criminal Justice*, 26: 441–52.

Lambert, E. and Clarke, A. (2004) 'Crime, capital punishment, and knowledge: are criminal justice majors better informed than other majors about crime and capital punishment?', *Social Science Journal*, 41: 53–66.

Lees, S. (2002) *Carnal Knowledge: Rape on Trial*, revised edn. London: Women's Press.

McGarrell, E.F. and Sandys, M. (1996) 'The misperception of public opinion toward capital punishment', *American Behavioral Scientist*, 39: 500–13.

Matthews, R., Hancock, L. and Briggs, D. (2004) *Jurors' Perceptions, Understanding, Confidence and Satisfaction in the Jury System: A Study in Six Courts*, Findings 227. London: Home Office Research and Statistics Directorate.

Mattinson, J. and Mirrlees-Black, C. (2000) *Attitudes to Crime and Criminal Justice. Findings from the 1998 British Crime Survey*, Home Office Research Study 200. London: Home Office Research and Statistics Directorate.

Mirrlees-Black, C. (2001) *Confidence in the Criminal Justice System. Findings from the 2000 British Crime Survey*, Research Findings 137. London: Home Office Research and Statistics Directorate.

Myhill, A. and Allen, J. (2002) *Rape and Sexual Assault of Women: The Extent and Nature of the Problem*, Home Office Research Study 237. London: Home Office Research and Statistics Directorate.

Orth, U. (2002) 'Secondary victimization of crime victims by criminal proceedings', *Social Justice Research*, 15: 313–25.

Peffley, M. and Hurwitz, J. (2002) 'The racial components of "race-neutral" crime policy attitudes', *Political Psychology*, 23: 59–75.

Riley, H. (2006) 'Does the Extent and Means of Acquisition of Criminal Justice System Knowledge Predict an Individual's Confidence in the Criminal Justice System?' Unpublished Masters dissertation.

St Amand, M.D. and Zamble, E. (2001) 'Impact of information about sentencing decisions on public attitudes toward the criminal justice system', *Law and Human Behavior*, 25: 515–28.

Salisbury, H. (2004) *Public Attitudes to the Criminal Justice System: The Impact of Providing Information to British Crime Survey Respondents*, Home Office Online Report 64/04. London: Home Office Research and Statistics Directorate.

Sampson, R.J. and Bartusch, D.J. (1998) 'Legal cynicism and (subcultural?) tolerance of deviance: the neighborhood context of racial differences', *Law and Society Review*, 32: 777–804.

Sidanius, J., Mitchell, M., Haley, H. and Navarrete, C.D. (2006) 'Support for harsh criminal sanctions and criminal justice beliefs: a social dominance perspective', *Social Justice Research*, 19: 433–49.

Soss, J., Langbein, L. and Metelko, A.R. (2003) 'Why do white Americans support the death penalty?', *Journal of Politics*, 65: 397–421.

Sprott, J. and Doob, A.N. (1997) 'Fear, victimization, and attitudes to sentencing, the courts, and the police', *Canadian Journal of Criminology*, 39: 275–91.

Temkin, J. (2002) *Rape and the Legal Process*. Oxford: Oxford University Press.

Tversky, A. and Kahneman, D. (1974) 'Judgement under uncertainty: heuristics and biases', *Science*, 185: 1124–131.

Tversky, A. and Kahneman, D. (1982) 'Availability: a heuristic for judging frequency and probability', in D. Kahneman, P. Slovic and A. Tversky (eds), *Judgment Under Uncertainty: Heuristics and Biases*. Cambridge: Cambridge University Press.

Ullman, S.E. and Townsend, S.M. (2007) 'Barriers to working with sexual assault survivors: a qualitative study of rape crisis centre workers', *Violence Against Women*, 13: 412–43.

Unnever, J.D. and Cullen, F.T. (2007) 'Reassessing the racial divide in support for capital punishment: the continuing significance of race', *Journal of Research in Crime and Delinquency*, 44: 124–58.

Walby, S. and Allen, J. (2004) *Domestic Violence, Sexual Assault and Stalking: Findings from the British Crime Survey*, Home Office Research Study 276. London: Home Office Research and Statistics Directorate.

Walker, N. and Marsh, C. (1988) 'Does the severity of sentences affect public disapproval? An experiment in England', in N. Walker and M. Hough (eds), *Public Attitudes to Sentencing: Surveys From Five Countries*. Aldershot: Gower.

Wemmers, J.M. (1999) 'Victim notification and public support for the criminal justice system', *International Review of Victimology*, 6: 167–78.

Whitehead, E. (2001) *Witness Satisfaction: Findings from the Witness Satisfaction Survey 2000*, Home Office Research Study 230. London: Home Office Research and Statistics Directorate.

Whitehead, J.T. (1998) '"Good ol' boys" and the chair: death penalty attitudes of policy makers in Tennessee', *Crime and Delinquency*, 44: 245–356.

Wortley, S. (1996) 'Justice for all? Race and perceptions of bias in the Ontario criminal justice system – a Toronto survey', *Canadian Journal of Criminology*, 38: 439–67.

Zamble, E. and Kalm, K.L. (1990) 'General and specific measures of public attitudes toward sentencing', *Canadian Journal of Behavioural Science*, 22: 327–37.

Zhang, L., Messner, S.F. and Lu, Z. (1999) 'Public legal education and inmates' perceptions of the legitimacy of official punishment in China', *British Journal of Criminology*, 39: 433–49.

Chapter 4

The myth of public support for capital punishment

Francis T. Cullen, James D. Unnever,
Kristie R. Blevins, Jennifer A. Pealer,
Shannon A. Santana, Bonnie S. Fisher
and Brandon K. Applegate

Americans today are ... familiar with the battery of results flowing from social science investigation, of *knowing that the majority of the nation supports the death penalty* or that half of all marriages end in divorce ... . Public life is awash in statistics documenting phenomena as diverse as consumer confidence and religious faith ... . Despite our daily immersion in social data, we generally do not inquire into how certain kinds of facts have achieved their prominence, their stability, and their seeming inevitability in public life. (Igo 2007: 2–3, emphasis added)

In *The Averaged American*, Sarah Igo (2007) wonderfully details the emergence and eventual prominence of surveys in the United States. She recounts how opinion polls, in particular, have been used to present a portrait of 'what America thinks'. This mode of depicting 'the public' draws special legitimacy from its ostensible reliance on scientific techniques and from its ostensible ability to advance democracy by conveying the will of the nation's citizenry. But as Igo (2007) shows, this quest to capture what the 'average' or typical citizen believes is pregnant with the risk of reductionism, of obscuring opinion differences and privileging a single way of understanding the public will. In the end, prominent surveys must be seen not only as a reflection of what the public thinks but also as an independent force in constructing the extant social reality. 'A history of surveyors' instruments', observes Igo (2007: 22), 'helps us appreciate how influential they have been in bounding and enforcing perceptions of social reality across the last century.' In particular, 'polls reified ... the soundness of the majority view' (2007: 149).

Indeed, consider the quote from Igo's *The Averaged American* used to introduce this chapter. It is ironic that Igo falls victim to the very phenomenon she has studied – the opinion poll. She unthinkingly announces that 'Americans know' that 'the majority of the nation supports the death penalty'. In fairness to Igo, this is not a wild claim but reflects the seemingly reliable finding that major opinion polls regularly report in the media. Even so, her statement is problematic precisely because it accepts the standard polling data – such as that produced by the Gallup Poll – as fully accurate. Thus, throughout her book, Igo is painstakingly sensitive to the marginalisation of minority views and to their exclusion when pollsters have constructed who 'we' are. But here, her implicit conception of 'Americans' averages out minorities, in that she ignores that disaggregated data show that a majority of African Americans oppose the use of capital punishment – an issue we address ahead (Cochran and Chamlin 2006; Unnever and Cullen 2007a). Especially relevant to the concerns in the current project, she fails to question what is meant by 'support for capital punishment' and whether this complex life-and-death policy can be measured with a single and simple query, as does the Gallup Poll: 'Are you in favour of the death penalty for a person convicted of murder?'

We do not wish to unduly criticise Igo for her passing reference to opinions about capital punishment. But citing her comments does serve to highlight just how fully the 'fact' that 'Americans support the death penalty' has become part of the existing social reality – taken for granted even by a scholar, Igo, typically self-conscious about such easy pronouncements. In this context, we can state the purpose of the current project: to deconstruct this ingrained social reality – this 'myth' about the public's supposed ready embrace of capital punishment. We hope to unravel its limits and to suggest its disquieting consequences.

In titling this chapter, we use the term 'myth' not to suggest an absence of public sentiments favourable to executing murderers, but rather to argue against the undifferentiated view that 'Americans support the death penalty'. In so doing, we present data from a national survey and from the extant research revealing that public opinion about capital punishment is complex and contingent. If anything, the public in the United States appears ambivalent, if not uncertain, about the state's use of lethal force against offenders; it is also divided by race. This empirical reality is potentially consequential in combating discourse that cites 'what the public wants' to support current death penalty policies. Indeed, there is the very real risk that 'bad science' will result in 'bad democracy'. In a policy domain in which lives literally are at stake, there is thus a pressing need for more finely calibrated social science data to challenge prevailing myths and to enrich ongoing discussions about the wisdom of capital punishment.

Constructing a myth: the role of public opinion polls

Public opinion polls in the United States were an invention of the 1930s. The genius of the opinion poll was that it promised to merge science and democracy. In a large and heterogeneous nation, polls could use scientific techniques to assess the 'will of the people'. From amid all the social diversity, they were a tool for distilling what 'the public' – Americans as a nation – believed about pressing socio-political issues. As Igo (2007: 141) notes, 'pollsters could bestow the people with a unitary voice, describing survey findings not as how citizens articulated their diverse views, but as how "America speaks"'. The tendency, observes Igo (2007: 141), was to 'slide into singular thinking about "the public" – even though the viewpoint in question often expressed a bare majority of respondents'.

Polls had the special power of capturing 'the public's opinion' with a single number. In 1936, the Gallup Poll first probed views toward capital punishment (Zeisel and Gallup 1989). This initial survey reported that 59 per cent favoured the death penalty 'for a person convicted of murder'; 38 per cent opposed this sanction while just 3 per cent expressed 'no opinion' (Gallup Poll News Service 2006). Over the next seven decades, the Gallup Poll – and other national surveys similar to it – implicitly claimed to represent 'public opinion' simply by recording the 'favour' versus 'oppose' answers to a single question. For most of this time, a majority of Americans expressed support for the death penalty. But in the midst of the Civil Rights movement of the 1960s, support declined, and in May 1966 more respondents opposed (47 per cent) than supported (42 per cent) capital punishment. Soon thereafter, however, the poll numbers for those endorsing the death penalty rose steadily, moving from 50 per cent in 1972 to 66 per cent in 1981, to a peak of 80 per cent in 1994. Since that time, support has slipped, and it now hovers in the mid-60 per cent. In 2006, 65 per cent of the public favoured the death penalty versus 28 per cent who did not (Gallup Poll News Service

2006). Other polls revealed similar patterns and numbers (Cullen *et al.* 2000). For example, a 2003 Harris Poll asked, 'Do you believe in capital punishment, that is the death penalty, or are you opposed to it?' In response, 69 per cent of a national sample of adults supported capital punishment whereas 22 per cent did not; 9 per cent either were 'not sure' or refused to give an answer (Taylor 2004).

The responses to these polls created the widely-held belief that 'the public supports the death penalty'. On the surface, the science seems indisputable. Do not polls show that about two-thirds of Americans embrace capital punishment? Is this not what 'Americans think'? Indeed, the notion of the punitive American public has become a powerful reality. To see it as merely a socially constructed reality – to depict it as a 'myth' – on the surface seems foolhardy (see also Cullen *et al.* 1988).

As Gottschalk (2006) points out, prior to the 1970s, death penalty opinions captured by the national polls were not highly consequential because capital punishment was not a pressing political issue. For a confluence of reasons, this situation changed in the early 1970s. In part a reaction to the socially tumultuous 1960s, 'law and order' had become a salient political issue. In this context, the US Supreme Court's *Furman* v. *Georgia* decision in 1972, which declared capital punishment unconstitutional and vacated over 600 death sentences, assumed inordinate significance. Capital punishment was suddenly embraced as a key symbolic issue – a dividing line in the emerging culture war between liberals and conservatives. In the ensuing debate, a key contention was whether 'evolving standards of decency' would render this sanction as 'cruel and unusual punishment' and thus as inherently and forever unconstitutional (see Sarat and Vidmar 1976). In fact, in the *Furman* case, the 'dissenting justices denied that the American public had repudiated the death penalty' (Gottschalk 2006: 218). This assertion elevated the significance of public opinion; among other factors, it would be an arbiter of the death penalty's constitutionality. 'Even though *Furman* was a muddled decision', observes Gottschalk (2006: 218–19), 'it was pivotal in steering the debate in this direction because the fiercest opponents and proponents did agree on one thing: public sentiment was critical' (see also Mallicoat and Radelet 2004; Roberts and Stalans 1997: 226).

At this critical juncture, the science of polling and democracy intersected in a consequential way. National opinion surveys, such as the Gallup Poll, seemed to settle the issue. Again, these polls had gained considerable legitimacy, implicitly promoting the view that public sentiments on key policy issues could be captured with a single question and the reporting of a single statistic (Igo 2007). This practice was not depicted in the media as hopelessly reductionistic but as an accurate portrayal of the will of the people. And in the aftermath of the *Furman* decision, the trend in public support for capital punishment (as noted above) appeared clear: it was on a steep upward trajectory (Rankin 1979; Zeisel and Gallup 1989). Thus, between March and November 1972, support jumped from 50 per cent to 57 per cent. By 1976, it was up to 66 per cent and by 1985 it had climbed to 75 per cent (Gallup Poll News Service 2006; see also Zeisel and Gallup 1989). These numbers thus reified the conclusion that 'Americans support the death penalty'. Indeed, many elected officials – especially Democrats – came to see opposing the death penalty as politically dangerous. As Firestone (2003: 5) notes, the 'Republican Party has long favoured executions and can point to national opinion polls showing three-quarters of Americans supporting capital punishment.'

The difficulty, however, is that this ostensible empirical reality is, in large part, a social construction of reality that rests on a shaky methodological artifact (Murray 2003; Niven 2002; see also Chapter 5, this volume, for an in-depth discussion of methodological issues). The bias – and arrogant danger – of the national opinion poll is the implicit assumption that the public will can be deduced through one question – or, at most, a few questions. What the consuming public is not told is that, in the case of capital punishment, only a slice of public thinking is captured by this methodology. In general, simple or single items tend to measure 'global attitudes' – overall, initial impressions. These attitudes are not false, given that knee-jerk reactions are, after all, still reactions. They may even inform voting decisions on broadly worded propositions (such as supporting 'three-strikes-and-you're-out' legislation that imposes life in prison for a third conviction). But as growing public opinion research has amply demonstrated, it is erroneous – a 'myth' to use our terminology – to assume that diverse, complex realities can be assessed so curtly. When more detailed questions are asked – when respondents are given more policy options and more information – their assessment of a policy, including the death penalty, takes on a new shape. Most often, information and deliberation lead citizens to a more nuanced, less punitive response (Applegate *et al.* 1996; Cullen *et al.* 2000; Hough and Roberts 1998; Murray 2003; Roberts and Stalans 1997).

In short, in cases of life and death – which is what the policy of capital punishment entails – it is problematic to boldly assume, based on polls reported in the media, that 'two in three' or 'the majority' of Americans favour state-imposed lethal sanctions. Such hubris is unwarranted because it is, in the end, unscientific. As we will see, the American public is far more uncertain about the death penalty than is commonly imagined.

Public uncertainty about capital punishment

Given the role of standard national public opinion polls in lending legitimacy to the constitutionality of capital punishment, scholars soon began to question the scientific adequacy of these surveys (see, for example, Ellsworth and Ross 1983; Harris 1986). This research showed that public sentiments were often based on faulty information and on 'emotion and symbolic attitudes' as opposed to 'rational reflection' (Roberts and Stalans 1997: 229). It also revealed that support for the death penalty was not rock solid but rather could decline markedly when the respondents were asked to consider different types of murders and types of offenders (e.g. juveniles and the mentally retarded) (Cullen *et al.* 2000; Roberts and Stalans 1997). Most instructive for the purposes of the current project (as we will see shortly), studies found that people's punitiveness was affected dramatically by the sentencing options presented to them. In particular, survey respondents often relinquished support for the death penalty when given the alternative of sentencing a convicted murderer to 'life in prison without the possibility of parole'.

More recently, another issue has become central in the debate over capital punishment: the possibility of putting innocent people to death. Largely due to advances in analysing DNA evidence, it became possible to demonstrate definitively that a person in prison – including on death row – was innocent of the crimes for which he or she had been convicted. Such evidence has now been used to free 200 offenders from US prisons. These offenders had spent an average of 12 years behind bars; 14 were on death row (Conway 2007). The very real prospect that an innocent person was executed in the past and could be executed in the future has the potential to undermine confidence in capital punishment.

Below, we use data from a national survey to show how the issues of sentencing alternatives and executing the innocent create uncertainty in support for the death penalty. Again, the purpose of this investigation is to illuminate the mythological status of the unqualified, reified view that 'Americans support the death penalty'.

The National Crime Policy Survey

In 2001, we conducted the National Crime Policy Survey (for a description, see Cullen *et al*. 2002; Cullen *et al*. 2007). Survey Sampling, Inc. provided a simple random sample of 1,000 phone and non-phone households, drawn from America's 50 states and the District of Columbia. The survey methodology was informed by Dillman's (1978) 'Total Design Method' and involved sending three waves of surveys, a pre-contact and reminder letter, a telephone reminder and a token (a free pen) for participation. Despite these efforts, participation in the study was limited. In all, 123 surveys were undeliverable due to invalid addresses. Of the eligible respondents, 349 surveys were returned, a response rate of 40 per cent. Of these, 329 surveys were usable.

The modest response rate raises concerns about the generalisability of the results. Two considerations, however, obviate these initial worries. First, the results to questions on the survey instrument regarding a range of crime-related policies are generally consistent with findings from the extant literature (Cullen *et al*. 2002; Cullen *et al*. 2007). In short, the sample's opinions seem 'normal' rather than counter-intuitive or inexplicable. Second, and relevant to the current study, the demographic composition of the sample would not obviously bias the responses against support for the death penalty; if anything, the sample's characteristics would make them more disposed to favour capital punishment. Thus, the sample appears to be disproportionately older (mean age 54.7), male (66.4 per cent), white (83.3 per cent) and Republican (38.1 per cent versus 26.9 per cent Independent and 34.9 per cent Democrat). Although the existing results are not always consistent, these characteristics tend to be either unrelated to or associated with higher levels of punitiveness (Applegate 1997; Unnever and Cullen 2007a).

The National Crime Policy Survey included a section devoted specifically to capital punishment. The section began with the following note to the respondents: 'Recently, there has been much attention given to the use of the death penalty in the United States. We would like to learn more about your opinion on this important matter.' The questions were mainly designed to explore two issues: first, whether giving the sentencing alternative of 'life in prison without the possibility of parole' would reduce support for the death penalty; and, second, how recent revelations of innocent offenders on death row might affect public opinion in this area (see Table 4.1). These questions and the responses to them will be discussed below.

Table 4.1 Public support for capital punishment versus life in prison without the possibility of parole (percentages reported)

Question	Percentage
Global question: Do you generally favor or oppose capital punishment – that is, the death penalty – in cases where people are convicted of murder?	
A. Strongly favor the death penalty	39.3
B. Somewhat favor the death penalty	34.7
C. Somewhat oppose the death penalty	12.7
D. Strongly oppose the death penalty	13.3
Alternatives to capital punishment questions: Some legislators are suggesting that capital punishment be replaced with the sentence of *life in prison without the possibility of parole* (that is, the offender would *never* be released from prison). Which option, then, would you generally favor for people convicted of murder?	
A. The death penalty	53.5
B. Life in prison without the possibility of parole	46.5
Another proposal is to replace the death penalty with life in prison without parole *and make the offender work in prison and pay money back to the victim's family.* Which option, then, would you generally favor for people convicted of murder?	
A. The death penalty	39.0
B. Life in prison without the possibility of parole and the offender works to pay back the victim's family	61.0

Overall support for capital punishment

To assess global support for the death penalty, the respondents were asked a question that mirrored the traditional Gallup Poll query of whether they supported the death penalty for those 'convicted of murder'. As can be seen from Table 4.1, 74.0 per cent of the respondents said that they either 'strongly favor' (39.3 per cent) or 'somewhat favor' (34.7 per cent) the death penalty. These results suggest that the members of the sample expressed punitive sentiments that rivalled or surpassed those of respondents in other polls. For example, in two Gallup Polls conducted in 2001, the percentage favouring capital punishment was 67 per cent (in February) and 68 per cent (in October) (Gallup Poll News Service 2006). Similarly, a 2001 Harris Poll found that 67 per cent of those surveyed said that they 'believed in' capital punishment (Taylor 2004).

At first glance, it appears that our data support the often-announced conclusion that 'the American public supports the death penalty'. However, an initial crack in this wall of public support can be seen when examining the degree to which the respondents endorse this sanction. Unlike most national polls, we did not measure 'support' with a dichotomous 'favor versus oppose' response set. Instead, four gradational choices were provided: 'strongly favor', 'somewhat favor', 'somewhat oppose' or 'strongly oppose' the death penalty. As can be seen in Table 4.1, this measurement strategy reveals that only four in ten sample members stated that they 'strongly favored' capital punishment. Framed in this way, six in ten respondents either opposed or only weakly embraced the execution of convicted murderers (see also Unnever *et al.* 2005).

To be sure, advocates and opponents of capital punishment could quibble over what these results mean. But that is the point. Once a more refined methodology is employed, the 'reality' that is depicted is blurred and thus is open to debate. It is possible to assert that nearly three in four in the sample favoured the death penalty or, by contrast, to point out that a clear majority did not strongly embrace this sanction. Reality is thus revealed as multifaceted and open to interpretation. The challenge is to employ more finely calibrated methods. And when this is done, Americans' support for capital punishment is shown to be contingent, not rigid, and to move oftentimes in a less punitive direction.

Considering alternative sanctions: life in prison without parole

Opinion polls contain a fundamental though typically overlooked flaw: the 'favour' response identifies precisely what sanction the murderer will receive (death), whereas the 'oppose' response leaves the nature of the subsequent penalty unspecified and open to speculation. For some respondents, the 'oppose' option is a good thing; it means that a life will not be taken by the state, which to them is a worthy end in and of itself. But for others answering a survey, saying that they 'oppose' a death sentence means that a convicted murderer might serve an inappropriately short prison term and perhaps be released into society 'to kill again'. For respondents wishing to avoid injustice to the victim and any untoward threat to public safety, the 'favour' response has a clear advantage: it ensures that the murderer will receive just deserts and never take another life.

As a result, the percentage of the respondents in a poll who favour the death penalty is likely to be artificially inflated by this methodological artifact. But what if the alternative to capital punishment was not simply 'oppose' but clearly spelled out? What if a respondent could choose between the death penalty and the next most severe sanction – 'life in prison without possibility of parole'? Might the percentage of the public expressing a preference for capital punishment decline?

Researchers have investigated this very issue (Cullen *et al.* 2000). The strategy has been first to ask the respondents if they favour the death penalty and then to see if they prefer this lethal sanction as opposed to (1) a life sentence without parole and (2) a life sentence without parole plus the offender working to pay restitution to the victim's family. The results across a variety of states and for both adult and juvenile offenders are remarkably consistent. When given an alternative sanction, support for capital punishment declines markedly. When selecting between the death penalty and life with no parole, support for capital punishment decreases to the point where the sample is nearly evenly split (usually, support for executing convicted murderers remains slightly higher). However, when the choice is between the death penalty and no parole plus restitution, a clear majority of the sample favours the non-death penalty option. As Bowers *et al.* (1994: 149) note, 'people will accept the death penalty unless or until they can have an alternative they want more' (see also Bohm *et al.* 1990; Cochran *et al.* 2003; Doble Research Associates 2004; Fox *et al.* 1990–1991; McGarrell and Sandys 1996; Moon *et al.* 2000; Vogel 2003; Vogel and Vogel 2003).

In our 2001 survey, we replicated these previous studies using a national sample. As reported in Table 4.1, the results closely align with the extant research findings. Although 74.0 per cent of the sample favoured the death penalty on the global question, support declined to just over half when the respondents could choose between 'the death penalty' (53.5 per cent) and 'life in prison without the possibility of parole' (46.5 per cent). When restitution was integrated into the no-parole option, a sufficient number of sample members switched preferences so that this non-death-penalty option was endorsed by six in ten respondents. Again, these results are consistent with previous research.

It would be erroneous to assume that the public would always choose the no-parole-restitution sentence over the death penalty. Support for this penalty might well dissipate if individuals were asked what sentence they preferred for an offender guilty of an especially heinous murder (see also Durham *et al.* 1996). Nonetheless, these findings suggest that members of the public are not wed inalterably to imposing lethal sanctions. Many might well prefer to spare an offender's life if they were assured that this person were never to walk the streets again. And others may prefer to avoid the death penalty if an offender's life could be put to good use and serve a higher purpose. In short, the findings illuminate that the level of support for capital punishment – for all its emotive and symbolic sources – also is reasoned and will change depending on the choices that are presented. Bowers *et al.* (1994: 142–3, 146) state the matter more forcefully:

These data suggest that public support for capital punishment is an illusion that has become a self-perpetuating political myth ... for a number of reasons: Pollsters have rested their assumptions on a single, misleading indicator of death penalty support; the media have reported this interpretation without reservations, qualifications or caveats; and politicians have used death penalty advocacy to capitalize on the public's fear of crime ... . The prevailing illusion of widespread, deep-seated public support for capital punishment has obscured this reality and its implication for change.

Second thoughts: the prospect of innocence

In the 1990s, the legitimacy of capital punishment was increasingly challenged by repeated revelations of innocent Americans sent to prison and to death row. In a study that spanned from 1989 to 2003, Gross *et al.* (2005) uncovered 340 cases in which convicted men (n = 327) and women (n = 13) were exonerated. More than half of this group had spent at least ten years in prison, while 80 per cent had served a term of at least five years. DNA evidence had been used to clear 114 individuals – a figure that has since climbed to 200 (Conway 2007; Gross *et al.* 2005). Of the 340 cases, most were in prison for rape (n = 121) or murder (n = 204). Notably, 74 individuals were under a death sentence (Gross *et al.* 2005: 529).

The steady stream of exonerated inmates saved from the death chamber and released from prison forced three stark conclusions. First, without concerted intervention by 'innocence projects' and teams of lawyers – and the advent of DNA evidence – tens of innocent people would have been executed. Second, in the absence of effective efforts at exoneration, many innocents in the past must have perished at the hands of the legal machinery; to argue otherwise strains credulity. Third, many more less fortunate innocents – either lacking effective counsel or for whom DNA evidence is unavailable – likely sit on death row and face execution. These disquieting realities make poignant the late Marvin Wolfgang's admonition that, with regard to capital punishment, the ethical and policy question is not '"Who deserves to die?" but rather "Who deserves to kill?"' (cited in Radelet and Borg 2000: 53).

This question emerged as especially salient in the state of Illinois where, in January 2000, Republican Governor George H. Ryan declared a moratorium on executions (Warden 2005). Two years later, the state of Maryland would do the same (Gottschalk 2006). After the *Furman* v. *Georgia* case in 1972, 18 of the 289 defendants sentenced to death in Illinois would eventually be exonerated and released. Three were exonerated in the first part of Governor Ryan's term in office (Warden 2005). Facing the reality that innocent people were being sent to death row, Ryan halted executions and appointed a 'fourteen-member Commission on Capital Punishment ... to review the administration of the capital punishment process in Illinois and recommend ways to improve the fairness and accuracy of the process' (Warden 2005: 407). A poll showed that 70 per cent of the state's residents approved of Ryan's actions (Warden 2005: 406). On 11 January 2003, saying that 'our capital system is haunted by the demon of error', Ryan took the next step of commuting the death sentences of all inmates under death sentences in Illinois – 167 individuals (Hall 2005: 371). As Hall (2005: 371-2) notes:

> This was arguably the most significant moment in the recent history of the capital punishment debate. Not since the landmark Supreme Court case of *Furman* v. *Georgia* had so many death sentences been set aside in a single instant, and never had an executive issued such a sweeping act of clemency in the death penalty context.

In short, the issue of innocence – the increasing evidence that people who had committed no crime would inevitably end up on death row – burst on the national scene and seemingly created second thoughts about the wisdom of capital punishment (see Prejean 2005). As just reviewed, these second thoughts were most apparent in Illinois. But would these doubts extend beyond this one state that was moved to action by highly publicised exonerations and a proactive governor? The responses to questions on our National Crime Policy Survey in 2001 suggest that, indeed, they have (see also Doble Research Associates 2004; Vollum *et al.* 2004).

As seen in Table 4.2, nearly three in four of the respondents favoured suspending the death penalty in light of the fact that DNA evidence had exonerated innocent capital defendants. Similarly, when asked to choose between an Illinois-type death penalty suspension or continuing to execute offenders on the presumption that no innocent people had been executed, nearly seven in ten favoured halting the 'death penalty until we can make sure that only guilty people are executed'. Finally, the respondents were asked how evidence that an innocent person had been executed would affect their view of the death penalty. A sizable minority – 41.9 per cent – would continue to endorse capital punishment 'even if this means executing an innocent person once in a great while'. But 39.0 per cent stated that 'I would have to oppose the death penalty', suggesting that concerns over innocence may depress support for this sanction (see also Unnever and Cullen 2005). And when combined with those who already have rejected capital punishment, a clear majority of the sample would be against future executions.

It would be an exaggeration to suggest that the United States is on the precipice of a complete transformation in public opinion about capital punishment. With regard to innocence, favouring a moratorium on executions is not the same as favouring the abolition of the death penalty. Implicit in endorsing a suspension is the view that the sanction would be reinstituted once adequate safeguards were in place – assuming that the prevention of error and the irrevocable execution of the innocent were ever feasible. Still, the issues of innocence and of how to deal with an inherently fallible machinery of justice reveal that the majority of Americans do not blindly embrace the death penalty. When asked to consider the reality of exonerations and to deliberate on the prospect of wrongfully executing a defendant, they pause and have second thoughts. Again, the point is that death penalty attitudes are not carved permanently in stone but are contingent. When faced with disquieting evidence, many Americans display uncertainty about capital punishment. In fact, the strong majority would prefer a moratorium to sort matters out to a continuation of a flawed execution process. This multifaceted perspective on the ultimate penalty is missed by polls that ask a

Table 4.2 Public support for suspending capital punishment and perceptions of innocence (percentages reported)

Question	Percentage
Suspend the death penalty: In several instances, criminals sentenced to be executed have been released based on new evidence or DNA testing. Based on this information, would you favor suspending the death penalty – not executing anyone for a limited period of time – until its fairness is studied?	
A. No	26.1
B. Yes	73.9
Suspend the death penalty in Illinois: Recently, the Governor of Illinois temporarily suspended the use of the death penalty because a number of people on Death Row who could have been executed were later proven to be innocent. In other states – such as Texas – the governors have not suspended the death penalty, saying that no innocent people have been executed in their states. Which position do you think is right?	
A. Temporarily suspend the death penalty until we can make sure that only guilty people are executed.	69.1
B. Keep executing convicted murderers because it is unlikely that any innocent people are really on Death Row.	30.9
Impact of executing an innocent citizen: If it were proven *absolutely* that an *innocent* person had been put to death for a crime they did not commit, *how would this affect your view of the death penalty?*	
A. I would continue to support the death penalty – it is better to execute convicted murderers, even if this means executing an innocent person once in a great while.	41.9
B. I would have to oppose the death penalty – if the death penalty means putting even one innocent person to death, we would be better off just giving all murderers life in prison.	39.0
C. I already oppose the death penalty.	19.2*

*Due to rounding, the total exceeds 100 per cent.

single 'favour–oppose' question and claim that Americans 'support the death penalty'.

Who really supports capital punishment? The question of race

As Igo (2007: 118) observes, from its inception the opinion poll was justified as a 'tool for democracy' – as a scientific means of discerning the people's will on policy issues. But in seeking to capture a single voice of the 'American public', pollsters often ignored the views of the disadvantaged. Early polls under-represented African Americans, instead falling 'back on the template of a white, educated, male populace when they set out in search of "the public"' (Igo 2007: 138). Equally problematic, the presentation of aggregated data to represent what 'the average American' believed glossed over differences rooted in race, class and gender. 'Social factors and social structures', notes Igo (2007: 140), 'were usually invisible in surveyors' presentation of their results, if not in the making of the polls.'

This problem has been particularly consequential with regard to death penalty attitudes where, as we will see shortly, white and African American sentiments diverge dramatically. Presenting an overall percentage – such as '66 per cent of Americans favour capital punishment' – is tantamount to presenting what whites in the US endorse, because the voices of minorities are muted – or statistically averaged out – due to their comparatively small numbers in the sample. In a democratic system, however, these voices should be heard, especially given that race is so deeply implicated in the justice system. African Americans comprise 12 per cent of the US's population but 42 per cent of those under a sentence of death (Snell 2006). In Gross et al.'s (2005: 547) study described above, 50 per cent of those exonerated between 1989 and 2004 on murder charges were black; the number climbed to 64 per cent for those charged with and incarcerated for rape. And as Steiker and Steiker (2005: 590) remind us, the death penalty has 'occupied a peculiar – and undoubtedly significant – role in American race relations. The American death penalty has disproportionately targeted African American offenders ... and executions (including extralegal executions – lynchings) have been an important mechanism for subordinating African Americans.' Blacks thus may have reason to fear the state's use of its most lethal sanction (Unnever and Cullen 2007a; Unnever et al., forthcoming; see also Prejean 2005). Not surprisingly, research reveals that compared to whites, African Americans are far more likely to believe that the US legal system is unjust (see, for example, Hagan and Albonetti 1982; Henderson *et al.* 1997).

The racial divide in support for capital punishment

There is now a substantial body of evidence showing that race is a robust predictor of death penalty attitudes (for a summary, see Unnever *et al.* forthcoming; see also Bobo and Johnson 2004). In multivariate analyses, 'being white' is positively and significantly related to support for capital punishment. This 'racial divide' persists even when a range of factors known to predict death penalty attitudes is systematically controlled (Cochran and Chamlin 2006; Unnever and Cullen 2007a).

Even more revealing, however, are statistics describing how large the gap is between white and black Americans. When national polling data are analysed by race, they typically show that African Americans' support for the death penalty is in the vicinity of 30 percentage points lower (Unnever *et al.* forthcoming). This divide has persisted for over three decades. Further, although the percentage of African Americans favouring the death penalty has occasionally crept above 50 per cent, in many years this has not been not the case. Recent Gallup polling data show that in 2006, only 43 per cent of blacks supported capital punishment; the comparable figure for whites was 70 per cent (Unnever *et al.* forthcoming; see also Saad 2007).

Note that for the entire adult sample – which includes blacks and whites – the Gallup Poll data from 2006 showed that 66 per cent favoured capital punishment, a finding that seemingly confirms that 'two-thirds of Americans support the death penalty'. But as we have just seen, this reading of the data is misleading. By focusing on what the 'average American' thinks, it masks the underlying racial conflict that exists. In this instance, averaging responses across the races privileges white views and silences black views. A reality is socially constructed that reifies the conclusion that 'Americans' endorse capital punishment. A more accurate and politically charged conclusion, however, would be: 'White Americans favour the death penalty; African Americans, who historically have been disproportionately put to death by the state, do not.'

It is noteworthy that the data from our 2001 study also support the finding of a clear racial divide in death penalty attitudes. Due to the small number of African Americans in the sample (n = 26), establishing reliable absolute percentages is difficult (e.g. percentages can fluctuate markedly when only a few respondents answer one way or the other). Still, the general pattern found in the Gallup Poll obtains. Whereas 77.0 per cent of the white respondents said that they 'strongly' or 'somewhat' favoured the death penalty, the comparable statistic for African Americans in the study was 50.0 per cent. Similar to previous studies, this shows a 27.0 per cent divide between the races in their support for capital punishment.

Which whites support capital punishment: the role of racial animus

The conclusion that 'Americans favour the death penalty' is further complicated by the fact that a key source underlying white support for state executions is animosity toward blacks. Scholars have used different terms to describe these negative, hostile feelings toward African Americans. Some use the term 'racial animus', others use the term 'racial resentment', and others more bluntly, but perhaps more accurately, describe it as 'white racism'. Regardless, the research is clear in showing that racial animus is a strong predictor of white support for capital punishment (see, for example, Barkan and Cohn 1994; Bobo and Johnson 2004; Soss *et al.* 2003; Unnever and Cullen 2007b; Unnever *et al.* 2005).

Equally instructive is how support for the death penalty is reconstructed when 'white racists' are removed from 'the American public'. Using 2002 General Social Survey data, Barkan and Cohn (2005: 41–2) note that 75.4 per cent of those who evidenced racial prejudice favoured capital punishment versus 59.0 per cent of those who did not. The combined percentage supporting the death penalty for non-prejudiced whites and African Americans was only 56.5. Although still a majority, this level of majority support is modest rather than seemingly incontrovertibly strong and thus places the policy of state executions on shakier grounds. Further, given that the constitutionality of the death penalty has been justified by the US Supreme Court as meeting 'evolving standards of decency' embraced by citizens, it will perhaps give jurists reason to pause when they consider that a key source of these standards is, ironically, indecent sentiments of racial animus (Unnever and Cullen 2007b: 1293).

Implications for Europe

In most respects, the issue of capital punishment in Europe is settled. All members of the European Union have abolished the death penalty, and any country seeking to be a member state cannot retain the sanction (Hill 2003; Radelet and Borg 2000). Capital punishment is now conceived by political elites as a violation of fundamental human rights and as antithetical to the essence of European citizenship (Hill 2003). At this time, there appears to be scant prospect of the death penalty being reinstituted.

Public opinion about capital punishment, however, is less settled. When nations such as Great Britain, France, and the Federal Republic of Germany abolished the death penalty, about two-thirds of each nation's populace opposed the policy shift (Steiker 2002). The subsequent decline in public support for state executions appears to have occurred as the result of, rather than the cause of, the abolition movement (Steiker 2002). Still, even today, there is a reservoir of popular sentiments amenable to capital punishment; in most European nations, it appears that, at the least, a sizable minority endorses using the death penalty on a global level (Hill 2003). Thus, a 1997 British poll found that 48 per cent either 'agreed' or 'strongly agreed' that 'Britain should bring back the death penalty', whereas a 1992 Spanish poll discovered that 47 per cent favoured reinstatement of the death penalty (Unnever *et al.* forthcoming). More recently, a 2006 national survey of 1,000 respondents in France reported that 42 per cent endorsed re-establishing capital punishment (TNS Sofres 2006).

Further, although the analysis is preliminary, Unnever *et al.* (forthcoming) have shown that, similar to the US, racial and ethnic animus predicts support for capital punishment in samples drawn from France, Great Britain, and Spain. This finding takes on significance given the extensive, if not growing, prejudice across Europe toward immigrants who differ racially and ethnically from the native-born citizenry (Pettigrew 1998; see also Tonry 1997). If animosity toward immigrants were to expand – for example, due to a string of terrorist attacks – it is conceivable that public opinion favourable to the death penalty could rise commensurately. Right-wing political groups could seek to capitalise on these sentiments by promising to reintroduce the death penalty to deal with the 'immigrant criminal threat'. Even if this policy were thwarted – as it likely would be – criminal justice penalties generally could shift decidedly in a punitive direction as progressive politicians scrambled to show the public that, despite their opposition to capital punishment, they were equally prepared to 'get tough on street crime'. In short, attitudes toward capital punishment could provide a context for broader political disputes that could lead to harsher sentencing policies (see Gottschalk 2006).

Conclusion: deconstructing the punitive public

The retention of capital punishment in the US – despite the abolition of the death penalty in most other western nations (Hill 2003) – is often referred to as a case of 'American exceptionalism' (Steiker 2002). The embrace of state executions is especially disquieting given that, as Steiker (2002: 97) points out, fellow world leaders in capital punishment in recent years 'are among the least democratic and worst human rights abusers in the world ... China, Iran, and Saudi Arabia' – nations that the US would not typically identify as sharing its core political and social values (see also Radelet and Borg 2000). Even so, 'American exceptionalism' should not mask the substantial 'American ambivalence' that surrounds the death penalty. In recent years, the annual number of executions in the US has been declining (Fagan and West 2005); in 2005, only 60 people were executed (Snell 2006), a figure which fell even further to 53 in 2006 (Tanner 2007). Equally instructive, since the death penalty was reinstated in 1976, the yearly number of executed offenders never surpassed 98 – a peak reached in 1999. It should also be recalled that thirteen states, including New Jersey in 2007, and the District of Columbia have abolished capital punishment. Of the other 38 states, only 16 held an execution in 2005. The use of the death penalty has been further circumscribed by US Supreme Court rulings declaring as unconstitutional the execution of the mentally retarded and juveniles under the age of 18 (Fagan and West 2005).

In this context, it is perhaps not surprising to discover that American public support for capital punishment is not high and intractable but contingent and malleable. Thus, we have shown that methodology matters – that when sentencing alternatives are contained in a survey, support for capital punishment declines markedly. We have shown as well that Americans are concerned about executing innocent offenders and are fully prepared to place a moratorium on the death penalty until it can be undertaken without mistake. And we have shown that no portrayal of 'Americans' support for the death penalty' will be accurate if the views of African Americans are washed out by the larger proportion of white respondents in any nationally 'representative' sample. We have seen that there is a clear racial divide, with blacks more likely to oppose the death penalty and whites – especially those harbouring racial animus – more likely to embrace the sanction.

Taken together, these observations confirm the conclusion that unerring American public support for capital punishment is a 'myth'.

Myths are potentially powerful, consequential social constructions of reality, especially when they derive legitimacy from a scientific enterprise. In the US, polling data have been used to justify capital punishment as an expression of the public will and to lure elected officials to support the policy of state executions. Bad science has thus led to bad democracy and has helped place the US at odds with the evolving international standards of decency and human rights. Indeed, the reified, widely-publicised view that 'two-thirds of Americans support capital punishment' undoubtedly has contributed to the deaths of defendants – most certainly guilty of their crimes, some perhaps not. With lives on the line, this myth merits systematic deconstruction. The continuing challenge is for researchers to present a nuanced, accurate picture of death penalty attitudes – one that does not cavalierly ignore genuine punitive sentiments but also one that illuminates the deep pockets of uncertainty Americans have about putting fellow citizens to death.

References

Applegate, B.K. (1997) 'Public Support for Rehabilitation: A Factorial Survey Approach'. Unpublished dissertation, University of Cincinnati.

Applegate, B.K., Cullen, F.T., Turner, M.G. and Sundt, J.L. (1996) 'Assessing public support for three-strikes-and-you're-out laws: global versus specific attitudes', *Crime and Delinquency*, 42 (4): 517–34.

Barkan, S.E. and Cohn, S.F. (1994) 'Racial prejudice and support for the death penalty by whites', *Journal of Research in Crime and Delinquency*, 31 (2): 202–9.

Barkan, S.E. and Cohn, S.F. (2005) 'On reducing white support for the death penalty: a pessimistic appraisal', *Criminology and Public Policy*, 4 (1): 39–44.

Bobo, L.D. and Johnson, D. (2004) 'A taste for punishment: black and white Americans' views on the death penalty and the war on drugs', *Du Bois Review*, 1 (1): 151–80.

Bohm, R.M., Flanagan, T.J. and Harris, P.W. (1990) 'Current death penalty opinion in New York State', *Albany Law Review*, 54 (3/4): 819–43.

Bowers, W.J., Vandiver, M. and Dugan, P.H. (1994) 'A new look at public opinion on capital punishment: what citizens and legislators prefer', *American Journal of Criminal Law*, 22 (1): 77–150.

Cochran, J.K. and Chamlin, M.B. (2006) 'The enduring racial divide in death penalty support', *Journal of Criminal Justice*, 34 (1): 85–99.

Cochran, J.K., Boots, D.P. and Heide, K.M. (2003) 'Attribution styles and attitudes toward capital punishment for juveniles, the mentally incompetent, and the mentally retarded', *Justice Quarterly*, 20 (1): 65–93.

Conway, C. (2007) 'The DNA 200', *New York Times*, 20 May, p. 14.

Cullen, F.T., Cullen, J.B. and Wozniak, J.F. (1988) 'Is rehabilitation dead? The myth of the punitive public', *Journal of Criminal Justice*, 16 (4): 303–17.

Cullen, F.T., Fisher, B.S. and Applegate, B.K. (2000) 'Public opinion about punishment and corrections', in M. Tonry (ed.), *Crime and Justice: A Review of Research*, Vol. 27. Chicago: University of Chicago Press, pp. 1–79.

Cullen, F.T., Pealer, J.A., Fisher, B.S., Applegate, B.K. and Santana, S.A. (2002) 'Public support for correctional rehabilitation in America: change or consistency?', in J.V. Roberts and M. Hough (eds), *Changing Attitudes to Punishment: Public Opinion, Crime and Justice*. Cullompton: Willan, pp. 128–47.

Cullen, F.T., Pealer, J.A., Santana, S.A., Fisher, B.S., Applegate, B.K. and Blevins, K.R. 2007 'Public support for faith-based correctional programs: should sacred places serve civic purposes?', *Journal of Offender Treatment*, 45 (3/4): 29–46.

Dillman, D.A. (1978) *Mail and Telephone Surveys: The Total Design Method*. New York: John Wiley.

Doble Research Associates (2004) *The Death Penalty in North Carolina: The Public Considers the Options*. Englewood Cliffs, NJ: Doble Research Associates.

Durham, A.M., Elrod, P. and Kinkade, P.T. (1996) 'Public support for the death penalty: beyond Gallup', *Justice Quarterly*, 13 (4): 705–36.

Ellsworth, P.C. and Ross, L. (1983) 'Public opinion and capital punishment: a close examination of the views of abolitionists and retentionists', *Crime and Delinquency*, 29 (1): 116–69.

Fagan, J. and West, V. (2005) 'The decline of the juvenile death penalty: scientific evidence of evolving norms', *Journal of Criminal Law and Criminology*, 95 (2): 427–97.

Firestone, D. (2003) 'Absolutely, positively for capital punishment', *New York Times*, 19 January, p. 5.

Fox, J.A., Radelet, M.L. and Bonsteel, J.L. (1990–1) 'Death penalty opinion in the post-*Furman* years', *New York University Review of Law and Social Change*, 18 (2): 499–528.

Gallup Poll News Service (2006) *The Gallup Poll: Death Penalty*. Princeton, NJ: Gallup Organization.

Gottschalk, M. (2006) *The Prison and the Gallows: The Politics of Mass Incarceration in America*. New York: Cambridge University Press.

Gross, S.R., Jacoby, K., Matheson, D.J., Montgomery, N. and Patil, S. (2005) 'Exonerations in the United States, 1989 through 2003', *Journal of Criminal Law and Criminology*, 95 (2): 523–60.

Hagan, J. and Albonetti, C. (1982) 'Race, class, and the perception of criminal injustice in America', *American Journal of Sociology*, 88 (2): 329–55.

Hall, B.R. (2005) 'From William Henry Furman to Anthony Porter: the changing face of the death penalty debate', *Journal of Criminal Law and Criminology*, 95 (2): 371–80.

Harris, P.W. (1986) 'Over-simplification and error in public opinion surveys on capital punishment', *Justice Quarterly*, 3 (4): 429–55.

Henderson, M.L., Cullen, F.R., Cao, L., Browning, S.L. and Kopache, R. (1997) 'The impact of race on perceptions of criminal injustice,' *Journal of Criminal Justice*, 26 (6): 1–16.

Hill, G. (2003) 'The death penalty: a European view', *Corrections Compendium*, 28 (3): 8–9.

Hough, H. and Roberts J. (1998) *Attitudes to Punishment: Findings from the British Crime Survey.* London: Home Office.

Igo, S.E. (2007) *The Averaged American: Surveys, Citizens, and the Making of a Mass Public.* Cambridge, MA: Harvard University Press.

McGarrell, E.F. and Sandys, M. (1996) 'The misperception of public opinion toward capital punishment', *American Behavioral Scientist*, 39 (4): 500–13.

Mallicoat, S.L. and Radelet, M.L. (2004) 'From the field: the growing significance of public opinion for death penalty jurisprudence', *Journal of Crime and Justice*, 27 (1): 119–30.

Moon, M.M., Wright, J.P., Cullen, F.T. and Pealer, J.A. (2000) 'Putting kids to death: specifying public support for juvenile capital punishment', *Justice Quarterly*, 17 (4): 663–84.

Murray, G.R. (2003) 'Raising considerations: public opinion and the fair application of the death penalty', *Social Science Quarterly*, 84 (4): 753–70.

Niven, D. (2002) 'Bolstering an illusory majority: the effects of the media's portrayal of death penalty support', *Social Science Quarterly*, 83 (3): 671–89.

Pettigrew, T.F. (1998) 'Reactions toward the new minorities of Western Europe', *Annual Review of Sociology*, 24: 77–103.

Prejean, S.H. (2005) *The Death of Innocents: An Eyewitness Account of Wrongful Executions.* New York: Random House.

Radelet, M.L. and Borg, M.J. (2000) 'The changing nature of death penalty debates', *Annual Review of Sociology*, 26: 43–61.

Rankin, J.H. (1979) 'Changing attitudes toward capital punishment', *Social Forces*, 58 (1): 194–211.

Roberts, J.V. and Stalans, L.J. (1997) *Public Opinion, Crime, and Criminal Justice.* Boulder, CO: Westview Press.

Saad, L. (2007) *Racial Disagreement Over Death Penalty Has Varied Historically.* Princeton, NJ: Gallup Organization. Available online at: http://www.galluppoll.com.

Sarat, A. and Vidmar, N. (1976) 'Public opinion, the death penalty, and the Eighth Amendment: testing the Marshall hypothesis', *Wisconsin Law Review*, 1976 (1): 171–206.

Snell, T.L. (2006) *Capital Punishment, 2005.* Washington, DC: Bureau of Justice Statistics, US Department of Justice.

Soss, J., Langbein, L. and Metelko, A.R. (2003) 'Why do white Americans support the death penalty?', *Journal of Politics*, 65 (2): 397–421.

Steiker, C.S. (2002) 'Capital punishment and American exceptionalism', *Oregon Law Review*, 81 (1): 97–130.

Steiker, C.S. and Steiker, J.M. (2005) 'The seductions of innocence: the attraction and limitations of the focus on innocence in capital punishment law and advocacy', *Journal of Criminal Law and Criminology*, 95 (2): 587–624.

Tanner, R. (2007) 'Under scrutiny, capital punishment falls to 30-year low', *Cincinnati Enquirer*, 5 January, p. A4.

Taylor, H. (2004) 'More than two-thirds of Americans continue to support the death penalty'. *Harris Interactive*. Retrieved from: http://www.harrisinteractive.com/harris_poll/index.asp?PID=431.

TNS Sofres (2006) 'L'évolution de l'opinion publique Française sur la pein de mort'. Retrieved from: http://www.tns-sofres.com.

Tonry, M. (1997) 'Ethnicity, crime, and immigration', in M. Tonry (ed.), *Ethnicity, Crime, and Immigration – Crime and Justice: A Review of Research*, Vol. 21. Chicago: University of Chicago Press, pp. 1–29.

Unnever, J.D. and Cullen, F.T. (2005) 'Executing the innocent and support for capital punishment: implications for public policy', *Criminology and Public Policy*, 4 (1): 3–37.

Unnever, J.D. and Cullen, F.T. (2007a) 'Reassessing the racial divide in support for capital punishment: the continuing significance of race', *Journal of Research in Crime and Delinquency*, 44 (1): 124–58.

Unnever, J.D. and Cullen, F.T. (2007b) 'The racial divide in support for the death penalty: does white racism matter?', *Social Forces*, 85 (3): 1281–301.

Unnever, J.D., Cullen, F.T. and Fisher, B.S. (2005) 'Empathy and support for capital punishment', *Journal of Crime and Justice*, 28 (1): 1–34.

Unnever, J.D., Cullen, F.T. and Jonson, C.L. (forthcoming) 'Race, racism, and support for capital punishment', in M. Tonry (ed.), *Crime and Justice: A Review of Research*, Vol. 37. Chicago: University of Chicago Press.

Unnever, J.D., Cullen, F.T. and Roberts, J.V. (2005) 'Not everyone strongly supports the death penalty: assessing weakly-held attitudes about capital punishment', *American Journal of Criminal Justice*, 29 (2): 187–216.

Vogel, B.L. (2003) 'Support for life in prison without the possibility of parole among death penalty proponents', *American Journal of Criminal Justice*, 27 (2): 263–75.

Vogel, B.L. and Vogel, R.E. (2003) 'The age of death: appraising public opinion of juvenile capital punishment', *Journal of Criminal Justice*, 31 (2): 169–83.

Vollum, S., Longmire, D.R. and Buffington-Vollum, J. (2004) 'Confidence in the death penalty and support for its use: exploring the value-expressive dimension of death penalty attitudes', *Justice Quarterly*, 21 (3): 521–46.

Warden, R. (2005) 'Illinois death penalty reform: how it happened, what it promises', *Journal of Criminal Law and Criminology*, 95 (2): 381–426.

Zeisel, H. and Gallup, A.M. (1989) 'Death penalty sentiment in the United States', *Journal of Quantitative Criminology*, 5 (3): 285–96.

Cases cited

Furman v. *Georgia*, 408 U.S. 228 (1972).

Chapter 5

Achieving accurate assessment of attitudes toward the criminal justice system: methodological issues

G. Tendayi Viki and Gerd Bohner

Introduction

The importance of people's attitudes towards the criminal justice system (CJS) cannot be overemphasised (see also Wood, this volume). As a system, the CJS is most functional when there is cooperation from members of the public, who report crimes, act as witnesses (during investigations and in court) and are often asked to be jurors. However, research shows that people's willingness to participate and cooperate with the criminal justice process partly depends on their attitudes toward the CJS (e.g. Kury and Ferdinand 1999; Viki *et al.* 2006; Wood and Viki 2004). The importance of public attitudes towards the CJS makes it essential to obtain accurate information using good research methods and tools.

There appears to be a view among politicians and policy decision-makers that the public hold punitive attitudes toward criminals. Whether the public's attitudes are as punitive as is often assumed has been a matter of debate (Kury and Ferdinand 1999; Roberts 1992; Wood and Viki 2004; see also Cullen *et al.*, this volume). Some critics have noted that conclusions that the public are punitive are often based on poorly designed surveys and polls (e.g. Kury and Ferdinand 1999). For example, in some research the public attitude constructs are poorly defined and operationalised. Indeed, some opinion polls of public attitudes employ broad or general measures. Roberts (1992) notes that broad measures of public attitudes often produce findings suggesting that the majority of people want harsher penalties for offenders. This is because in this research there is no opportunity for participants to consider different types of offenders or alternative sentences. Such criticism highlights the importance of measuring public attitudes accurately using items that evaluate specific aspects of the CJS. Reliable and valid measurement instruments are self-evidently necessary in this process. Political debate and criminal justice policy decision-making need not be based on poorly conducted research.

The goal of this chapter is to discuss some of the methodological issues that arise when attempting to measure people's attitudes. We will discuss how researchers may *develop* reliable and *valid* measures of public attitudes to the CJS. *Reliability* refers to a measurement instrument's ability to measure the attitude object consistently. *Validity* refers to whether the instrument measures the attitude it is designed to measure (and not some other construct; Bohner and Wänke 2002; Himmelfarb 1993). First, the concept of attitude measurement will be described. We will contrast qualitative and quantitative attitude measures and also describe the different types of quantitative measurement. Second, we will focus on how to design direct measures of attitudes. We will consider issues such as item selection, number of items, question order and response format. Third, we will discuss the concepts of reliability and validity and how they may be used to evaluate the quality of an attitude measure. Finally, we will consider the potential role of indirect attitude measures in dealing with issues that may constrain the validity of direct measures (e.g. motivated response distortions). The ultimate goal of the chapter is to provide a general discussion of issues that may help researchers avoid the pitfalls of poor measurement design.

Attitude measurement

When assessing public attitudes researchers may use qualitative measures (King 2004). Within this methodology, researchers may employ open-ended questions during in-depth interviews (written or taped) in which participants' responses are not restricted to a particular response scale but recorded verbatim. These data are then analysed using qualitative data analysis techniques such as content, discourse and conversational analyses (Forrester 1999; Forrester and Ramsden 2000). Qualitative measures can provide in-depth and detailed information about people's attitudes. Some researchers argue that this method may actually be the best approach to use in certain circumstances (see King 2004, for a full review of when and how

97

to use qualitative methods). However, qualitative measures often require a large investment of time and effort for both researchers and participants. This is especially the case when researchers want to conduct large-scale surveys. The level of detailed analysis that is necessary with qualitative data becomes very time-consuming and costly for researchers conducting surveys with over 500 participants (Krosnick 1999). As such, the most popular measurement tools that are used in surveys concerning public attitudes are quantitative measures (see Wood and Viki 2004, for a review). Due to their popularity and usefulness, the present chapter focuses on how to develop reliable and valid quantitative measures to assess public attitudes toward the CJS.

What is measurement?

Measurement using quantitative instruments refers to the assignment of numbers to events or objects in such a way that the numbers are able to reflect relationships amongst those objects and/or events (Bohner and Wänke 2002; Himmelfarb 1993; Stevens 1946). With regard to attitudes, measurement means the assignment of numbers to reflect the presence and/or intensity of attitudes towards particular objects or events. Such measurement can be based on various scales, the lowest of which is the *nominal scale*. Within nominal scales, the numbers reflect only equality or difference in the qualitative properties being assessed (Bohner and Wänke 2002). An example of a nominal scale is when numbers are assigned to various religious categories (e.g. 1 = Muslim, 2 = Christian and 3 = Buddhist). Dichotomous measures (e.g. 1 = no and 2 = yes) are also examples of nominal scales. With regard to attitudes towards the CJS, nominal scales would only be able to tell us if people's attitudes are the same or different (e.g. supporting vs. not supporting the death penalty; also see Cullen *et al.*, this volume, for a discussion of the limitations of dichotomous scales). For example, in a recent MORI poll participants were asked to select three factors that they thought would most likely reduce crime. Their choices were nominal and included factors such as more police on the beat, more offenders in prison and better parenting (MORI 2006).

Nominal scales can provide useful and informative data. However, such scales are only effective if the list of choices that is offered to the participants is fully comprehensive (Krosnick 1999). Pilot testing using open-ended questions may be necessary to ensure that a comprehensive list of options is obtained. Furthermore, researchers may be interested not only in categorising people, but in knowing how people compare to one another along a certain continuum. For example, public attitude researchers may want to know whose attitudes are more favourable and whose are less favourable. *Ordinal scales* provide a means of ranking participants in terms of most favourable to least favourable attitudes (or vice versa). On these scales, the number assignment reflects a certain order (e.g. first to last), hence the term ordinal scaling. A good example of ordinal scaling in research relevant to the CJS is a recent study by Lieberman *et al.* (2003). Surveying 186 Californian undergraduates, Lieberman *et al.* (2003) asked participants to rank order 19 sexual acts from least to most morally wrong. In such a study, the researchers are then able to provide ranking data in terms of which act is deemed the most morally wrong (this was incest behaviour in Leiberman *et al.*'s research).

Although ordinal scales provide useful ranking information, the numbers cannot tell researchers by how much people's attitudes actually differ. Furthermore, ranking may compel participants to choose between two or three choices they feel the same way about (Krosnick 1999). In order to get information about the order and the size of attitude differences researchers have to use *interval scales*. Such scales have equal distances between measurement points. Examples of interval scales are Celsius and Fahrenheit degrees of measuring temperature. Because interval scales have equal distances between measurement points, we can interpret the relative difference between scale points as reflecting a comparable difference in attitude. If person A (John) has an attitude score of 5 towards the police, person B (Peter) has an attitude score of 7 and person C (Laura) has an attitude score of 8, this could be interpreted as indicating that the difference between Peter's and John's attitude towards the police is twice as large as the difference between Laura's and Peter's attitude. When analysing interval scale data positive linear transformations are possible because they maintain the ranking information in the data, as well as the equal distances between measurement points on the scale (Bohner and Wänke; 2002).

The highest level of measurement is a *ratio scale* (Himmelfarb 1993). This scale is similar to the interval scale but it has the added advantage of having a meaningful, absolute zero point (e.g. height, weight and number of sweets). In attitude measurement ratio scales are used in computer-based studies that employ differences in response time as an indicator of attitude, for example the Implicit Association Test (IAT; see Nosek *et al.* 2007). Both interval and ratio scales are often referred to as continuous measures. As we will note later, most attitude researchers use responses scales that approximate interval scales (Krosnick 1999). Participants are usually presented with various statements about the CJS and they have to indicate their level of agreement on Likert-type scales or semantic differential scales (Himmelfarb 1993). The strength of such measures is that they allow for researchers to compute descriptive statistics that indicate people's relative standing on a particular attitude construct and the magnitude of differences between measurements (Wegener and Fabrigar 2004). Using data that approximate interval scales also allows researchers to perform parametric statistical analyses such as correlations, regressions and analyses of variance (Wegener and Fabrigar 2004).

Specifying measurement goals

According to Wegener and Fabrigar (2004) the first task that researchers should perform when designing quantitative measures is '... to specify the goals of the measure and to formulate the theoretical assumptions that [will] guide its construction' (p. 146). This issue is particularly pertinent to research on public attitudes towards the CJS. One of the greatest limitations of media opinion polls is that the research questions are often poorly defined. When we speak of public attitudes toward the CJS what exactly do we mean? The CJS has many branches and processes, and involves several types of offenders. Kury and Ferdinand (1999) note that opinion polls that report the public to be highly punitive use broad attitude measures such as 'In your view are sentences too harsh, about right, or not harsh enough?' (p. 375). Such questioning often results in the research finding that people think that sentencing is not harsh enough (Roberts 1992). However, it is not clear exactly what respondents are referring to when answering such questions about sentencing. Is it sentencing for murder, rape or drunk driving? It is distinctly possible that people feel that sentencing for rape is too lenient whereas sentencing for petty theft is too harsh (Hough and Roberts 1998). In this regard, broad attitude measures such as the one above may not be useful.

Another problem with using broad measures of attitudes is that general attitude measurement often does not produce good attitude–behaviour correlations (Eagly and Chaiken 1993). Assuming that the ultimate goal of measuring attitudes towards the CJS is to predict people's behaviour (e.g. cooperating with police investigations), it becomes imperative for researchers to be specific about the aspects of the CJS they are investigating. For example, people's views about the sentencing of sex offenders could be assessed separately from attitudes towards murderers (Brown 1999). Indeed, some researchers have developed measures of people's attitudes towards various aspects of the CJS including attitudes towards: prison inmates (Gerstein *et al*. 1987), correctional work (Robinson *et al*. 1992), rehabilitation, deterrence and retribution (Applegate *et al*. 1997; Chung and Bargozzi 1997;), the court system (Kaukinen and Colavecchia 1999) and the death penalty (McGarell and Sandys 1996).

The above noted differentiated measures of attitudes have allowed researchers to reach more nuanced conclusions about people's attitudes towards the CJS. For example, and contrary to widely held assumptions, Applegate *et al*. (1997) found strong support for the rehabilitative functions of the CJS. When Mattison and Mirrlees-Black (2000) asked specific questions about first-time and repeat offenders they found that people were more in favour of punitive sanctions for repeat offenders (vs. first-time offenders). Jacoby and Cullen (1998) found that people do not favour prison sentences for all types of offenders, but they do for violent and sex offenders. Other researchers have found that of all the branches of the CJS, local police forces receive the most positive evaluations (e.g. Peek *et al*. 1978). All the above research findings support the argument that, before designing instruments assessing public attitudes towards the CJS, researchers need to be more specific about what aspects of the criminal justice process they are investigating.

Direct measurement of attitudes

Once the research goals have been specified, researchers can then proceed to develop the scales with which to measure attitudes towards the CJS. Most attitude surveys use the simple approach of just asking people what their attitudes are. This is referred to as the direct measurement of attitudes (Bohner and Wänke 2002; see also this volume). For example, participants may be asked to simply indicate their agreement with various statements about the police (e.g. 'The police in my town are efficient'). When presented with such statements respondents have to make sense of them before responding. In the example question above, respondents may know who the police are, but they may not have a clear idea how to interpret the word 'efficient'. This could mean that the police carry out investigations well or even that they are quick when responding to people's calls. These participant decision-making processes highlight the need for researchers to construct specific and clear questions for their surveys. When respondents have made sense of the question and identified the attitude object, they will then need to access their attitudes in order to respond. This is only possible if the respondents have already formed an opinion about the issue. If they have not formed an opinion or they cannot access their attitude at the moment (due to various factors), they may have to generate an attitude on the spot (Schwarz and Bohner 2001; see also Bohner and Wänke, this volume). From these 'retrieved' or 'generated' attitudes participants can then respond to the attitude question.

As will be noted later, the process of direct measurement can be problematic. For example, if participants have not formed an opinion toward the question, their responses may be influenced by the context in which they are responding (Strack *et al.* 1991; Sudman *et al.* 1996). In fact, context may even influence participants' willingness to report attitudes that they are aware of due to social desirability concerns. Bohner and Wänke (2002) differentiate two potential problems that may cause errors in direct measures of attitudes (i.e. *reactivity*). In the first instance, errors in measurement occur due to participants being motivated to distort their responses within the measurement context. The second type of error occurs due to the way that attitudes are being measured (e.g. question wording, number of items, question order). In this section, ways to deal with reactivity issues relating to measurement design and process will be discussed first. Issues relating to motivated response distortions will be discussed later under the section concerning indirect and implicit measures.

Generating items

Selecting the appropriate content and wording of items is paramount if the measurement scale is to meet its research goals. According to Wegener and Fabrigar (2004), if the conceptual basis of the scale has been clearly defined then researchers can write items that have good face validity reflecting the defined measurement criteria. For example, if researchers decide that they are going to focus specifically on people's attitudes towards the rehabilitation of offenders, a range of items can be developed specifically for this purpose (e.g. Cullen *et al.* 1989). This range of items should be designed to cover all facets of the specified attitude (e.g. rehabilitation is morally good, rehabilitation works, rehabilitation is easy to do). Ideas for further items could also be obtained from previous measures of similar constructs, although researchers must be careful not to just accept the theoretical assumptions made by past researchers (Wegener and Fabrigar 2004).

When generating the content of the attitude scale researchers must also be careful with their wording (Janada 1998). Ambiguous items that use vague and incomprehensible words should be avoided. Items containing words that could have multiple meanings should also be avoided. Researchers should generate items that have simple wording structures; they should avoid items that contain double negatives or double barrelled items. Especially important when researching attitudes towards to the CJS is for researchers to avoid leading questions, items that are likely to indicate particular biases of the researcher and items whose wording conveys that a particular choice is the best. An example item might be asking participants to indicate their level of agreement with a statement such as, 'For the safety of children, it is best to imprison child sex-offenders for lengthy sentences'. Besides having the ambiguous wording (i.e. 'lengthy sentences'), the first part of the question could bias participants' responses since no one wants to be seen as being against child safety.

Researchers need to make decisions about the number of items that should be included in the measurement scale. Researchers agree that multiple-item measures have better psychometric properties than single-item measures (Wegener and Fabrigar 2004). This is because any single item assessing attitudes has some level of measurement error, ambiguity and bias. The advantage of having multiple items is that the various sources of error are assumed to cancel each other out (Wegener and Fabrigar 2004). A further advantage of having multiple items, highlighted above, is that multiple items allow researchers to cover different aspects of the attitude object under study. If the measurement goals of the scale are clearly articulated this should provide guidance as to how many items are needed to cover the various aspects of the attitude object. It is important to note that although multi-item scales are superior, single-item measures can also be useful. This is because single-item measures are economical and often have reasonable levels of reliability and validity (Jaccard et al. 1975). Indeed, single items may be preferable to multiple items when assessing attitude accessibility rather than valence is the goal of the research (Bohner and Wänke 2002).

Researchers also have to make decisions about the order of the questions in the scale. It is commonly advised that researchers begin with items that are relatively easy for participants to understand and respond to (Krosnick 1999). It is not advisable to begin with questions that are sensitive and complex as this may result in uncomfortable or unmotivated participants. If researchers are measuring several constructs, the advice is to keep all items measuring one construct together (Wegener and Fabrigar 2004). This is effective because it allows participants to think about one issue at a time, rather than responding to random questions about several issues. It is important to note that early questions can influence how participants respond to later questions (Tourangeau and Rasinski 1988). Therefore, researchers may want to randomly rotate questions within particular blocks and also rotate the blocks of questions within the questionnaire (this has to be done keeping in mind the earlier advice about starting with simpler questions).

Format of response scales

After the content, wording, order and number of items has been decided, researchers then need to make decisions about how participants are going to respond to the questions. One of the popular response formats used in research on attitudes towards the CJS is the semantic differential scale (Osgood *et al.* 1957). The semantic differential scale consists of five to ten items with bipolar adjectives at either end of each item. The scale is often used to evaluate a single attitude object (e.g. participants may be asked to think of the police or child sex offenders). The end points of each item typically have words that are evaluatively opposite in meaning (e.g. happy–sad, slow–fast, love–hate). As such, this technique is most useful when researchers can find word pairs of opposite meaning to assess the attitude object of interest. Participants are typically asked to respond on a seven-point scale. The total or average score is computed for each participant and represents their attitude score. An example of a semantic differential scale measure of attitudes toward the CJS is Gerstein *et al.*'s (1987) measure of attitudes toward the average inmate. Participants are asked to think of prison inmates and then they rate them on qualities such as friendly vs. unfriendly, warm vs. cold and moral vs. immoral.

The other highly popular response format is the Likert scale (also known as the Likert Method of Summated Ratings; Likert 1932). Participants are presented with various attitude statements and asked to indicate their level of agreement with each statement. These responses are usually recorded using a five-point or seven-point scale (e.g. 1 = *strongly disagree* to 5 = *strongly agree*). The statements to which participants respond would have been designed using methods described above. These statements typically reflect evaluations of or beliefs about the attitude object. As with semantic differentials, the total or average score is computed for each participant and represents their attitude score. An example of a scale that uses the Likert response format is the Rehabilitation Orientation Scale by Cullen *et al.* (1989). Participants are asked to indicate their level of agreement with statements such as, 'The rehabilitation of adult criminals just does not work'. Participants indicate their responses on a seven-point scale (1 = *very strongly agree* to 7 = *very strongly disagree*).

A less popular method among researchers who examine attitudes towards the CJS is Thurstone's method of equal-appearing intervals. In the first step of scale development (stimulus scaling), judges are presented with various statements about the attitude object that represent different degrees of extremity in evaluating the attitude object. The judges are then asked to sort the statements into a specified number of equal-spaced categories (e.g. ranging from 1 (= *least favourable*) to 5 (= *most favourable*). Each statement is then assigned a value that corresponds to the median score it received from the judges. A final subset of items is then selected for use in the final scale based on two criteria: (1) high agreement among the judges regarding each item's positivity or negativity; (2) the items selected reflect the whole range of the evaluation continuum. In the second stage (person scaling), participants are asked to select those items with which they agree. Their final score is then computed as the median of the items they have selected. Although Thurstone's method is hardly used in research on attitudes towards the CJS, this technique could be very useful because it uses the criterion of equal intervals as an explicit basis of item selection (Wegener and Fabrigar 2004).

So how do researchers decide which response format to use? The choice of response format is determined by the researcher's goals. According to Bohner and Wänke (2002), semantic differential scales have the advantage that the same set of evaluative items can be used across a range of attitude objects. This can be beneficial for researchers who want to compare people's evaluations of various attitude objects. For example, researchers may want to compare people's views of various branches of the CJS (e.g. courts, police, prison service) or various types of offenders (murderers, rapists, burglars). In contrast, both Likert scales and Thurstone scales have to be designed for each attitude object. Because participants are presented with attitude statements to which they indicate their agreement, some pilot work is usually necessary before scale construction is completed.

Researchers also need to decide on the number of points that their rating scales should have. According to Krosnick (1999), for bipolar scales or scales that run from positive to negative and have a neutral point in the middle, reliability and validity is highest with seven response points. For unipolar scales that have zero at one end (e.g. reflecting different levels of agreement), five point scales are more reliable. Measures that use magnitude scaling with high numbers of points (e.g. 101 points) are the least reliable and valid. Krosnick and Berent (1993) also note that the quality of obtained data is better when each scale point is labelled with words. However, when selecting these words researchers must ensure that the words they use are capable of dividing the scale into a format that approximates equal units (Klockars and Yamagishi 1988).

There are some researchers of attitudes towards the CJS who chose to offer participants response options that are nominal in nature (e.g. agree/disagree, true/false or yes/no; e.g. Robinson *et al.* 1992). Such measures are useful because they are relatively easy for participants to use. However, Krosnick (1999) recommends against using such measures due to the acquiescence problem. Acquiescence refers to the tendency of participants to endorse the assertion made by a statement without considering its content (Krosnick 1999). Researchers have documented high levels of acquiescence with dichotomous scales such that statements in the same scale that should be strongly negatively correlated only display weak negative correlations. Consequently, Krosnick (1999) recommends to avoid dichotomous measures and to use rating scales or other forced-choice formats (e.g. ranking) instead.

How to evaluate the quality of a measure

Evaluating the quality of a measure can actually begin during the item generation and development process. As the scale is being con-structed researchers can engage in the evaluation of items' quality and usefulness. For example, judges' ratings, as in the Thurstone method, can be used by researchers to select items. Using this method, researchers can select items for which there is most agreement among the judges since these are likely to contain the least amount of measurement error. Once the items have been selected and the scale has been designed, measure quality can be evaluated in terms of *reliability* and *validity*. Classical test theory conceives of a person's response on a scale as a combination of 'true score' plus 'error' (Lord and Novick 1968). Measurement error can be from random factors (i.e. *random error*) such as participant mood, participants misreading one or two questions or coding errors when data are entered by researchers. Random error introduces variance in data but is not highly problematic because such errors are expected to cancel each other out, especially in multi-item measures. A person's attitude score can also be influenced by *systematic errors* resulting from the measure tapping into other constructs that are not part of its stated measurement goals. A good example is when participants consistently assume that the researcher expects them to respond to questions in a certain manner. Attitude scores from a measure with such levels of systematic error would reflect both the construct of interest and participants' motivation to please the researcher (Bohner and Wänke 2002).

Researchers should aim to reduce the influence of both systematic and random error within their measures. By reducing random error, researchers are able to demonstrate that their scale measures consistently whatever it measures (i.e. *reliability*). By reducing both random and systematic error, researchers are able to demonstrate that their scale measures the construct it claims to measure (i.e. *validity*). It is important to note that a scale can have high levels of reliability but have very low levels of validity. In this case, the scale would produce consistent scores but would not be measuring the construct it claims to measure. In other words, reliability is not an indicator of validity, but a scale cannot achieve high levels of validity unless it is reliable.

Reliability

The reliability of a scale can be assessed in two main ways; these are *test-retest* and *internal consistency*. Internal consistency is the most popular indicator of reliability that is reported by researchers. The term internal consistency refers to the degree to which items in a scale correlate to each other (Wegener and Fabrigar 2004). One way to assess internal consistency is via the *split-half reliability* method. In this method, the scale is split into two halves and the correlation between the two halves is analysed. The problem with the split-half method is that a scale can be split in half in many ways, and the way the scale is split affects the correlation scores one obtains. To deal with these issues researchers often analyse internal consistency using Cronbach's alpha (Cronbach 1951). This coefficient can take on a maximum value of 1, with higher scores indicating a higher level of internal consistency. Cronbach's alpha can be described as the mean of all possible split-half coefficients that could be computed for a particular scale. It is important to note that the more items one has in a scale the larger the alpha coefficient one is likely to obtain. As such, multi-item scales are more likely to be reliable since with more items random error is assumed to be cancelled out.

Test-retest reliability is a measure of the stability of the scale. This is usually computed by correlating the test scores of the same measure administered to the same people at different times. The larger the correlation between the two measurement points the greater the stability (or consistency) of the measure. In addition to indicating the reliability of a measure, the test-retest coefficient also reflects the stability of the construct being assessed. In this regard, the test-retest method is most useful when the construct being assessed can be assumed to be relatively stable. A potential problem with the test-retest method is that the testing itself may affect people's attitudes and these may change between tests. Attitudes towards the CJS can be viewed as relatively stable in comparison to other constructs such as mood. However, it is possible that these may change between measurements (e.g. after exposure to news about current levels of crime). A low correlation between the two measurement points would then not be a reflection of an unreliable measure but of an actual change in people's attitudes (see also Bohner and Wänke, this volume). The above problems with the test-retest method are the reasons why researchers prefer to report Cronbach's alpha when assessing reliability (e.g. Chung and Bagozzi 1997; Cullen et al. 1989; Robinson et al. 1992).

Validity

A reliable scale is one whose scores are not strongly influenced by random error. However, this does not indicate that the scale is not being influenced by systematic forms of error that result from the measure tapping into other constructs that it is not intended to measure. Previously, researchers have differentiated various types of validity, including face validity, content validity and criterion validity. All of these aspects, however, can be placed under one heading of construct validity (Wegener and Fabrigar 2004). This is because all the different forms of validity are concerned with issues of systematic error. Wegener and Fabrigar (2004) note that, within construct validity, the important differentiation is between associative and dissociative forms of validity.

Associative forms of validation provide evidence of the utility of the measure by showing that it is associated with other measures and constructs in ways that would be predicted by theory. This is sometimes referred to as *convergent validity* (Campbell and Fiske 1959). Campbell and Fiske (1959) recommend the use of what they refer to as the multitrait-multimethod approach to associative validation. This means that measures of attitude can be validated by checking their associative relationships with various measures of similar constructs. These constructs may be assessed using different methods and measures (e.g. questionnaires and physiological measures). If a researcher develops a scale assessing public attitudes towards prisoner rehabilitation, this scale should be related to other published measures of attitudes towards rehabilitation. The scale can also be expected to be related with other attitudes that can be assumed to be antecedents or consequences of the attitudes towards prisoner rehabilitation. For example, attitudes towards rehabilitation may be reasonably expected to be related to liberal political attitudes. Indeed, one way to validate the scale would be to administer it to two groups who may be expected to have different attitudes towards the rehabilitation (e.g. conservatives vs. liberals). Attitudes towards rehabilitation may also be reasonably expected to be related to the willingness to work as a volunteer on an offender rehabilitation programme. The ultimate goal of this validation exercise would be to demonstrate that the scale is related to other measures and constructs in the manner that it is theoretically expected to be.

Dissociative forms of validation can be used to define the limits of the scale. It is important not only to show a scale's relationship with similar constructs, but to also show that the scale has no relationship with variables that it is *not* expected to be related to (Wegener and Fabrigar 2004). This is similar to what Campbell and Fiske (1959) described as *divergent validity*. For example, our scale of attitudes toward rehabilitation may not be expected to be related to a scale assessing sexist attitudes. The scale may also be unrelated to people's willingness to volunteer to work with the elderly and infirm. Factor analyses can also be performed to demonstrate that the scale is conceptually distinct from other measures of attitudes toward the CJS (e.g. attitudes toward the police or attitudes toward retribution; see Chung and Bagozzi (1997) for an example of such analyses). Ultimately, the combination of associative and dissociative forms of validation helps to show that the scale is tapping into the construct of interest and not other unrelated constructs.

Indirect measures of attitudes

The use of direct measures of attitudes is based on the assumption that people are *willing* and *able* to inform researchers of their views on particular issues. However, this is not always the case. Contextual cues in the research situation may alter respondents' perceptions of what is required of them and influence their responses (i.e. *demand characteristics*). For example, respondents may complete a questionnaire in a manner they think is in line with the experimenter's expectations or hypotheses. In addition to responding to demand characteristics, participants may also be motivated to present themselves in a particular manner to the researchers (i.e. *impression management*). For example, participants may not be willing to reveal their true opinions to embarrassing questions about their sexual preferences. These potential problems with direct measures have motivated researchers to come up with ways to gain access to participants' 'true' attitudes (but cf. Bohner and Wänke, this volume).

Several researchers have suggested that a potential way to deal with impression management is to have participants complete measures of the tendency to self-enhance. These measures include negative statements that are true for almost everyone (see Crowne and Marlowe's (1960) social desirability scale). Participants who do not endorse such statements can thus be viewed as self-enhancing. By completing measures of social desirability and measures assessing the attitudes of interest, researchers can then control for the effects of self-enhancement statistically. However, controlling for the effect of impression management post hoc may not be completely effective. This is because there is no clear way of knowing how participants would have responded if they had been telling the 'truth' (Krosnick 1999).

Other researchers have created ways to motivate participants to respond truthfully. One such technique is the bogus pipeline technique (Jones and Sigall 1971). When this method is used, participants are attached to a convincing looking lie-detector machine. Participants then complete the attitude measure that the researchers are interested in. This method has been found to reduce participants' motivation to distort their responses. In a recent study, Gannon *et al.* (2007) found that child molesters who were attached to a bogus pipeline endorsed more cognitive distortions in comparison to child molesters who were not attached to a bogus pipeline. This finding indicates that child molesters may have the tendency to depress their cognitive distortion scores in order to appear good to researchers and clinicians. They only report their 'real' attitudes when they are motivated to respond truthfully. Although the bogus pipeline method may work as a research tool, this method may be too costly and time-consuming when researchers want to conduct surveys with large sections of the population. Also, the method may not be useful when participants cannot easily access their attitudes (Roese and Jamieson 1993).

Another solution proposed by researchers is to use indirect measures of attitudes. Using this technique, participants respond to the researcher's questions but they are unaware that their attitudes are being measured. For example, in Hammond's (1948) error-choice method, participants are presented with two forced-choice responses to a question that is ostensibly designed to measure their knowledge. However, neither of the two choices is factually correct; instead they reflect biases in opposite directions. For example, the two options presented to participants may be: (a) drug offences in the UK increased by 17 per cent in 2006; or (b) drug offences in the UK increased by 1 per cent in 2006. The correct answer according to Home Office statistics is about 9 per cent (Nicholas *et al.* 2007). As such, both answers are equally wrong in either direction. A respondent's choice in this situation is then seen as a reflection of their own attitudes towards the issue (Hammond 1948).

A similar method of using logical reasoning errors as indicators of attitude was first suggested by Thistlethwaite (1950) and successfully applied to measuring racial attitudes by Saucier and Miller (2003; see also Heitland and Bohner 2008). Projective techniques in which participants interpret ambiguous stimuli have also been used by researchers, especially in market research (Fram and Cibotti 1991). It is important to note that the utility of the above techniques when studying public attitudes towards the CJS may be limited. The error-choice method can probably be used to study biased views of crime rates and sentencing practices. However, such a method may also reveal people's lack of knowledge about the CJS rather than their biases. As for projective tests, obtaining ambiguous stimuli that are relevant to the CJS may be difficult and time-consuming.

Some other interesting forms of indirect attitude measurement are the non-reactive measures. When researchers use these techniques, participants are often completely unaware that a measurement is taking place. These techniques include behavioural observation and the use of archival records. When collecting such data, researchers can observe participants' behaviour in natural settings and use that as an indicator of their attitudes. However, in reaching such conclusions researchers should be wary of situational pressures on people's behaviour. Also, there may be ethical issues that arise when people are observed and measured without their consent. Archival records can also be good indicators of public attitudes towards social issues (e.g. studying letters to editors of newspapers). However, archival records are most useful when studying past events and may be subject to interpretational biases by researchers. A special case of observational data are physiological measures (e.g. event-related brain potentials, galvanic skin response); although these cannot be taken unobtrusively, they are non-reactive in the sense that they are outside of respondents' voluntary control. Research along these lines has made significant progress in recent decades (for a review, see Ito and Cacioppo 2007).

Measuring implicit attitudes

As already noted above, people may be unwilling to inform researchers of their true attitudes. This may be because of situational factors or self-presentation concerns. It is also possible, however, that people may be unable to access their attitudes even if they want to be truthful to researchers. Some aspects of an attitude may be implicit and influence people's behaviour without their awareness (Greenwald *et al.* 2002). Greenwald and Banaji (1995) define implicit attitudes as evaluations whose origin a person cannot identify and that affect various responses (see Bohner and Wänke 2002). In order to circumvent both the 'willingness' and 'awareness' problems in attitude research, social psychologists have developed several implicit attitude measures (for reviews, see Wittenbrink and Schwarz 2007). These procedures are non-reactive because participants are not directly asked to indicate their attitude towards the attitude objects. We discuss here two of the most widely used response-time based measures: priming procedures and implicit association tests.

Priming

In this type of implicit measure, participants are primed with the attitude object of interest. The effects of the prime on participants' responses to certain stimuli are then observed (Bargh 2003, 2006; Fazio *et al.* 1986). For example, participants are informed that their task is to categorise evaluatively unambiguous target words (e.g. 'wonderful', 'horrible') into 'good' and 'bad' by pressing a key as quickly as possible (Fazio *et al.* 1986). Prior to each target word being categorised, participants are shown the primes (e.g. politicians or white/black faces; Fazio *et al.* 1995). Differences in participants' reaction times when categorising good versus bad words after seeing different types of prime are taken as an indicator of their evaluation of the prime. For example, if a participant is faster categorising good (vs. bad) words after seeing white (vs. black) faces, this would be taken to indicate a more positive attitude toward whites than toward blacks. It is important to note that primes may have these effects even if they are presented subliminally, i.e. below the threshold of conscious recognition, so that participants are not aware of the fact that they have been primed with the attitude object.

The implicit association test (IAT)

This is the most well known implicit measure in psychology and was developed at Yale University by Anthony Greenwald and his colleagues (Greenwald *et al.* 1998; Greenwald and Farnham 2000; Nosek *et al.* 2007). The measure is based on the notion that attitudes, stereotypes and even self-esteem can be viewed in terms of associations between particular concepts. The IAT was developed to measure the strength of these associations. For example, the first IAT measured the relative association between flower versus insect (the attitude objects) and positive versus negative words. Greenwald and colleagues found that flowers were more strongly associated than insects with positive rather than negative words (Greenwald *et al.* 1998).

The IAT measures how quickly people categorise words and/or pictures. For example, imagine a person who likes the police force but dislikes prison guards. Our task would be to gauge the person's relative association of the police (vs. prison guards) with positive versus negative characteristics. For each of the above four categories (the police, prison guards, positive and negative) we identify words or pictures to use as exemplars. For example, we might choose pictures of police officers or prison guards and words such as 'competent' or 'inept' to represent relevant categories. In the first block of the IAT, the person is simply asked to press computer keys as quickly as possible to categorise police versus prison guard pictures that appear individually on the computer screen (e.g. press 'q' for the police and 'p' for prison guards). In a second block, the person will then be asked to use the same keys to categorise positive vs. negative words (e.g. press 'q' for positive and 'p' for negative).

After completing these first two blocks, participants then take part in the first critical block in which stimuli from all four categories are presented. Participants are asked to press 'q' if the stimulus is the police or a positive word and to press 'p' if the stimulus is prison guards or a negative word. In this block, the police and positive words share the same key and prison guards and negative words share the same key. This is called the compatible block (assuming the person likes the police better than prison guards). In the next block, participants then practice a reversed categorisation of police versus prison guard pictures (now: press 'q' for prison guards and 'p' for the police), after which they take part in the final, incompatible block. Here, participants are presented with the four concepts and asked to press 'q' if the stimulus is prison guard or a positive word and to press 'q' if the stimulus is the police or a negative word. Now, the police and negative words share the same key and prison guards and positive words share the same key.

Before each critical block, participants perform several practice trials that are similar to the critical trials they are about to undertake. Participants' IAT scores are computed by subtracting the mean response time per trial of the compatible block from the mean response time per trial of the incompatible block. A person who really likes the police should be faster at categorising the police and positive when these responses share the same key (as well as prison guard and negative). This person's IAT score would thus be positive. Generally, the sign and magnitude of IAT scores is taken as an indicator of the relative strength of the association of the two target categories (police vs. prison guards) with negativity or positivity.

The IAT has been used to study several issues including race, age, self-esteem and dehumanisation (Nosek *et al.* 2007). It has also been found to have good internal consistency and to predict specific types of social behaviour (for a review, see Lane *et al.* 2007). Both the IAT and the priming procedures are relatively difficult to design and implement (in comparison to questionnaires). Because they measure response time, both procedures require the use of a computer (and sometimes the Internet). This makes the procedures easier to execute in laboratories than in field surveys. In the field, IAT and priming may be used if researchers carry laptop computers. However, the time it takes to set up and collect data may make it difficult and costly to conduct large-scale surveys of social attitudes. Indeed, most of the attitudes that are measured in surveys about the CJS may not require implicit measurement. This may be the reason why implicit measures are not highly popular among CJS researchers. However, researchers examining attitudes towards the CJS may want to consider using implicit measures, especially when examining sensitive topics such as sexual behaviour. Implicit measures can also be used on smaller samples to complement larger attitudinal surveys.

Conclusion

In this chapter, we attempted to provide a brief guide concerning some of the methodological issues researchers should consider when designing studies to assess public attitudes towards the CJS. For more detailed analyses of each specific issue, readers may refer to the articles that are referenced in this chapter. It is critical for researchers to consider carefully each issue we have described as this may strongly influence the reliability and validity of the data they obtain. Developing measures that assess specific aspects of the criminal justice process is an excellent way to discover whether or not people are as punitive towards offenders as is often claimed. Media polls that use general measures may not provide valid indicators of public attitudes. These considerations along with the consideration of other issues concerning item selection and design, choice of response format and question order should result in good measures being developed. Researchers interested in public attitudes towards the CJS may also want to consider the use of indirect and implicit attitude measures to complement more traditional procedures.

References

Applegate, B.K., Cullen, F.T. and Fisher, B.S. (1997) 'Public support for correctional treatment: the continuing appeal of the rehabilitative ideal', *Prison Journal*, 77: 237–58.

Bargh, J.A. (2003) 'Why we thought we could prime social behavior', *Psychological Inquiry*, 14: 216–18.

Bargh, J.A. (2006) 'What have we been priming all these years? On the development, mechanisms, and ecology of nonconscious social behavior', *European Journal of Social Psychology*, 36: 147–68.

Bohner, G. and Wänke, M. (2002) *Attitudes and Attitude Change*. Hove: Psychology Press.

Brown, S. (1999) 'Public attitudes towards the treatment of sex offenders', *Legal and Criminological Psychology*, 4: 239–52.

Campbell, D.T. and Fiske, D.W. (1959) 'Convergent and discriminant validation by the multitrait-multimethod matrix', *Psychological Bulletin*, 56: 81–105.

Chung, W. and Bagozzi, R. (1997) 'The construct validity of measures of the tripartite conceptualization of punishment attitudes', *Journal of Social Service Research*, 22: 1–25.

Cronbach, L.J. (1951) 'Coefficient alpha and the internal structure of tests', *Psychometrika*, 16: 297–334.

Crowne, D.P. and Marlowe, D.A. (1960) 'A new scale of social desirability independent of psychopathology', *Journal of Consulting Psychology*, 24: 349–54.

Cullen, F., Lutze, F., Link, B. and Wolfe, N. (1989) 'The correctional orientation of prison guards: do officers support rehabilitation?', *Federal Probation*, March: 33–42.

Eagly, A.H. and Chaiken, S. (eds) (1993) *The Psychology of Attitudes*. Fort Worth, TX: Harcourt Brace Jovanovich.

Fazio, R.H., Jackson, J.R., Dunton, B.C. and Williams, C.J. (1995) 'Variability in automatic activation as an unobtrusive measure of racial attitudes: a bona fide pipeline?', *Journal of Personality and Social Psychology*, 69: 1013–27.

Fazio, R.H., Sanbonmatsu, D.M., Powell, M.C. and Kardes, F.R. (1986) 'On the automatic activation of attitudes', *Journal of Personality and Social Psychology*, 50: 229–38.

Forrester, M.A. (1999) 'Conversation analysis: a reflexive methodology for critical psychology', *Annual Review of Critical Psychology*, 1: 34–49.

Forrester, M.A. and Ramsden, C. (2000) 'Discursive ethnomethodology: analysing power and resistance in talk', *Psychology, Crime and Law*, 6: 281–304.

Fram, E.H. and Cibotti, E. (1991) 'The shopping list studies and projective techniques: a 40-year view', *Marketing Research*, 3: 14–22.

Gannon, T.A., Keown, K. and Polaschek, D.L.L. (2007) 'Increasing honest responding on cognitive distortions in child molesters: the bogus pipeline revisited', *Sexual Abuse: A Journal of Research and Treatment*, 19: 5–22.

Gerstein, L., Topp, C. and Correll, G. (1987) 'The role of the environment and person when predicting burnout among correctional personnel', *Criminal Justice and Behavior*, 14: 352–69.

Greenwald, A.G. and Banaji, M.R. (1995) 'Implicit social cognition: attitudes, self-esteem, and stereotypes', *Psychological Review*, 102: 4–27

Greenwald, A.G. and Farnham, S.D. (2000) 'Using the Implicit Association Test to measure self-esteem and self-concept', *Journal of Personality and Social Psychology*, 79: 1022–38.

Greenwald, A.G., Banaji, M.R., Rudman, L.A., Farnham, S.D., Nosek, B.A. and Mellott, D.S. (2002) 'A unified theory of implicit attitudes, stereotypes, self-esteem, and self-concept', *Psychological Review*, 109: 3–25.

Greenwald, A.G., McGhee, D.E. and Schwartz, J.K.L. (1998) 'Measuring individual differences in implicit cognition: the Implicit Association Test', *Journal of Personality and Social Psychology*, 74: 1464–80.

Hammond, K.R. (1948) 'Measuring attitudes by error-choice and indirect method', *Journal of Abnormal and Social Psychology*, 43: 38–48.

Heitland, K. and Bohner, G. (2008) 'A German Version of the Racial Argument Scale'. Unpublished manuscript, University of Bielefeld.

Himmelfarb, S. (1993) 'The measurement of attitudes', in A.H. Eagly and S. Chaiken (eds), *The Psychology of Attitudes*. Fort Worth, TX: Harcourt Brace Jovanovich, pp. 23–87.

Hough, M. and Roberts, J. (1998) *Attitudes to Crime and Punishment: Findings from the British Crime Survey*. London: HMSO.

Ito, T.A. and Cacioppo, J.T. (2007) 'Attitudes as mental and neural states of readiness: using physiological measures to study implicit attitudes', in B. Wittenbrink and N. Schwarz (eds), *Implicit Measures of Attitudes*. New York: Guilford Press, pp. 125–58.

Jaccard, J., Weber, J. and Lundmark, A (1975) 'Multitrait-multimethod analysis of four attitude assessment procedures', *Journal of Experimental Social Psychology*, 11: 149–54.

Jacoby, J.E. and Cullen, F.T. (1998) 'The structure of punishment norms: applying the Rossi-Berk model', *Journal of Criminal Law and Criminology*, 89: 245–305.

Janada, L.H. (1998) *Psychological Testing: Theory and Applications*. Boston: Allyn & Bacon.

Jones, E.E. and Sigall, H. (1971) 'The bogus pipeline: a new paradigm for measuring affect and attitude', *Psychological Bulletin*, 76: 349–64.

Kaukinen, C. and Colavecchia, S. (1999) 'Public perceptions of the courts: an examination of attitudes toward the treatment of victims and accused', *Canadian Journal of Criminology*, 41: 365–85.

King, L.A. (2004) 'Measures and meanings: the use of qualitative data in social and personality psychology', in C. Sansone, C. Morf and A. Panter (eds), *The Sage Handbook of Methods in Social Psychology*. New York: Sage, pp. 173–94.

Klockars, A.J. and Yamagishi, M. (1988) 'The influence of labels and positions in rating scales', *Journal of Educational Measurement*, 25: 85–96.

Krosnick, J.A. (1999) 'Maximizing questionnaire quality', in J.P. Robinson, P.R. Shaver and L.S. Wrightsman (eds), *Measures of Political Attitudes*. New York: Academic Press, pp. 37–57.

Krosnick, J.A. and Berent, M.K. (1993) 'Comparisons of party identification and policy preferences: the impact of survey question format', *American Journal of Political Science*, 37: 941–64.

Kury, H. and Ferdinand, T. (1999) 'Public opinion and punitivity', *International Journal of Law and Psychiatry*, 22: 373–92.

Lane, K.A., Banaji, M.R., Nosek, B.A. and Greenwald, A.G. (2007) 'Understanding and using the Implicit Association Test: IV. What we know (so far)', in B. Wittenbrink and N.S. Schwarz (eds), *Implicit Measures of Attitudes: Procedures and Controversies*. New York: Guilford Press, pp. 59–102.

Lieberman, D., Tooby, J. and Cosmides, L. (2003) 'Does morality have a biological basis? An empirical test of the factors governing moral sentiments relating to incest', *Proceedings of the Royal Society of London. Series B, Biological Sciences*, 270: 819–26.

Likert, R. (1932) 'A technique for the measurement of attitudes', *Archives of Psychology*, 140: 1–55.

Lord, F.M. and Novick, M.R. (1968) *Statistical Theories of Mental Test Scores*. Reading, MA: Addison-Wesley.

McGarell, E.F. and Sandys, M. (1996) 'The misperception of public opinion toward capital punishment: examining the spuriousness explanation of death penalty support', *American Behavioural Scientist*, 39: 500–14.

Mattison, J. and Mirrlees-Black, C. (2000) *Attitudes to Crime and Criminal Justice: Findings from the 1998 British Crime Survey*. London. HMSO.

MORI (2006) 'Public attitudes to parenting'. Available at: http://www.ipsos-mori.com/polls/2006/respect.shtml.

Nicholas, S., Kershaw, C. and Walker, A. (2007) *Crime in England and Wales 2006/07*. London. HMSO.

Nosek, B.A., Greenwald, A.G. and Banaji, M.R. (2007) 'The Implicit Association Test at age 7: a methodological and conceptual review', in J.A. Bargh (ed.), *Automatic Processes in Social Thinking and Behavior*. Hove: Psychology Press, pp. 265–92.

Osgood, C.E., Suci, G.J. and Tannenbaum, P.H. (1957) *The Measurement of Meaning*. Chicago: University of Illinois Press.

Peek, C.W., Alston, J.P. and Lowe, G.D. (1978) 'Comparative evaluation of the local police', *Public Opinion Quarterly*, 42: 370–9.

Roberts, J.V. (1992) 'Public opinion, crime and criminal justice', in M. Tonry (ed.), *Crime and Justice: A Review of Research*. Chicago: University of Chicago Press.

Robinson, D., Porporino, F. and Simourd, L. (1992) *Staff Commitment in the Correctional Service of Canada*, NCJ Document Number: 148402. Ottawa: Canada Correctional Service.

Roese, N.J. and Jamieson, D.W. (1993) 'Twenty years of bogus pipeline research: a critical review and meta-analysis', *Psychological Bulletin*, 114: 363–75.

Saucier, D.A. and Miller, C.T. (2003) 'The persuasiveness of racial arguments as a subtle measure of racism', *Personality and Social Psychology Bulletin*, 29: 1303–15.

Schwarz, N. and Bohner, G. (2001) 'The construction of attitudes', in A. Tesser and N. Schwarz (eds), *Blackwell Handbook of Social Psychology*, Vol. 1: *Intraindividual Processes*. Oxford: Blackwell, pp. 436–57.

Stevens, S.S. (1946) 'On the theory of scales of measurement', *Science*, 103: 667–80.

Strack, F., Schwarz, N. and Wänke, M. (1991) 'Semantic and pragmatic aspects of context effects in social and psychological research', *Social Cognition*, 9: 111–25.

Sudman, S., Bradburn, N.M. and Schwarz, N. (1996) *Thinking about Answers: The Application of Cognitive Processes to Survey Methodology*. San Francisco: Jossey-Bass.

Thistlethwaite, D. (1950) 'Attitude and structure as factors in the distortion of reasoning', *Journal of Abnormal and Social Psychology*, 45: 442–58.

Tourangeau, R. and Rasinski, K. (1988) 'Cognitive processes underlying context effects in attitude measurement', *Psychological Bulletin*, 103: 299–314.

Viki, G.T., Culmer, M.J., Eller, A. and Abrams, D. (2006) 'Race and willingness to co-operate with the police: the roles of quality of contact, attitudes towards the behaviour and subjective norms', *British Journal of Social Psychology*, 12: 285–302.

Wegener, D.T. and Fabrigar, L.R. (2004) 'Constructing and evaluating quantitative measures for social psychological research: conceptual challenges and methodological solutions', in C. Sansone, C.C.C. Morf and A.T. Panter (eds), *The Sage Handbook of Methods in Social Psychology*. New York: Sage, pp. 145–72.

Wittenbrink, B. and Schwarz, N. (eds) (2007) *Implicit Measures of Attitudes*. New York: Guilford Press.

Wood, J. and Viki, G.T. (2004) 'Public attitudes towards crime and punishment', in J. Adler (ed.), *Forensic Psychology: Debates, Concepts and Practice*. Cullompton: Willan, pp. 16–36.

Part 2

Public Opinion: Victims and Offenders

Chapter 6

The typical rape: factors affecting victims' decision to report

Margaret Wilson and Angela Scholes

Introduction

This chapter examines victims' view of the criminal justice system (CJS) and how those views impact on decisions to report victimisation. It focuses specifically on rape victims and their perceptions of how they are likely to be treated within the CJS. It reports research findings showing that negative views result in victims not coming forward to report rape. It goes on to discuss the implications of such views in terms of the adequate functioning of the CJS. This chapter closes with a discussion of how the under-reporting of rape may send a message to potential offenders and affect one of the main aims of the CJS – general deterrence.

Attrition

It has been suggested that as few as 5 per cent of all rapes reported in the UK result in a conviction, and given that the vast majority of rapes occurring are not even reported (Gross *et al.* 1998), this amounts to a very serious failure for the criminal justice system (CJS). The most salient reason for attrition comes in the first stages of the process, where the victim does not make a formal complaint (Feist *et al.* 2007; Lea *et al.* 2003; see also Gilchrist, this volume). Indeed, some studies show that as few as 6 per cent of all rapes are reported to the police (Ahmed and Bright 2000; Rape Crisis Federation 2004). Awareness of the problem of under-reporting has been growing since the 1960s, since it became obvious that there are large disparities between official police figures for the frequency of rape and sexual assault and those reported by the British Crime Survey (BCS; Durston 1998).

The decision to report is actually quite a complex one to study, as it involves not only the victims' perceptions of the crime, but their perceptions of others' perceptions of the crime and of how they will subsequently react to it. A large part of this involves victims' preconceptions about the CJS itself and how being involved in the system will affect them and those who know them.

The second stage of possible attrition is withdrawal. Many victims who do report sexual assaults later withdraw their complaint (Kelly et al. 2005; Lea et al. 2003; Pino and Meier 1999). In one study, victims withdrew their support in 39 per cent of cases, with the majority being withdrawn in the police investigation stage. A further 10 per cent of withdrawals took place after the offender was charged, with the commonest reasons being the victim's desire to carry on with their life, or not wanting to go through the investigative or court process (Feist et al. 2007).

Attrition may also result from the decision of the police or the Crown Prosecution Service (CPS) not to proceed with the case. The highest proportion of cases fall out of the system during the police investigation, and a third are filtered out before referral to the CPS (Kelly et al. 2005). Prosecutors may decide not to take the case forward because of a lack of evidence (Lea et al. 2003) and finally, of course, even cases that end up in court may not result in a conviction.

Perceptions of the CJS are important at each stage. When the decision is in the hands of the victim, their view of how they will be treated is central. The actual actions of the CJS in relation to the treatment of victims of sex offenders feeds back into people's conceptualisations of the process. And finally, the interaction between the victim's and the jury's experience in court reinforces the link between lay attitudes and outcomes.

This review will consider research relating to both stranger and acquaintance rape and male and female victims. These subsets of victims face different levels and versions of similar issues.

Offence behaviour and rape myth acceptance

Central to much of the research to be addressed in this chapter is the notion of what constitutes a 'typical rape' and the degree to which the incident matches those stereotypes, in both the mind of the victim and for those within the CJS who subsequently deal with the case. Research has identified what constitutes a 'classic rape scenario', and the match or mismatch to these factors contributes to all of the subsequent decisions that affect attrition, from reporting right through to the conviction of the offender. In the 'classic rape' the victim is a female, attacked by a male stranger in a dark alley, with force used to control her (Williams 1984).

In common with many other forms of unusual experiences such as fires (Sime 1990) and hostage incidents (Wilson and Smith 1999), those who have no professional experience of rape have vague or quite inaccurate views of likely events. Even those who have been a victim themselves will have little knowledge of what constitutes typical or frequent behaviour. Sime (1990), Donald and Canter (1992) and Wilson and Smith (1999) have discussed the theoretical issues surrounding the way people construct a 'typical scenario', so within the scope of the present review it will suffice to say that people's image of what constitutes typical is probably derived from media portrayals. With respect to the factual media, they are more likely to report on the 'typical rapes', and those are the ones likely to have been reported to the police and resulted in conviction, creating a self-perpetuating cycle of belief. With respect to the fictional media, descriptions of criminal activity are notoriously inaccurate and usually 'sensational'. Wherever the misinformation comes from, the result is the same. People have a distorted view of what constitutes a 'typical rape'.

First, the typical rape involves a female victim. And yet 1,150 male rapes were reported to police in England and Wales in the year 2006/2007 (Nicholas et al. 2007), representing approximately 8 per cent of the total rapes that year. Second, a 'typical rape' is carried out by a stranger, whether they attack the victim outdoors or break into her house. And yet it is well established that the majority of all reported rapes are carried out by an offender known to the victim (e.g. Feist et al. 2007). Of the unreported rapes, it is even more likely that they are acquaintance rapes as will be discussed below. The 'typical' victim will fight her assailant and sustain physical injuries. These factors are more frequently reported in made-up accounts than in genuine cases (Rainbow 1996). Even if we take the subset of rapes that are carried out by strangers, the actual behaviours displayed by the majority of rapists are not consistent with the lay 'prototype'.

Examining what actually went on in 125 stranger rapes involving female victims in the UK, Wilson et al. (1996) identify three broad types. The most frequently occurring style in their sample (38.4 per cent) was that labelled 'criminality'. In these cases the victim is attacked by someone who appears to have planned the attack and controls the victim by threat and restraint (e.g. tying, gagging, blindfolding). They may use a disguise and they may steal unidentifiable goods to sell on.

The second most prevalent style is that of 'intimacy' (32.8 per cent). While the lay view may incorporate a masked man who ties up his victim, the majority have very little expectation of the 'intimacy' style offender. These offenders tend to talk to the victim and ask her questions about her life. They may stay with her after the attack is completed and sometimes reveal details about themselves. They may compliment the victim, or apologise, and their sexual behaviour may involve kissing. Such is the deviation of this style from our expectations that even very experienced detectives have been shown to consistently underestimate the likely occurrence of these behaviours. Wilson *et al.* (1996) asked 52 senior detectives to estimate the percentage occurrence of a series of rape behaviours for UK stranger rapes. The results showed that the intimacy behaviours were underestimated while the more 'prototypical' features such as disguise, and threats were consistently overestimated.

The final type of rapes are described as 'aggression' and it is here that the media portrayals find their closest fit, with verbal and physical violence directed toward the victim. But this subset of stranger rapes only accounts for 28.8 per cent of the sample. Although it is recorded that over 80 per cent of victims resisted their attacker, this includes verbal resistance, such that 'please don't' may be counted. In reality, most victims report that they are too frightened to put up any physical resistance.

The classic rape scenario is one aspect of a set of beliefs collectively known as 'rape myths', which have been consistently found to be endorsed by a large proportion of the population. Rape myths can be defined as 'prejudicial, stereotyped or false beliefs about rape, rape victims and rapists' (Burt 1980: 217). Rape myths not only define what constitutes a typical – and therefore 'genuine' – rape but also add another layer of belief about the victim's role in 'bringing it on herself' and the offender's justifications for thinking that the victim consented. For example, female rape victims are often considered to have been 'wanting it' and male rape victims are thought to have been 'asking for it' (Koss and Harvey 1991; Mezey and King 1992). Rape myths, such as 'all women secretly want to be raped' or 'women who wear short skirts are asking for it', are incorporated in the belief systems of both lay people and professionals (Barber 1974; Burt 1978;

Feild 1978; Kalven and Zeisel 1966). Many attitudes towards rape are strongly connected to other pervasive attitudes, such as sex role stereotyping, adversarial sexual beliefs and a general acceptance of interpersonal violence (Burt 1980).

The rape myth acceptance (RMA) literature is vast and outside the scope of this review, but there are some trends worth summarising here. Overall, men are more likely to believe rape myths related to victim-blaming, and often have more limited definitions of rape than women (Kleinke and Meyer 1990; McLendon *et al.* 1994). There is also evidence that men are more likely than women to assume that the victim of a sexual assault provoked the attack in some way and blame them for their victimisation (Foley *et al.* 1995; Kleinke and Meyer 1990; Whatley and Riggio 1993). However, other demographic differences in RMA are less clear. In Lonsway and Fitzgerald's (1994) meta-analysis of RMA research there was no conclusive evidence regarding who is more accepting, in terms of ethnicity, age or educational/occupational variables. Nevertheless, regardless of sub-group differences, the absolute levels are still unacceptably high. Even more concerning is the finding that RMA is prevalent within the CJS (Rape Crisis Federation 1999, 2001). Those working in the CJS (such as police officers, prosecutors and judges) showed a tendency to agree that rape occurs because women dressed or behaved in a seductive manner, because women were a poor judge of character, or because of a stereotype of women as sex objects (Feldman-Summers and Palmer 1980). Most astonishing, perhaps, is that officials also agreed that the number of rapes could be reduced by altering the behaviour of potential victims (Feldman-Summers and Palmer 1980).

The issues that arise with respect to attrition at every stage of the CJS relate to the notions of typical rape and the extent of the divergence between this and the crime in question. There are two areas of concern for victims who have decided to report the crime to the police; first whether they will be believed and treated as a victim of crime, and second, the way in which they may be treated in general during their interactions with the CJS.

Will I be believed?

Being believed has been found to be the most important factor for victims reporting their assault to the police (Bachman 1998; Solórzano 2007; Williams 1984). Even in those cases where the offender was subsequently found guilty, if the victim felt that the officer they dealt with did not believe them, they rated their experience negatively (Temkin 1999). In studies of victims' experiences of reporting victimisation, women have often stated that they felt they were not believed by police officers and that they lacked support from officers (Chambers and Millar 1986; Hall 1985; Wright 1984).

Whether the victim is believed of course relates to the nature of the attack and whether it fits the predetermined criteria. The closer the fit the more likelihood that the victim will feel they have been taken seriously. Rape myths lead people to minimise or avoid acknowledging the injuries a victim has incurred, or even blame the victim for their injuries or for the attack itself (e.g. Calhoun et al. 1976; Jones and Aronson 1973; Lerner 1970; Lerner et al. 1976; Smith et al. 1976; Weis and Borges 1973). The following sections examine the key aspects that diverge from false notions of the 'typical' rape: victim gender, the offender–victim relationship and the presence of serious physical injury.

Male victims

Being a male victim is perhaps the greatest divergence from the typical rape and explains why so very few male victims report (Calderwood 1987; Hodge and Canter 1998; King and Woolett 1997; Mitchell et al. 1999; Walker et al. 2005). Research shows that women are significantly more likely to report rape than men (Pino and Meier 1999), and that males find it harder to report rape than women (Groth and Burgess 1980; Kaufman et al. 1980; McMullen 1990; Stanko and Hobdell 1993). During the 1990s male victims of sexual abuse both in childhood (Hunter 1990; Mendel 1995; Violato and Genius 1993) and in adulthood (Ashworth 1995; McMullen 1990) began to receive greater recognition. Nevertheless, male victims of rape are still largely misunderstood (Rentoul and Appleboom 1997; Stanko and Hobdell 1993). Male rape was only legally recognised with the introduction of the Criminal Justice and Public Order Act 1994. This incorporated male rape into the traditional definition of rape by including anal penetration as part of rape. Thus rape is now defined as an offence if a man has vaginal or anal penetrative sex with an individual (male or female) who does not give their consent.

Being believed is a serious issue for male victims (Gunn and Linden 1997), and it is generally agreed that there is a perception of 'implausibility' around male victims of sexual assault (Pino and Meier 1999). For male victims, others' perceptions are arguably even more salient since there are stereotypes surrounding what a 'victim' is which are pervaded by assumptions about gender, with victims typically being women or children (Seabrook 1990). The gender of the victim also influences male views of rape with men less likely to class a scenario as rape when a victim is a homosexual male rather than a heterosexual woman (Rentoul and Appleboom 1997).

Acquaintance rape

In cases where the offender is previously known to the victim, under-reporting is even more prevalent (Ford *et al.* 1998). The first and most obvious stage of the decision to report is the victim's own perceptions of whether a crime has been committed. If the victim him or herself does not believe that the act constituted a crime then reporting will not be considered. If the victim knows their attacker they are less likely to identify themselves as a rape victim (Oros *et al.* 1980). The victim may fear that they led the attacker on, meaning they were not really raped and so believe there is no crime to report (Schwendinger and Schwendinger 1980; Weis and Borges 1973).

Studies have found that women who were attacked by a stranger were most likely to receive a sympathetic response from the police, and that sympathy increased with the level of physical injury experienced by the victim (Feldman-Summers and Norris 1984; Koss *et al.* 1985; Williams 1984). If the victim and offender are current or former partners, the police are most likely to take a 'no further action' (NFA) decision (Lea *et al.* 2003).

Therefore it seems that victims are right to consider the believability of the incident to be important and, in accordance with this, women are more likely to report a rape if it corresponds with the 'classic rape' scenario (Weis and Borges 1973). As previously mentioned, a number of researchers have found that rapes are more likely to be reported to the police when the offender is a stranger rather than someone known to the victim (Feldman-Summers and Ashworth 1981; Greenberg and Ruback 1992; Lizotte 1985; McDermott 1979; Williams 1984). Given that the majority of male rapes are acquaintance rapes (Mezey and King 1992), this further exacerbates the reporting problem for male victims.

Therefore, the relationship to the offender can be an important factor in the decision to report (Bachman 1998; Williams 1984) although there is disagreement over which way this factor works. Some have found that victims who were assaulted by someone they already knew were less likely to report a rape (Solórzano 2007), while others have found that victims assaulted by someone known to them are more likely to report (Bachman 1998). Further, those assaulted by parents, relatives or acquaintances are less likely to withdraw than those assaulted by partners or ex-partners (Feist *et al*. 2007). These apparent contradictions may arise from treating all acquaintance rapes as one homogenous group when in reality acquaintance rape includes a whole range of victim–offender relationships from platonic friends to ex-partners to someone seen regularly in a shop (Wilson and Leith 2001).

There has been some suggestion that if there is a previous relationship, the victim may be reluctant to report with the knowledge that the rapist may be sent to prison (Schwendinger and Schwendinger 1980) or that the offender will be given a harsh sentence (Fox and Scherl 1972). Victims may wish to protect their friends/family or the friends/family of the offender (Weis and Borges 1973).

Physical harm

Many victims experience great difficulty in accepting and admitting they have been a victim of a crime (Hagan 1986; Mezey and King 1992). The degree of force a victim is subjected to is the main factor in deciding how victims label their experience (Williams 1984). Victims are more likely to view themselves as a rape victim if they experienced a high level of violence and are physically injured (Amir 1971). Being choked, tied up, locked up or subjected to some other type of high violence will encourage women to see themselves as rape victims (Oros *et al*. 1980). Those women who are beaten, hospitalised, become pregnant or contract a sexually transmitted disease are also more likely to identify themselves as a rape victim and so more likely to report a rape (Baker and Peterson 1977).

Greenberg and Ruback's model of Victim Decision-Making (1992) confirms that one way in which victims determine the seriousness of their crime is by the amount of physical harm they experienced. For example, if the offender had a weapon, the victim was subjected to degrading acts or the victim sustained physical injuries, the attack appears significantly more likely to be reported to the police, a finding backed up by other studies (Amir 1971; Bachman 1998; Feldman-Summers and Norris 1982). However, in reality, Feist *et al*. (2007) report that just 30 per cent of victims were subjected to physical or emotional threat during or prior to the assault, and only a third of victims actually experienced physical assault. Here again, it is not just the decision to report that is affected by the typical rape myth; if there is no violence or threat of violence, cases are likely to be no-crimed by the police, or a 'no further action' decision is likely to be made (Harris and Grace 1999).

Greenberg and Ruback's (1992) study also found that the location of the attack influenced the victim's decision to report, with more victims reporting attacks that occurred outdoors, while Lizotte (1985) found that a victim is more likely to report when the offender has less right to be at the scene of the attack. These two factors are possibly related to the image that the victim was accosted by someone who was not part of their normal routine and that they were therefore less 'responsible' for the attack, but might also be explained by the non-reporting of those who went somewhere with an offender and who subsequently felt that because of this they were somehow to blame.

Many victims will blame themselves for the attack, or worry that they will be blamed by their family and friends or the police (Williams 1984). Victims of acquaintance rape are more likely to self-blame than victims of stranger rape and see their 'role' in the incident as a factor that will prevent them from being believed.

It is not just the single factors of gender, violence and relationship that independently contribute to perceptions of the attack; the factors frequently co-occur to accentuate the disparity between an attack and the typical rape.

It is assumed that a male victim should be able to fight off an attacker, as there is a social expectation that men are able to protect themselves (Ashworth 1995; McMullen 1990). Consequently, men are more likely to report rape when they can show that they could not have protected themselves (Pino and Meier 1999). Male victims of sexual assault have an expectation that they are powerful and able to defend themselves. This expectation influences the way male victims are seen by their friends and family, as well as healthcare and criminal justice officials (Huckle 1995; Mezey and King 1987, 1989).

A close victim–offender relationship prior to the attack usually means the attack will be less violent, with a lower likelihood of injury or less need for medical treatment (Williams 1984). This results in a lack of evidence that will allow the victim to identify themselves as a rape victim. Women who are raped by someone they have just met romantically or socially ('date rape') are most likely to be subject to the intimacy-style rape behaviours which are seen as atypical of rape in general (Wilson and Leith 2001). However, in Wilson and Leith's (2000) study it was the ex-partners who reported the most violent and abusive style rapes. This raises some complications in predicting reporting. The rapes studied in Wilson and Leith's research were reported to the police, so it may have been the violence that overcame the reluctance of ex-partners to report. Such are the problems for researchers studying a relatively hidden phenomenon.

How will I be treated?

Alongside fear of not being taken seriously, fear of poor treatment by the police and/or others within the CJS has been found to affect victims' decision to report an offence (Hagan 1986; Mezey and King 1992; Schultz 1975). Research shows that many rape victims will not have had any contact with the police until they have to report their own victimisation (Davies 2000) and therefore have very little to go on when constructing an image of what their experience will entail. The actions and behaviours of the people that a rape victim interacts with immediately after the assault are critical to the victim's ultimate psychological health. Sexual assault victims need to be treated with acceptance, empathy and support (Koss and Harvey 1991). Reporting a rape or sexual assault to the police is a qualitatively different process to reporting an assault because police treat victims of sexual assaults differently to victims of other crimes, showing a tendency towards scepticism (Myers and LaFree 1982). The primary factors which discourage reporting by female rape victims are embarrassment (MacDonald 1971), humiliation and guilt (Hecht 1993, 1996; Wiehe and Richards 1995).

Inconsistencies in the behaviour of police officers dealing with victims of sexual offending was first discovered in the 1970s and 1980s, and exists both across forces and between cases (Estrich 1987; Holmstrom and Burgess 1978; Medea and Thompson 1974; Smith 1989). The police force area in which an attack took place also appears to influence rates of withdrawal of complaint, with the implication being that some forces are better at dealing with rape victims than others, and therefore better at reducing the likelihood of withdrawal on the part of the victim (Feist et al. 2007). In the past, the police and court system were identified as engaging in practices which were considered to discourage reporting (Lowe 1984) and some have gone as far as to say that female victims would be less likely to report assaults if they truly understood the difficulties rape victims experience as they go through the criminal justice process (Lizotte 1985). However, in recent years there have been a number of initiatives introduced to improve the victim's experience of the CJS (Jordan 2001), for example the introduction of separate rape examination suites (Lees 1997).

Nevertheless, female victims of sexual assault still do not report because they do not believe that they will be dealt with in confidence (Bachman 1998) and male victims may fear that their sexual preferences will be criticised or questioned by both their friends and families or officials such as healthcare workers or the police (King 1995). They may fear that their sexuality will be questioned, that they will be labelled homosexual themselves (Goyer and Eddleman 1984; Huckle 1995; Mezey and King 1989; Rentoul and Appleboom 1997). Male victims of sexual assault are particularly concerned about the impact on their own masculinity and consequent confusion they experience regarding their sexuality (King 1995).

For male victims, as for females, the actual act of reporting an assault is distressing in itself (Groth and Burgess 1980). Shock and embarrassment may mean that men are discouraged from reporting sexual crimes against them (McMullen 1990) and subsequently getting themselves help (Stanko and Hobdell 1993). Victims may fear further degradation by the authorities (Gunn and Linden 1997), and may fear that they will experience homophobia from the police (Goyer and Eddleman 1984; Huckle 1995; Mezey and King 1989). Homosexual male victims may be even more reluctant to report rape than heterosexual victims, with many not reporting because they feel that the police will be unsympathetic and believe they were 'asking for it' (Mezey and King 1992).

The attitudes of criminal justice workers influence reporting (Pollard 1992). Negative attitudes create lower levels of reporting, leading to more offenders going undetected and victims missing out on the support they need (Davies 2002). It is therefore vital that victims have confidence that they will be treated well by the CJS in order to reduce crime and safeguard the welfare of victims.

How will others perceive me?

Apart from the reactions of the CJS professionals that a victim will encounter, beliefs about the opinions of others are also relevant to the decision to report. Many victims feel that it will become known that they have been a victim of rape and that this will influence the way they are treated by colleagues, friends and family. The notoriety or stigma that goes along with being a rape victim may put a victim off reporting the assault to the police (Amir 1971).

The research suggests that rape victims are right to be concerned about the reactions of others to their having been a victim. People tend to react differently to victims of rape than they do to victims of other types of assault (Bachman 1998). Rape victims are often viewed with suspicion and doubt (Allison and Wrightsman 1993) and may experience negativity and disbelief. In one study of the views of almost 600 people, over half of the participants believed 50 per cent or more of reported rapes are not genuine. Instead, participants believed that an allegation of rape was made as an act of anger or revenge or to cover up an illegitimate pregnancy (Burt 1980).

Some other reasons for non-reporting have also been suggested by the research. Some victims have said that they are too busy to participate in a prosecution (Amir 1971). In the US, victims who did not report their assault most often said it was a private or personal matter that they dealt with outside of the official channels (Bachman 1998). Victims have also expressed fears that there may be retaliation by the offender or their friends/family. In the US, the annual National Crime Victimization Survey of 101,000 respondents showed that one in ten victims did not report an attack because they feared reprisals by the offender (Bachman 1998).

Will it result in a conviction?

If the case reaches trial, there are two main issues that affect the victim – first the way they feel they may be treated during the trial and second whether the outcome will be worth enduring the process.

Victims of sexual assault experience all the same reactions as victims of other crimes, such as a desire for justice and a wish to see the offender apprehended (Schultz 1975). This is therefore a strong reason for reporting the crime; however, it is mediated by the victim's perceptions of how likely it is that the offender will really be convicted. Some victims lack confidence that the CJS will apprehend or punish the offender (Ashworth and Feldman-Summers 1978; Law Enforcement Assistance Administration 1974; McDermott 1979). These factors are therefore part of the balance of costs and benefits that the victim must assess: whether all the perceived negatives about reporting the crime and experiencing the process will be worth the benefit of seeing the offender brought to justice. Part of this decision is also influenced not only by a victim's desire to see justice for their own crime, but in order to protect others from being victims in the future, although some victims of sexual assault report feeling pressured to report assaults to the police in order to protect other women from undergoing an assault at the hands of the same offender (Schultz 1975).

During the 1960s and 1970s there was increasing concern that a rape trial commonly turned into a cross-examination of the victim and her lifestyle (Durston 1998; Holmstrom and Burgess 1983; Weis and Borges 1973; Williams and Holmes 1981). In the UK, the Sexual Offences (Amendment) Act 1976 was introduced as a response to the poor treatment of rape victims at the hands of the CJS. Nevertheless, the lifestyle of the victim may still be called into question in relation to the crime. For example, prostitutes often face insensitivity and incredulity when reporting rape, largely because they are already perceived as promiscuous (Miller and Schwartz 1995).

There has been a significant fall in the conviction rate for rape in England and Wales in the past 20 years, from 24 per cent in 1985 to just 9 per cent in 1997 (Harris and Grace 1999). Other studies report figures such as 13 per cent (Feist et al. 2007) and 18 per cent (Brown et al. 2007). Here again, the relationship between the 'template' of a classic rape and the details of the actual crime under consideration come back into play. There will be many who will say that the decision to prosecute has nothing to do with perceptions of the victim or the crime but with 'evidence', and that the amount of defence or prosecution evidence relates to the jury's decision (LaFree 1980).

But what is considered evidence necessarily relates to the crime, and evidence that is perceived as strong includes the offender being a stranger, a weapon being used and the victim suffering injuries that require medical attention (Lizotte 1985). Other factors that relate to the typical rape also appear again with respect to convictions; for example, convictions are less likely when the attack occurs in the victim's home, and decrease in likelihood the longer the victim takes to report the crime, presumably increasing the perception that reporting was done as cover-up or revenge (LaFree 1980).

If the victim's medical history was taken at the reporting stage or forensic evidence was recovered after the attack the likelihood of getting the case to court and achieving a conviction is significantly increased (Feist et al. 2007). If there is evidence that the assault is linked to another sexual offence, this strengthens the case enormously (Feist et al. 2007), as does the involvement of more than one offender (LaFree 1980). The chance of the case proceeding to court and achieving a conviction is significantly increased if the offender threatened the victim and if witnesses were present (Feist et al. 2007).

Deterrence

There are two forms of deterrence: general deterrence which refers to society's attitude towards crime, and specific deterrence whereby an individual may consider what would happen to them personally if they break the law. Research has suggested that would-be rapists are deterred by the threat of formal sanctions (Antunes and Hunt 1973; Bachman *et al.* 1992; Tittle 1969). According to deterrence theory, the sole factor that will deter potential offenders from crime is the certainty that they will be caught and subsequently punished for their crime (Bachman 1998). Deterrence underpins the CJS, but in order for punishment to be effective it must be 'certain, severe and swift' (Blackburn 1993).

However, at present there is a lot of discussion in the popular media about falling apprehension and conviction rates for sex offending and that very few sexual offenders are actually punished for their crime, thus undermining the aim of the CJS. There have also been a number of cases in which offenders have been given lenient sentences for serious offences. Reports such as these reinforce the idea that the CJS does not take a harsh view of sexual offending and may lead potential offenders to believe that they will not be punished. In addition to these factors undermining the CJS's attempts to deter offenders, they may also deter victims. A key factor in the decision to report an offence is the belief that the offender will be punished. With this kind of media coverage appearing on a regular basis, victims may begin to believe that there is simply no point in reporting their crime. This may lead to a self-fulfilling prophecy in which victims do not report because they do not believe the offender will be punished and offenders commit crimes because they do not perceive a strong deterrent.

However, there are two arguments against this hypothesis and both relate to the causes of sexual crime. A common objection to deterrence theory is that many crimes are impulsive or emotionally driven and as such lack reasoning about the consequences (Blackburn 1993). The deterrent effect of the CJS is more likely to exist with instrumental crimes such as burglary (Blackburn 1993) in which offenders are commonly seen to complete a profit/cost calculation before offending (Cornish and Clarke 1986). This is not necessarily the case in sexual offences. Finkelhor (1984) identified four preconditions to sexual offending. Crucially, the offender must be motivated to sexually offend. They have to overcome their internal inhibitors to offending such as their own conscience and convince themselves that their desires are acceptable. Once the offender has convinced themselves that their desires are acceptable, they must overcome external inhibitors such as limited access to their target. Offenders may employ detailed strategies to do this, such as staking out dark alleys or locations where women are likely to be alone. Finally, the offender must overcome the victim's resistance to the assault, potentially with violence or threats.

In the Finkelhor model the threat of punishment as a deterrent plays a very small role. The offender moves through the four stages before committing the assault, and rather than conducting a conscious risk/benefit analysis they convince themselves that their desires are acceptable. Subsequently sexual offenders often do not believe that their offence is actually a crime (Lord 2003). Sex offenders have been shown to deny that they have committed a crime (Nichols and Molinder 1984), and so the traditional deterrent aspect of the CJS and the use of punishment as a deterrent is lacking with these offenders.

The first argument then relates to the sexual predator. The second concerns those offenders who 'genuinely' did not believe the act was a crime at all and concerns those rapes that have been attributed to 'miscommunication'. In these rapes, then, the man believes that consent has been given or implied, even when not specifically verbalised. The most frequently cited example is where the victim is drunk and there is some uncertainty over whether they are capable of giving consent. These types of rape have been the focus of a recent campaign aimed specifically at young men, informing them of the importance of ensuring that their partner has given 'active consent' before having sex. Naturally, there has been some controversy over the miscommunication perspective, with some researchers claiming that men are quite capable of determining lack of consent, even in its most subtle non-verbal forms (e.g. O'Bryne et al. 2006).

The role of deterrence then, depends on the type of offender and contains a great deal of complexity that may not be addressed by simply telling 'would-be rapists' that they will not get away with their crimes. Nevertheless, the message is important for victims who need to know that they will be believed and treated with sympathy and respect. In order that they are believed, both the public and those involved in the CJS would benefit from a better understanding of rape behaviour in general in order to counteract people's reliance on 'typical rape' stereotypes.

References

Ahmed, K. and Bright, M. (2000) 'Women angry as "rapists go free"', *The Observer*, 30 July.

Allison, J.A. and Wrightsman, L.S. (1993) *Rape: The Misunderstood Crime.* Newbury Park, CA: Sage.

Amir, M. (1971) *Patterns in Forcible Rape.* Chicago: University of Chicago Press.

Antunes, G.E. and Hunt, A.L. (1973) 'The deterrent impact of criminal sanctions: some implications for criminal justice policy', *Journal of Urban Law*, 51 (2): 145–61.

Ashworth, A. (1995) *Principles of Criminal Law*, 2nd edn. Oxford: Oxford University Press.

Ashworth, C.D. and Feldman-Summers, S. (1978) 'Perceptions of the effectiveness of the criminal justice system', *Criminal Justice and Behavior*, 5 (3): 227–40.

Bachman, R. (1998) 'The factors related to rape reporting behavior and arrest', *Criminal Justice and Behavior*, 25 (1): 8–29.

Bachman, R., Paternoster, R. and Ward, S. (1992) 'The rationality of sexual offending: testing a deterrence/rational choice conception of sexual assault', *Law and Society Review*, 26 (2): 343–72.

Baker, A.L. and Peterson, C. (1977) 'Self-blame by rape victims as a function of the rape's consequences: an attributional analysis', *Crisis Intervention*, 8 (3): 92–104.

Barber, R. (1974) 'Judge and jury attitudes to rape', *Australia and New Zealand Journal of Criminology*, 7: 157–72.

Blackburn, R. (1993) *The Psychology of Criminal Conduct.* Chichester: Wiley.

Brown, J.M., Hamilton, C. and O'Neill, D. (2007) 'Characteristics associated with rape attrition and the role played by scepticism or legal rationality by investigators and prosecutors', *Psychology, Crime and Law*, 13 (4): 355–70.

Burt, M. (1978) 'Attitudes supportive of rape in American culture', in House Committee on Science and Technology, Subcommittee on Domestic and International Scientific Planning, Analysis and Cooperation, *Research into Violent Behavior: Sexual Assaults.* Hearing, 95th Congress, 2nd Session, 10–12 January 1978. Washington, DC: Government Printing Office, pp. 277–322.

Burt, M.R. (1980) 'Cultural myths and supports for rape', *Journal of Personality and Social Psychology*, 38 (2): 217–30.

Calderwood, D. (1987) 'The male rape victim', *Medical Aspects of Human Sexuality*, 21: 181–9.

Calhoun, L.G., Selby, J.W. and Warring, L.J. (1976) 'Social perception of the victim's causal role in rape: exploratory examination of four factors', *Human Relations*, 29: 517–26.

Chambers, G. and Millar, A. (1986) *Prosecuting Sexual Assault*. Edinburgh: Scottish Office Central Research Unit.

Cornish, D.B. and Clarke, R.V. (1986) *The Reasoning Criminal: Rational Choice Perspectives on Offending*. New York: Springer.

Davies, M. (2000) 'Male sexual assault victims: a selective review of the literature and implications for support services', *Aggression and Violent Behavior*, 6: 1–12.

Davies, M. (2002) 'Male sexual assault victims: a selective review of the literature and implications for support services', *Aggression and Violent Behavior: A Review Journal*, 7: 203–14.

Donald, I.J. and Canter, D. (1992) 'Intentionality and fatality during the King's Cross Underground fire', *European Journal of Social Psychology*, 22 (3): 203–18.

Durston, G. (1998) 'Cross-examination of rape complainants: ongoing tensions between conflicting priorities in the criminal justice system', *Journal of Criminal Law*, 62: 91.

Estrich, S. (1987) *Real Rape*. Cambridge, MA: Harvard University Press.

Feild, H.S. (1978) 'Attitudes toward rape: a comparative analysis of police, rapists, crisis counsellors, and citizens', *Journal of Personality and Social Psychology*, 36: 156–79.

Feist, A., Ashe, J., Lawrence, J., McPhee, D. and Wilson, R. (2007) *Investigating and Detecting Recorded Offences of Rape*, Home Office Online Report 18/07. London: Home Office.

Feldman-Summers, S. and Ashworth, C.D. (1981) 'Factors related to intentions to report a rape', *Journal of Social Issues*, 37 (4): 53–70.

Feldman-Summers, S. and Norris, J. (1982) 'Differences Between Rape Victims who Report and Those Who Do Not Report to a Public Agency'. Unpublished paper, Psychology Department, University of Washington, Seattle, WA.

Feldman-Summers, S. and Norris, J. (1984) 'Differences between rape victims who report and those who do not report to a public agency', *Journal of Applied Social Psychology*, 14 (6): 562–73.

Feldman-Summers, S. and Palmer, G.C. (1980) 'Rape as viewed by judges, prosecutors and police officers', *Criminal Justice and Behavior*, 7 (1): 19–40.

Finkelhor, D. (1984) *Child Sexual Abuse: New Theory and Research*. New York: Free Press.

Foley, L.A., Evancic, C., Karnik, K., King, J. and Parks, A. (1995) 'Date rape: effects of race of assailant and victim and gender of subjects on perceptions', *Journal of Black Psychology*, 21: 6–18.

Ford, T.M., Liwag-McLamb, M.G. and Foley, L.A. (1998) 'Perceptions of rape based on sex and sexual orientation of victim', *Journal of Social Behaviour and Personality*, 13 (2): 253–63.

Fox, S.S. and Scherl, D.J. (1972) 'Crisis intervention with victims of rape', *Social Work*, 17 (1): 37–42.

Goyer, P.F. and Eddleman, H.C. (1984) 'Same-sex rape of non-incarcerated men', *American Journal of Psychiatry*, 134: 1239–43.

Greenberg, M.S. and Ruback, R.B. (1992) *After the Crime: Victim Decision-Making*. New York: Plenum.

Gross, A.M., Weed, N.C. and Lawson, G.D. (1998) 'Magnitude scaling of intensity of sexual refusal behaviours in a date rape', *Violence Against Women*, 4: 329–39.

Groth, A.N. and Burgess, A.W. (1980) 'Male rape: offenders and victims', *American Journal of Psychiatry*, 137 (7): 806–10.

Gunn, R. and Linden, R. (1997) 'The impact of law reform on the processing of sexual assault cases', *Canadian Review of Sociology and Anthropology*, 34: 155–74.

Hagan, F. (1986) *Introduction to Criminology: Theories, Methods and Criminal Behaviour*. Chicago: Nelson-Hall.

Hall, R. (1985) *Ask Any Woman: A London Inquiry into Rape and Sexual Assault*. Bristol: Falling Wall Press.

Harris, J. and Grace, A. (1999) *A Question of Evidence? Investigating and Prosecuting Rape in the 1990s*, Home Office Research Study No. 196. London: Home Office.

Hecht, S.L. (1993) 'Writing and reading about rape: a primer', *St Johns Law Review*, 66: 979–1061.

Hecht, S.L. (1996) 'Topics of our times: rape is a major public health issue', *American Journal of Public Health*, 86: 15–17.

Hodge, S. and Canter, D. (1998) 'Victims and perpetrators of male sexual assault', *Journal of Interpersonal Violence*, 13 (2): 222–40.

Holmstrom, L.L. and Burgess, A.W. (1978) *Four to Six-Year Follow up of Rape Victims*, address by Ann Wolbert Burgess. University of Illinois at Chicago Circle, May.

Holmstrom, L.L. and Burgess, A.W. (1983) *The Victim of Rape: Institutional Reactions*. New York: Transaction Press.

Huckle, P.L. (1995) 'Male rape victims referred to a forensic psychiatric service', *Medicine Science Law*, 35 (3): 187–92.

Hunter, M. (1990) *The Sexually Abused Male: Volume 1. Prevalence, Impact and Treatment*. Lexington MA: Lexington.

Jones, C. and Aronson, E. (1973) 'Attribution of fault to a rape victim as a function of respectability of the victim', *Journal of Personality and Social Psychology*, 26: 415–19.

Jordan, J. (2001) 'Worlds apart? Women, rape and the police reporting process', *British Journal of Criminology*, 41: 679–706.

Kalven, H. and Zeisel, H. (1966) *The American Jury*. Chicago: University of Chicago Press.

Kaufman, A., Divasto, P., Jackson, R., Voorhes, D. and Christy, J. (1980) 'Male rape victims: noninstitutionalised assault', *American Journal of Psychiatry*, 137 (2): 221–23.

Kelly, L., Lovett, J. and Regan, L. (2005) *A Gap or a Chasm? Attrition in Reported Rape Cases*, Home Office Research Study No. 293. London: Home Office.

King, M. (1995) 'Sexual assaults on men: assessment and management', *British Journal of Hospital Medicine*, 53: 245–6.

King, M.B. and Woolett, E. (1997) 'Sexually assaulted males: 115 men consulting a counselling service', *Archives of Sexual Behaviour*, 26: 579–88.

Kleinke, C.L. and Meyer, C. (1990) 'Evaluation of a rape victim by men and women with a high and low belief in a just world', *Psychology of Women Quarterly*, 14: 343–53.

Koss, M. and Harvey, M. (1991) *The Rape Victim: Clinical and Community Interventions*. Newbury Park, CA: Sage.

Koss, M.P., Dinero, T.E., Seibel, C. and Cox, S. (1985) 'Stranger and acquaintance rape: are there differences in the victim's experience?', *Psychology of Women Quarterly*, 12: 1–23.

LaFree, G. (1980) 'Variables affecting guilty pleas and convictions in rape cases: toward a social theory of rape processing', *Social Forces*, 58 (3): 833–50.

Law Enforcement Assistance Administration (1974) *Crime in the Nation's Five Largest Cities. Advance Report*. Washington, DC: US Department of Justice, National Criminal Justice Information and Statistics Service.

Lea, S.J., Lanvers, U. and Shaw, S. (2003) 'Attrition in rape cases: developing a profile and identifying relevant factors', *British Journal of Criminology*, 43: 583–99.

Lees, S. (1997) 'In search of gender justice', in S. Lees (ed.), *Ruling Passions: Sexual Violence, Reputation and the Law*. Buckingham: Open University Press, pp. 175–90.

Lerner, M.J. (1970) 'The desire for justice and reactions to victims', in J. McCauley and L. Berkowitz (eds), *Altruism and Helping Behavior*. New York: Academic Press, pp. 205–29.

Lerner, M.J., Miller, D.T. and Holmes, J.C. (1976) 'Deserving versus justice: a contemporary dilemma', in L. Berkowitz and E. Walster (eds), *Advances in Experimental Social Psychology*, Vol. 9. New York: Academic Press, pp. 133–62.

Lizotte, A.J. (1985) 'The uniqueness of rape: reporting assaultive violence to the police', *Crime and Delinquency*, 31: 169–90.

Lonsway, K.A. and Fitzgerald, L.F. (1994) 'Rape myths: in review', *Psychology of Women Quarterly*, 18 (2): 133–64.

Lord, A. (2003) 'Working with personality-disordered offenders', *Forensic Update*, 73: 31–9.

Lowe, M. (1984) 'The role of the judiciary in the failure of the Sexual Offences (Amendment) Act to improve the treatment of the rape victim', in J. Hopkins (ed.), *Perspectives on Rape and Sexual Assault*. London: Harper & Row, pp. 67–88.

MacDonald, J.M. (1971) *Rape Offenders and Their Victims*. Springfield, IL: Charles C. Thomas.

McDermott, M.J. (1979) *Rape Victimization in 26 American Cities*. Washington, DC: US Department of Justice, Law Enforcement Assistance Administration, National Criminal Justice Information and Statistics Service, US Government Printing Office.

McLendon, K., Foley, L.A., Hall, J., Sloan, L., Wesley, A. and Perry, L. (1994) 'Male and female perceptions of date rape', *Journal of Social Behavior and Personality*, 9: 421–8.

McMullen, R.J. (1990) *Male Rape: Breaking the Silence on the Last Taboo*. London: GMP.

Medea, A. and Thompson, K. (1974) *Against Rape*. New York: Farrar, Straus & Giroux.

Mendel, P. (1995) *The Male Survivor: The Impact of Sexual Abuse*. Newbury Park, CA: Sage.

Mezey, G. and King, M. (1987) 'Male victims of sexual assault', *Medicine, Science and the Law*, 27: 122–4.

Mezey, G. and King, M. (1989) 'The effects of sexual assault on men: a survey of 22 victims', *Psychological Medicine*, 19: 205–9.

Mezey, G.C. and King, M.B. (1992) *Male Victims of Sexual Assault*. Oxford: Oxford University Press.

Miller, J. and Schwartz, M.D. (1995) 'Rape myths and violence against street prostitutes', *Deviant Behavior*, 16: 1–23.

Mitchell, D., Hirschman, R. and Nagayama-Hall, G.C. (1999) 'Attributions of victim responsibility, pleasure and trauma in male rape', *Journal of Sex Research*, 36 (4): 369–73.

Myers, M.A. and LaFree, G.D. (1982) 'Sexual assault and its prosecution: a comparison with other crimes', *Journal of Criminal Law and Criminology*, 73 (3): 1282–305.

Nicholas, S., Kershaw, C. and Walker, A. (eds) (2007) *Crime in England and Wales 2006/2007*, Home Office Statistical Bulletin. London: Home Office.

Nichols, H.R. and Molinder, L. (1984) *The Multiphasic Sex Inventory*. Tocomo, WA: Self-published.

O'Bryne, R., Rapley, M. and Hansen, S., (2006) '"You couldn't say 'no', could you?": young men's understandings of sexual refusal', *Feminism and Psychology*, 16 (2): 133–54.

Oros, C.J., Leonard, K. and Koss, M.P. (1980) 'Factors related to a self-attribution of rape by victims', *Personality and Social Psychology Bulletin*, 6 (2): 193.

Pino, N.W. and Meier, R.F. (1999) 'Gender differences in rape reporting', *Sex Roles*, 40 (11/12): 979–90.

Pollard, P. (1992) 'Judgements about victims and attackers in depicted rapes: a review', *British Journal of Social Psychology*, 31: 309–26.

Rainbow, L. (1996) 'False Rape Allegations: First Steps in a Multidimensional Approach to Detection of Deception in Rape Statements'. Unpublished MSc thesis, University of Liverpool.

Rape Crisis Federation (2004) *Rape, Statistics, Police Reporting, Court Procedures and the Law*. Nottingham: Rape Crisis Federation of Wales and England.

Rape Crisis Federation: Wales & England (1999) *Annual Report 1998–1999*. Nottingham: Rape Crisis Federation of Wales and England.

Rape Crisis Federation: Wales & England (2001) *Annual Report 1999–2001*. Nottingham: Rape Crisis Federation of Wales and England.

Rentoul, L. and Appleboom, N. (1997) 'Understanding the psychological impact of rape and serious sexual assault of men: a literature review', *Journal of Psychiatric and Mental Health Nursing*, 4: 267–74.

Schultz, C. (1975) *Rape Victimology*. Springfield, IL: Charles C. Thomas.

Schwendinger, H. and Schwendinger, J. (1980) 'Rape victims and the false sense of guilt', *Crime and Social Justice*, 13: 4–17.

Seabrook, J. (1990) 'Power lust', *New Statesman and Society*, 27 April, pp. 20–2.

Sime, J. (1990) 'The concept of panic', in D. Canter (ed.), *Fires and Human Behaviour*, 2nd edn. London: David Fulton, pp. 63–81.

Smith, L. (1989) *Concerns about Rape*, Home Office Research Study No. 106. London: HMSO.

Smith, R.E., Keating, J.P., Hester, R.K. and Mitchell, H.E. (1976) 'Role and justice considerations in the attribution of responsibility to a rape victim', *Journal of Research in Personality*, 10: 346–57.

Solórzano, B.H. (2007) 'A comprehensive review of the influences on reporting of sexual assaults', *Psychology of Women Quarterly*, 31 (2): 225–6.

Stanko, E.A. and Hobdell, K. (1993) 'Assault on men', *British Journal of Criminology*, 33: 400–15.

Temkin, J. (1999) 'Reporting rape in London: a qualitative study', *Howard Journal*, 38 (1): 17–41.

Tittle, C.R. (1969) 'Crime rates and legal sanctions', *Social Problems*, 16 (4): 409–23.

Violato, C. and Genius, M. (1993) 'Problems of research in male child sexual abuse: a review', *Journal of Child Sexual Abuse*, 2: 33–54.

Walker, J., Archer, J. and Davies, M. (2005) 'Effects of rape on male survivors: a descriptive analysis', *Archives of Sexual Behavior*, 34: 69–80.

Weis, K. and Borges, S. (1973) 'Victimology and rape: the case of the legitimate victim', *Issues in Criminology*, 8 (2): 71–115.

Whatley, M.A. and Riggio, R.E. (1993) 'Gender differences in attributions of blame for male rape victims', *Journal of Interpersonal Violence*, 8: 502–11.

Wiehe, V.R. and Richards, A.L. (1995) *Intimate Betrayal: Understanding and Responding to the Trauma of Acquaintance Rape*. Thousand Oaks, CA: Sage.

Williams, J.A. and Holmes, K.A. (1981) *The Second Assault: Rape and Public Attitudes*. Westport, CT: Greenwood Press.

Williams, L.S. (1984) 'The classic rape: when do victims report?', *Social Problems*, 31 (4): 459–67.

Wilson, M.A. and Leith, S. (2001) 'Acquaintances, lovers and friends: rape within relationships', *Journal of Applied Social Psychology*, 31 (8): 1709–26.

Wilson, M.A. and Smith, A. (1999) 'Roles and rules in terrorist hostage taking', in D. Canter and L. Alison (eds), *The Social Psychology of Crime: Groups, Teams and Networks*. Ashgate: Aldershot.

Wilson, M.A., Canter, D. and Jack, K. (1996) *The Psychology of Rape Investigation: A Study in Police Decision Making*, Final Report to the ESRC.

Wright, R. (1984) 'A note on attrition of rape cases', *British Journal of Criminology*, 24 (4): 399–400.

Chapter 7

Attitudes towards victims of crime: a double-edged sword?

Elizabeth Gilchrist

Introduction

Victimisation experience significantly affects the lives of those involved. Research in Scotland identified that 20 per cent of victim respondents reported still being preoccupied with their victimisation experience even twelve months after it occurred (MacLeod *et al*. 1996). Additionally, the response of others to the victim can have as great an effect as the original victimisation experience. Thus it is clearly important to explore public attitudes to victims of crime and to probe what factors affect these attitudes. It is also crucial to explore how attitudes to victims impact on judgments of victims and to consider the effect this can have on the criminal justice process.

Some key questions considered throughout the chapter are: (1) whether or not strong beliefs about victims and appropriate victim behaviour and demeanour create stereotypes of the 'deserving victim' (Richardson and May 1999); (2) whether victim behaviours that do not fit with widely held beliefs regarding appropriate victim behaviour create public tension; and (3) whether victim characteristics unrelated to their victimisation affect how victims are seen and treated within the criminal justice system (CJS).

What is the role of the victim in the criminal justice system?

The role of the victim in the CJS has always been equivocal. With many types of crime, the role of the victim is central, in the opportunity for the offence to occur, the reporting of the offence and then the subsequent prosecution of the offender(s). In other types of crime, the 'victim' is less central and indeed sometimes less identifiable (e.g. so-called victimless crime such as drug-taking and prostitution). The role of the victim also varies according to the philosophy of the prosecution system of the country. In a 'public law' system, the role of the victim is less influential as criminal prosecutions are pursued by the Crown on behalf of society and as such the victim has the role of being a key witness to the offence (Gilchrist 1995). In countries where a 'private law' mentality is more influential, the victim has a slightly different role, with their views as 'the complainant' carrying great weight in initiating and sustaining a prosecution. In England and Wales, although there is now a public prosecution service, historically criminal proceedings were private matters. Even the police prosecuted as private bodies on behalf of the victims. Also, while the right is not always exercised and it is possible for the Crown Prosecution Service to 'take over' a private prosecution case and discontinue it, it is still possible in England and Wales for a victim to pursue a private prosecution through the criminal courts. In this system, particularly in sexual offences and offences from within a domestic setting, the victim has a more central role. However, although it is common to hear that victims have 'dropped the charges', charges can only be dropped with the consent of the Crown Prosecution Service. If the CPS does not consent then the prosecution goes ahead.

Later in criminal proceedings the victim again plays a very important role. The importance of the role at this stage is influenced less by philosophy and more by offence type. The victim's evidence can be a crucial aspect of proving a case. This is particularly true in cases of interpersonal violence and cases involving family members, child victims and sexual and domestic offences. It has been suggested that for some offences, for example cases of rape, it can appear that it is the victim rather than the defendant who is being assessed in terms of their credibility, which is closely linked to whether they present as a 'deserving victim'.

Later in the process, at sentence, there is a further role for the victim. Until recently the victim has been considered in an indirect manner – and again the role is influenced by the philosophy of the CJS. The Scottish system would perhaps consider the nature of the act, assess the criminality behind this and assign an appropriate penalty accordingly while the system in England and Wales might also consider the impact of the act, in addition to the actual criminality involved, and assign a sentence on the basis of both aspects. Thus the influence of the victim varies by jurisdiction. Recently, however, there have been changes which have given the victim more say in the sentencing process (Gilchrist 1995). For example, victims in England and Wales are requested to produce a Victim Personal Statement (VPS) which is considered, alongside reports as to the offenders' circumstances and character, at the point of sentence. This was introduced in 2001 (as a political measure) to respond to the request for greater input from victims into the criminal justice process (Woolf 2001).

A further recent development to increase the input of victims is the introduction of the public protection advocate to the parole process in England and Wales. There has been concern that the Parole Board appeared to favour the perpetrators and not fully consider the victim's perspective. To remedy this, the Home Secretary suggested that victims ought to be represented on the Parole Board which, after several responses were suggested, resulted in the appointment of public protection advocates who attend hearings. A scheme was also implemented whereby the National Probation Service would ensure that a VPS was available for consideration at parole hearings thus giving the victim and the public a greater role in public protection (National Probation Service 2007).

Given the centrality of the role of the victim within the CJS and the influence of non-evidentiary factors on judgments of personal credibility and reliability in this setting, it is vitally important to consider how victims, particularly victims of specific offences, are viewed in order to identify potential areas of bias and unfairness within the process and to consider how concern about victims might affect attitudes to offenders. To this end this chapter will review factors shaping attitudes to victims of crime and explore factors affecting judgments of the victim within the courtroom.

How are victims generally viewed?

One might assume that we would generally hold positive and sympathetic views of victims of crime and to an extent this is true. However, there are many general stereotypes as to what the victim of crime should look like and how they ought to act. Sensational offences such as stranger rapes and extreme violence in public places are over-represented in media reports of crime (Ardovini-Brooker and Caringella-MacDonald 2002). This skewed media reporting creates a skewed view of which people are victims of crime, where they are at risk and from whom. It also contributes to the prevalence of stereotypes about victim characteristics.

Additionally, it has been suggested that perhaps due to a need to create a sense of predictability and control over the frightening and otherwise random threat of crime, people may look for aspects of victim behaviour that could have contributed to their victim status. Seeking reasons for victimisation which could then be managed (e.g. behaviours that could be controlled or situations which could be avoided) may go some way towards explaining the sometimes negative and judgmental responses to victims of crime.

Social psychology has proposed a variety of theories to explain attitudes to 'victims'. It has been suggested that if misfortune was seen as being related to stable personal attributes then negative affect towards the individual would be greater. The 'fundamental attribution error', that is the tendency to view others' behaviour as deriving from stable internal causes, has been proposed as explaining some variation in attitude to victims, in that victims who are held to be responsible for their own victimisation elicit less positive responses from respondents. Weiner *et al.* (1971) proposed that attitudes to victims varied as a function of the stability of the cause of the victimisation, whether the misfortune was attributed internally to the person or externally to the environment and whether the action was deemed to be intentional or unintentional.

Schneider *et al.* (1994) explored attitudes to rape victims and perpetrators and found that female victims were judged more harshly than male victims and that the severity of the sentence endorsed increased when there had been injury caused and the victim was the same gender as the respondent. Anderson and Lyons (2005) found that male and female respondents made different attributions about rape victims: men blamed rape victims more than women; however, this was mediated by gender-role beliefs, such that traditional gender-role beliefs accounted for much of the gender-related differences. Social support available also impacted on attitudes to victims with socially supported victims receiving less blame than unsupported women. This study also identified that while gender of victim had no impact on attributions towards victims, it did affect attributions about offenders. Smirles (2004) also found no differences in attribution of responsibility by gender of the victim. They found instead that the gender of the respondent affected the attribution of responsibility. This was mediated by other factors. For example, the attributions of female respondents were affected by the victim's reaction but this was not the case for males.

Clements *et al.*'s (2006) recent work has identified that attitude to victims varies by victim type; for example, victims of spouse abuse were held to be more blameworthy than those victimised by strangers. They identified an interaction with gender of respondent citing work which found that females were more negative about victims of spousal abuse than males. Overall they considered that, perhaps because there had tended to be a focus on specific victim types, the understanding of attitudes and concerns about victims more generally remained rather disjointed. Also, while offence-specific scales had been developed – for example, Ward (1988) had developed an 'attitudes towards rape victims scale' – little had been done to unify the approach to all victims, leaving the theory development disjointed. Clements *et al.* (2006) developed a tool to assess concerns about victims of crime more generally and to explore how far general empathy and crime-related beliefs linked with concern about victims. The Victim Concern Scale (VCS) that they developed consisted of four factors: general concern for victims, concern for vulnerable victims and victims of violent crime, concern for victims of property crimes and concern for 'culpable' victims (i.e. drug takers, prostitutes). Using this scale, they found that attitudes to victims varied with the age and gender of the respondent, with older respondents and female respondents expressing a higher level of concern for victims, including culpable victims. However, contrary to previous work they did not find a link between attributions regarding crime causation (internal versus external attributions) and concern for victims. They also established that while empathy correlated with concern for victims it did appear to involve unique facets so that concern for victims encompassed more than empathy, and also there was no relationship between concern for victims and other crime-related attitudes, for example authoritarianism. An interesting finding was that those high on victim concern also endorsed offender rehabilitation attitudes. As the authors identified, this challenges the notion of individuals being either pro-victim or pro-offender. Thus perhaps balancing the rights of victims and offenders is an erroneous way of conceptualising this area? This work is an important progression in the approach to understanding attitudes to victims of crime and it is hoped that further studies making use of the VCS and exploring connections to potentially theoretically linked concepts will follow.

Lyons (2006) suggested that individuals are affected by general attitudes towards minority status – either 'stigma' (overly generalised negative attitude) – or 'sympathy' (overly generalised positive attitude) and that this would predict response to minority victims. Lyons found that black victims were blamed less than white victims (i.e. sympathy), but gay and lesbian victims were held more accountable than heterosexual victims (i.e. stigma). Thus Lyons suggested that it was respondents' attitudes towards particular groups and characteristics which shaped attributions of blame rather than victim characteristics alone. Richardson and May (1999) suggested that this gendered notion of 'deserving' victim and the sexualised aspects of it serve to deny those who are 'other' (i.e. women or non-heterosexuals) the right to full access to justice.

Viki and Abrams (2002) have argued that social psychological theory in the form of benevolent sexism (Glick and Fiske 1996) can help to explain some types of reaction to victims of sexual assault. Glick and Fiske (1996) suggest that benevolent sexism (sexist attitudes that appear positive in tone) and hostile sexism combine to form the broader construct 'ambivalent sexism' where sexist prejudice can appear to operate in a benign way or a more aggressive way. It might be thought that benevolent sexism could only operate in a positive manner. However, Viki and Abrams have suggested that classifying women who conform to traditional norms as 'good' women can be as negative as classifying those who challenge these norms as 'bad'. Both impose rigid expectations on women's behaviour and in turn on victims' behaviour, leading to victim blaming when expectations of gender or behaviour have been violated. This type of thinking also enables one to hold women victims to be responsible for their own rape experiences, especially in non-stranger rapes (see also Abrams et al. 2003).

Research in Canada with professionals involved in the care and assessment of sexually abused young persons found that they held strong beliefs about the victim status of children which was affected by whether the child's behaviour was considered to be problematic (e.g. had they run away, taken drugs or stolen?). If deemed to be 'problem' children the professionals appeared to find it more difficult to see the child as a credible victim. Thus professionals do need to be aware of the variety of ways in which sexual abuse might affect a child's behaviour and view behaviours in this light rather than identifying children as credible or non-credible victims (Hicks and Tite 1998).

Research with New Zealand police officers shows that professionals employ stereotyped definitions of 'real rape' and 'deserving' victim when making judgments about the credibility of rape victims. Jordan (2004) identified that in cases that the police had decided were false, they tended to see alternative motives driving forward the 'false' allegation, such as avoiding negative consequences of engaging in consensual sexual activity or seeking revenge for being spurned. Delayed reporting of incidents or initially concealing aspects of the incident (e.g. having been drunk) were aspects of cases which raised police scepticism about the veracity of the complaint (Jordan 2004). Jordan concluded that the police needed to move away from a framework of suspicion and disbelief and approach the victims of rape with an understanding of the reality of rape and the concerns victims have when reporting incidents which deviated from stereotypical rape scripts. Additionally, Jordan suggested that law reforms seeking to address attrition focused on the courtroom might be limited due to the early filtering effect of the traditional police approach (Jordan 2004).

A UK study of attrition in rape cases suggested that there were various processes and various professional judgments that contributed to the high level of attrition in these cases (see also Wilson and Scholes, this volume). Gregory and Lees (1996) suggested that the police 'no crimed' cases where they had difficulty in believing the victim, and this was more common in cases where there had been a prior relationship between the victim and the perpetrator. The police also initiated the withdrawal of a complaint in some stranger rape cases where they considered that obtaining further corroborative evidence would be difficult. Later in the process the police did not report a high percentage of rape cases to the public prosecuting authorities which was explained by the police as being due to CPS-led guidelines about the need for a good prospect of conviction. The 'reasonable prospect of conviction' and 'public interest' considerations that inform CPS decisions also have a negative impact on the numbers of cases proceeding through the criminal justice process. The first consideration tends to be greatly influenced by judgments of the credibility of the victim which is clearly influenced by non-legal and broader judgments of victims. The second involves a measure of cost-benefit analysis which requires the prosecutor to weigh up the potential sentence if found guilty and the cost of the trial, and perhaps look to prosecute a lesser offence on the basis that conviction is so uncertain in rape and sexual assault cases (again linking to the perceived credibility of the victim). In other words, a guilty plea to a lesser offence is seen to serve the public interest more (Gregory and Lees 1996).

Research into how victims are represented in the media has identified that cases ranked highest for victim blame tended to involve acquaintances. The lowest ranked cases were where the victim and offender were strangers and where the offence had occurred in a public space outdoors. Ardovini-Brooker and Caringella-MacDonald (2002) concluded that it was in cases that fitted best with the stereotyped image of a 'real rape' that offenders were blamed (see also Wilson and Scholes, this volume).

George and Martinez (2002) also found that the race of the victim and the perpetrator had an effect on attributions of responsibility, but they found this affected both black and white victims and all types of rape. Irrespective of their ethnicity, all victims of interracial rapes were held to be more culpable. Also racist attitudes affected judgments as to sentence in both stranger and acquaintance rapes. Black women's victimisation experiences were seen less seriously and black men were held more responsible as perpetrators. George and Martinez concluded that stereotyped attitudes to race and rape persist and subtle aspects of racial prejudice may still influence decisions across the criminal justice process in a way that requires challenge (see also Bottoms *et al.* 2004).

The evidence as to whether more generally biased attitudes have an influence is equivocal. An important finding emerging from the data does appear to be that, within the CJS, ethnic minority individuals, whether victim or offender, do tend to be held more responsible for their behaviour and experiences.

Victims in court

Speech

There is a considerable body of work suggesting that many 'extra-legal' factors affect the decision-making of both lay and professional people in the CJS at various points. The courtroom is one of the most often researched arenas and it is clear that there are many aspects of the courtroom which can be affected by other than strictly 'legal' factors.

Various features of victims and defendants affect the court process. Victim characteristics such as physical attractiveness, gender-related speech patterns and ethnicity have an effect on jurors' attributions of guilt, responsibility and credibility. But it is not just judgments of the victim which are affected by 'extra-legal' factors. For example, it has been shown that the defendant's demeanour can have a significant effect on judgments of guilt and decisions about appropriate sentence (Pryor and Buchanan 1984). Aspects of judicial behaviour appear also to be influential. A study of mock jurors identified that the participants were certainly aware of, and perhaps influenced by, non-verbal cues from the judges, and in particular of negative non-verbal signals (Burnett and Badzinski 2005).

One key feature of the courtroom is the presentation of oral evidence. Often one of the most influential factors in a case is the judgment as to the credibility of those giving oral evidence. Often the key evidence is from the victim of the offence. We know from other areas in psychology that judgments about others in any setting are affected by factors that are not consciously considered (e.g. O'Hair *et al.* 1988). Robinson and colleagues used an innovative synthetic speech methodology to test out how gender affected credibility. Their study of 46 raters found that both male and female raters judged female speakers as more credible (Robinson *et al.* 1998). Quina *et al.* (1987) asked 151 students to rate the authors of hypothetical interviews where both the gender of the hypothetical author and the 'gender' of the linguistic style of writing were varied. They found that author gender did not significantly affect judgments but that the gender of the linguistic style did. 'Non-feminine' linguistic style was rated as being higher in competence but lower in warmth than a more feminine style. Furthermore, certain speech patterns have been identified as being powerful and others powerless. Hosman (1989) found that speech containing hedges (for example, 'kind of'), hesitations (for example, 'um') and intensifiers (for example, 'really') were seen as being powerless and those using this style of speech seen as lacking in authority but being more sociable. Importantly, this study found that status of the speaker interacted with speech style. A high-status speaker using powerless speech was judged negatively on character and a low-status speaker using powerful speech was judged positively on sociability. Hosman (1989) suggested that if speakers want to be seen as powerful they should avoid certain styles of speech. This is unlikely to be information that is known to many within the courtroom but highly likely to affect how they are judged.

Physical characteristics

It has been suggested that, similar to the application of the 'halo effect' in other settings, those who are physically attractive are seen as being more credible, more deserving and less culpable than their less attractive counterparts (Thornton and Ryckman 1983). In an early study of over one hundred undergraduate students in the USA,

Thornton and Ryckman (1983) found many interaction effects from other variables affecting the attribution of responsibility to victims of rape. In general male respondents assigned more responsibility to victims and tended to identify some behaviour that the victim had engaged in prior to the assault as being an influence. Also, they were more likely to identify a victim's appearance as being linked to the assault. A main effect was found for attractiveness with the less attractive victims being held to be more responsible for their experience than the more attractive victim. Thornton and Ryckman suggested that this could be understood as reflecting thoughts that an unattractive female was an unlikely victim therefore she must have presented herself in a provocative manner. A further finding was that while respondents did not think victim attractiveness would influence the amount of time it would take to recover from the experience, they did consider that the unattractive victim may face a greater degree of social rejection. Interestingly, victim attractiveness and gender of respondent did not appear to affect the view of the offender.

Behaviour

Additionally, women who are portrayed as having physically resisted an attack, and possibly suffered injury as a result, are seen as more credible victims than those who have not (Kerr and Kurtz 1977). There are issues about what is expected of deserving victims (Richardson and May 1999) and appropriate victim behaviour prior to, during and following an offence appears to have a strong influence on later decisions by police and lay people alike. Recent media reports in Scotland have highlighted the fact that a high proportion (40 per cent) of the general adult population who would qualify as potential rape trial jurors would attribute blame to a victim of rape if the women were considered to have put themselves in a risky position, for example going home with a man, and a significant minority believed that certain behaviours contributed to the rape (e.g. intoxication or provocative clothing; Rape Crisis Scotland 2007).

One factor which has had an influence on rules of evidence in criminal proceedings in the UK (Burman et al. 2007) is a victim's previous sexual experience which appears to negatively impact the attribution of offence responsibility (Brown et al. 1992). A study of mock jurors using undergraduate students found that the respondents who heard evidence about an alleged rape victim's prior sexual involvement with the offender saw the victim as being less credible and blamed her more. Further, telling respondents to disregard this information had little effect (Schuller and Hastings 2002). This is interesting in the light of the fact that alternative work in this area has suggested that the impact of prejudicial thinking about rape victims would be mitigated by the provision of expert testimony as to the reality of rape (Tetrault 2006).

In general, acquaintance rape, while being more likely, tends to result in victims being more harshly judged and perpetrators less harshly judged (Bridges 1991). Additionally, in acquaintance rape, research has identified that respondents have reported being less sure of the perpetrator's guilt (Szymanski et al. 1993) and less sure of the issue of victim consent which ultimately links to shorter recommended sentences (Willis 1992). Additionally, factors which affect how far respondents identify with victims have also been implicated in affecting blame judgments. Kaplan and Miller (1978) identified that parents of female only children were more pro-conviction in rape cases, whereas parents of male children were less so. The authors of this early study suggested that defensive attribution might explain these findings.

A further problem for victims of rape has been the ability to introduce information on the victim's sexual history in court. This resulted in some defendants who had chosen not to be legally represented subjecting their victims to long, detailed and humiliating cross-examination regarding previous sexual history and sexual preferences. At best many have suggested that the criminal justice process subjects victims of sexual assault to 'secondary victimisation' through having to relive their ordeal in public. Specific provisions to prevent the introduction of irrelevant personal information, often referred to as 'rape shield' laws, were introduced in many Western jurisdictions (e.g. the Sexual Offences Act (Criminal Procedure; Scotland) 2002) in order to protect the victims of rape. These laws variously restrict information about the reputation of the victim, prior sexual experience of the victim and other potentially prejudicial information from being introduced in evidence or even referred to in court. A recent evaluation of how these 'rape shield' laws were operating in one jurisdiction, Scotland, has concluded, however, that the provisions are ineffective, that in fact a higher proportion of cases involved applications to introduce sexual history and character evidence since the 'new' legislation (Burman et al. 2007). Furthermore, seven out of ten victims of serious sexual assault in the study period would be questioned about sexual history.

A further issue that arises in rape trials is that the expectations that are held about appropriate victim behaviour, which link to attributions as to credibility and responsibility of victims, do not accord with what clinicians and data from victims would suggest is actually *normal* in a victimisation situation. For example, whether a victim immediately reports the offence to the police is linked to credibility, with any delay in the reporting of an offence reducing the credibility of the victim (Balogh *et al.* 2003). However, we know that it is highly likely that victims will initially look for help from a friend or family member (Ahrens *et al.* 2007). For example, child victims of sexual abuse typically delay for between a week and two years prior to disclosing abuse and a large proportion of child abuse victims disclose only when prompted (Hershkowitz *et al.* 2007).

Alcohol and the drunkenness of victims have been found to have a negative effect on the perceived credibility of the victim with responsibility for the offence often being attributed to the victim (Schuller and Wall 1998). Research exploring the impact of substance misuse has also identified that this has an impact on the judgments made of victims of sexual assault. In a study of students in the USA, Wenger and Bornstein (2006) found that illegal substances and both legal and illegal alcohol use resulted in respondents judging the victims of alleged sexual assault as being less credible. Thus far fewer guilty verdicts were recorded in cases involving any intoxicant than in the 'sober' condition. This study also explored the impact of prior relationship and the possible interaction between prior relationship and intoxication, and contrary to earlier findings did not identify an interaction effect. However, they did identify that those lower in rape myth acceptance judged victims to be more credible and women tended to see victims as more credible. Wenger and Bernstein (2006) suggest that aspects of jury decision-making in real life might mitigate individual prejudice (see later) but also draw attention to the fact that different standards appear to operate in judging males and females.

Research exploring the impact of victim emotion on judgments of credibility suggest that, prior to juror discussions, emotions displayed strongly influence the judgments made. However, following mock juror discussions the effect of the displayed emotions on the judgment of credibility is lessened (Dahl *et al.* 2007). Dahl *et al.* (2007) suggest that this fits with broader research in social psychology that suggests that prejudice and the influence of stereotypes can be reduced following group interaction. This study used groups of 5–7 mock jurors to explore the impact of the emotion displayed by victims in rape cases, and varied the emotion so that it was 'congruent, neutral or incongruent' with the testimony being delivered. They compared this work to earlier work which had explored simply the effect of congruence of emotion displayed and its effect on individual decisions without discussion (Kaufmann *et al.* 2003). This earlier work, based on data from 169 students, had found that those who watched congruent testimony (as measured by cues such as facial expression and speech rate) tended to view the victim as being more credible and tended to reach more guilty verdicts (Kaufmann *et al.* 2003). One important finding from this research was that the participants were not consciously aware of the effect of the emotion cues and tended to ascribe their decisions to the content of the testimony as opposed to any other factor.

More recent research exploring the effect of victim emotion on the judgment of judges in rape cases has provided some reassuring evidence suggesting that perhaps training can mitigate the effects of prejudice and bias. Wessell *et al.* (2006) found that judgments of the credibility of rape victims made by Norwegian judges did not appear to be influenced by the varied emotions presented to them and nor were their verdicts. The authors suggest that the experience and professional training of judges mean that they are better at filtering out irrelevant information. This is an improvement on previous research which suggested that specific instructions to ignore prejudicial information was ineffective (Tanford and Penrod 1984) as it implies that while instructions to ignore information might not be helpful in a courtroom, education and general exposure to the reality of criminal cases might be.

So far, this chapter has concentrated mostly on how rape victims are perceived but there are two other categories of victim whose credibility and blameworthiness is highly influential in the criminal setting: victims of child abuse and victims of domestic violence. As there are aspects of the nature of these offences which mirror those of victims of adult rape, it might be assumed that similar factors are at play in these cases, but there are certain aspects, such as beliefs about developmental influences on memory and views of 'domestic' conflict, which deserve particular attention.

Child victims

There are equivocal findings as to the impact of age on credibility, with children being seen as less credible, more credible or similar to adult victims (Bottoms and Goodman 1994). The specific age of the child appears to have an impact with younger children being seen as more credible in cases of child sexual abuse. Nightingale (1993) found that the numbers of guilty verdicts proposed and the perceived credibility of the victim decreased with age and that the blame attributed to the victim increased with age. It was suggested that perhaps this linked to beliefs about the honesty of children. Ross *et al.* (2003) conducted a study in this area to explore what particular features affected outcomes in child abuse cases. They used data from 300 mock jurors to explore a model that they proposed in which both the cognitive ability of child victims and the honesty of child victims would influence judgments made about their cases. They suggested that lack of cognitive ability might interact with an ability to fabricate accounts of sexual abuse and thus enhance credibility. They did identify two factors in ratings of child witnesses – 'honesty' and 'cognitive ability' – but found that only the perceived honesty of the victims affected the subsequent judgments while assessment of cognitive ability did not. Alternative research exploring the interaction between type of offence and child victim credibility suggested that age of victim had no impact on credibility ratings but type of offence did, so that children were seen as being more credible, more honest and able to recall better in sexual assault cases than in robbery cases (McCauley and Parker 2000). This research suggests that alternative dimensions affect judgments of credibility and honesty where child victims are involved and indicate a need for some more comprehensive research in this area.

Recent research established an interaction between respondent gender and the effect of age in the assessment of credibility of victims in child abuse cases. Rogers and Davies (2007) found that younger victims were perceived to be more credible, but that women respondents were more pro-victim in general and male respondents were more greatly affected by age (tending to blame older victims more).

The expression of emotion by child victims and the demeanour of children in the courtroom have an effect similar to that of rape victims. Children who look frightened or cry when confronting their alleged abuser are seen as more credible. The authors suggest that pre-trial preparation designed to help the child witness face the courtroom scene without suffering unduly might in fact have a negative effect on the trial outcome (Regan and Baker 1998). Furthermore, juror education around normal behaviour in response to abuse might be appropriate.

Thus it appears that again, similar to the situation in cases of rape, many factors interact to affect the assessment of credibility in child abuse victims. It is clear that these factors, which are typically out of the victim's control, carry great weight in the criminal justice setting where lay judgments are of true influence, and in this case there is a need to research further in this area and develop more sophisticated theoretical thinking.

Victims of domestic violence

As in rape cases, attrition on domestic violence cases is high. Often the reason proffered for the failure of many cases to proceed through the criminal justice process is that the victim did not wish to proceed. Until relatively recently the decision of the victim to withdraw charges was routinely accepted without question, even in the context of an abusive relationship.

It is impossible to do justice to the range of negative attributions that have been made about victims of domestic violence within a few paragraphs, nor to reflect the complexity of domestic violence. However, some key issues can be raised. Across many areas, victims of domestic violence are routinely seen as contributing to their abuse by staying, held responsible for any threat to their children by not leaving and potentially as contributing to their own victimisation by failing to behave in appropriate ways (Gilchrist 2006). However, much of this attribution links to poor understanding of the nature of the violence and the misattribution of the abuse to momentary explosions of anger in the context of a relationship.

Researchers have identified that the gender of the respondent seems to operate in different ways to that found with other victim types, with Kristiansen and Giulietti (1990) reporting that male respondents hold female victims of domestic violence less responsible for their victimisation than female respondents (contrary to that found in rape cases). This would support a 'defensive attribution theory' (Shaver 1970) more than the 'just world hypothesis' (Lerner 1980) as the reason that women blame women more might arise from the need for women to defend themselves from victim status which would be increased by the perceived similarity between self and victim.

Research in the USA (Kingsnorth *et al.* 2001) has identified that victim violence and victim cooperation, but not victim or perpetrator race, affect police responses to domestic violence. Incidents where the victim is cooperative and is not and has not been confrontational or abusive are more likely to result in positive action (e.g. arrest). However, in a similar way to rape cases, research has identified that those who hold traditional views tend to blame women victims of domestic violence more, and particularly women who challenge stereotyped notions of appropriate female behaviour. Thus women who do not fit with the notion of 'good' women or 'deserving' victims are held more responsible for their victimisation (Hillier and Foddy 1993).

More recent work by Stewart and Maddren (1997) has identified that the gender of the victim also has an impact on blame attribution in cases of family violence. They found that police officers attributed more blame to male victims and, in a similar way to findings in attributions about rape victims (see earlier), to intoxicated victims. Overall, Stewart and Maddren (1997) suggest that police are typically reluctant to get involved in 'family violence', perhaps reflecting historic notions of domestic abuse being a 'private' issue and not appropriate for formal intervention, or perhaps reflecting the endorsement of beliefs supportive of domestic violence generally in society. Interestingly, police are even more reluctant to become involved when the victim is male. This may reflect a more general debate as to differences between male-to-female and female-to-male violence (Johnson 2006) or perhaps merely prove too great a challenge to police stereotypes of victims and views of masculinity.

While domestic violence victims are often held responsible for the failure of their case to be processed via the criminal courts, it is suggested that the scepticism with which professionals approach these cases has a significant effect. For example, victims of domestic violence are required to affirm on many more occasions than victims of other crimes that they do indeed wish to pursue a prosecution. Also prosecutors 'defer' to the desires of the victims in domestic violence cases far more than in any other type of case (Gilchrist 1995). Thus, in addition to individual factors biasing responses to this type of victim, perhaps the notion of family violence as 'private' violence is also influential.

Summary and conclusions

It is clear that there are many factors that affect the judgments made of victims. These vary by gender of both respondent and victim, by race, by sexuality and by type of offence. The judgments are also affected by features of the victims such as attractiveness, speech patterns, displayed emotions and even adherence to traditional sex roles. Throughout the criminal justice process professionals and lay people make attributions on dimensions such as credibility, blame and deservingness on the basis of their previous, often unconscious judgments. Broader beliefs about the nature of violence and/or public and private demarcations also influence attitudes to victims of certain crimes.

Ethnic minorities, women who challenge gender roles, those who can be held to have engaged in complicit behaviours or those who express inappropriate emotion are held more responsible for their victimisation than others. Rigid beliefs about gender roles, both benevolent and hostile, and attributions of positive and negative identity appear to play a part in shaping these responses. Specific instructions to ignore potentially prejudicial information and legislative rules to exclude such information do not as yet appear to protect victims from these reactions. It is suggested that broader education for decision-makers around the realities of victimisation and typical victim responses, and possibly focused preparation and advice for victims to prepare them for the courtroom, might be beneficial.

As yet what research has achieved is to highlight the need for further research and further change in this area. It is hoped that with the breadth and depth of research available and with the current political will to involve victims positively in the criminal justice process at all points, the limited progress made in altering attitudes and removing prejudice from the CJS can be addressed.

References

Abrams, D., Viki, G.T., Masser, B. and Bohner, G., (2003) 'Perceptions of stranger and acquaintance rape: the role of benevolent and hostile sexism in victim blame and rape proclivity', *Journal of Personality and Social Psychology, 84:* 111–25.

Ahrens, C.E., Campbell, R., Ternier-Thames, N.K, Wasco, S.M. and Sefl, T. (2007) 'Deciding whom to tell: expectations and outcomes of rape survivors' first disclosures', *Psychology of Women Quarterly,* 31: 38–49.

Anderson, I. and Lyons, A. (2005) 'The effect of victims' social support on attributions of blame in female and male rape', *Journal of Applied Social Psychology,* 35: 1400–17.

Ardovini-Brooker, J. and Caringella-MacDonald, S. (2002) 'Media attributions of blame and sympathy in ten rape cases', *Justice Professional,* 15: 3–18.

Balogh, D.W., Kite, M.E., Pickel, K.L., Canel, D. and Schroeder, J. (2003) 'The effects of delayed reporting and motive for reporting on perceptions of sexual harassment', *Sex Roles: A Journal of Research*, 48: 337–48.

Bottoms, B. and Goodman, G. (1994) 'Perceptions of children's credibility in sexual assault cases', *Journal of Applied Social Psychology*, 24: 702–32.

Bottoms, B.L., Davis, S.L. and Epstein, M. (2004) 'Effects of victim and defendant race on jurors' decisions in child sexual abuse cases', *Journal of Applied Social Psychology*, 34: 1–33.

Bridges, J.S. (1991) 'Perceptions of date and stranger rape: a difference in sex role expectations and rape-supportive beliefs', *Sex Roles*, 24: 291–307.

Brown, B., Burman, M. and Jamieson, J. (1992) *Sexual History and Sexual Character Evidence in Scottish Sexual Offence Trials*. Edinburgh: Scottish Office Central Research Unit.

Burman, M., Jamieson, L., Nicholson, J. and Brooks, O. (2007) 'Impact of aspects of the law of evidence in sexual offence trials: an evaluation study', *Scottish Government Social Research 2007: Crime and Justice*. Scottish Government, Edinburgh: Blackwell.

Burnett, A. and Badzinski, D.M. (2005) 'Judge nonverbal communication on trial: do mock jurors notice?', *Journal of Communication*, 55: 209–24.

Clements, C.B., Brannen, D.N., Kirkley, S., Gordon, T.M. and Church, W.T. (2006) 'The measurement of concern about victims: empathy, victim advocacy and the Victim Concern Scale (VCS)', *Legal and Criminological Psychology*, 11: 283–95.

Dahl, J., Enemo, I., Drevland, G.C., Wessel, E., Eilertsen, D.E. and Magnussen, S. (2007) 'Displayed emotions and witness credibility: a comparison of judgements by individuals and mock juries', *Applied Cognitive Psychology*, 21: 1145–55.

George, W.H. and Martinez, L. (2002) 'Victim blaming in rape: effects of victim and perpetrator race, type of rape, and participant racism', *Psychology of Women Quarterly*, 26: 110–19.

Gilchrist, E. (1995) 'Fairness in prosecutorial decision-making', *Scottish Journal of Criminal Justice Studies*, 1: 25–32.

Gilchrist, E. (2006) 'Domestic violence and child protection: can psychology inform legal decisions?', in B. Brooks-Gordon, and M. Freeman (eds), *Law and Psychology: Current Legal Issues Volume 9*. Oxford: Oxford University Press, pp. 242–57.

Glick, P. and Fiske, S. (1996) 'The ambivalent sexism inventory: differentiating hostile and benevolent sexism', *Journal of Personality and Social Psychology*, 70: 491–512.

Gregory, J. and Lees, S. (1996) 'Attrition in rape and sexual assault cases', *British Journal of Criminology*, 36: 1–17.

Hershkowitz, I., Lanes, O. and Lamb, M.E. (2007) 'Exploring disclosure of child sexual abuse with alleged victims and their parents', *Child Abuse and Neglect*, 31: 111–23.

Hicks, C. and Tite, R. (1998) 'Professionals' attitudes about victims of child sexual abuse: implications for collaborative child protection teams', *Child and Family Social Work*, 3: 37–48.

Hillier, L. and Foddy, M. (1993) 'The role of observer attitudes in judgments of blame in cases of wife assault', *Sex Roles*, 29: 629–44.

Hosman, L.A. (1989) 'The evaluative consequences of hedges, hesitations, and intensifiers', *Human Communication Research*, 1: 383–406.

Johnson, M.P. (2006) 'Conflict and control gender symmetry and asymmetry in domestic violence', *Violence Against Women*, 12 (11): 1003–18.

Jordan, J. (2004) 'Beyond belief? Police, rape and women's credibility', *Criminal Justice*, 4: 29–59.

Kaplan, M.F. and Miller, L.E. (1978) 'Effects of jurors' identification with the victim depend on likelihood of victimisation', *Law and Human Behavior*, 2: 353–68.

Kaufmann, G., Drevland, G., Wessel, E., Overskeid, G. and Magnussen, S. (2003) 'The importance of being earnest: displayed emotion and witness credibility', *Applied Cognitive Psychology*, 17: 21–34.

Kerr, N.L. and Kurtz, S.T. (1977) 'Effects of victim's suffering and respectability on mock juror judgements: further evidence on the just world theory', *Representative Research in Social Psychology*, 8: 42–56.

Kingsnorth, R.F., MacIntosh, R.C., Berdahl, T., Blades, C. and Rossi, S. (2001) 'Domestic violence: the role of interracial/ethnic dyads in criminal court processing', *Journal of Contemporary Criminal Justice*, 17: 123–41.

Kristiansen, C. and Giulietti, R. (1990) 'Perceptions of wife abuse: effects of gender, attitudes towards women and just world beliefs among college students', *Psychology of Women Quarterly*, 14: 177–89.

Lerner, M.J. (1980) *The Belief in a Just World: A Fundamental Delusion*. New York: Plenum Press.

Lyons, C.J. (2006) 'Stigma or sympathy? Attributions of fault to hate crime victims and offenders', *Social Psychology Quarterly*, 69: 39–59.

McCauley, M.R. and Parker, J.F. (2000) 'When will a child be believed? The impact of the victim's age and juror's gender on children's credibility and verdicts in a sexual abuse case', *Child Abuse and Neglect*, 25: 523–39.

MacLeod, M., Prescott, R.G.W. and Carson, L. (1996) *Listening to Victims of Crime: Victimisation Episodes and the Criminal Justice System in Scotland: An Examination of White and Ethnic Minority Crime Victim Experience*, Crime and Criminal Justice Research Findings No. 13. Edinburgh: Scottish Office.

National Probation Service (2007) *Victim Representation at Parole Hearings*, Probation Office Circular PC 27: 2007. London: National Probation Service.

Nightingale, N.N. (1993) 'Juror reactions to child victim witnesses: factors affecting trial outcome', *Law and Human Behavior*, 17: 679–94.

O'Hair, D., Cody, M., Goss, B. and Krayer, K. (1988) 'The effect of gender, deceit orientation and communicator style on macro-assessments of honesty', *Communication Quarterly*, 36: 77–93.

Pryor, B. and Buchanan, R.W. (1984) 'The effects of a defendant's demeanour on juror perception of credibility and guilt', *Journal of Communication*, 34 (3): 92–9.

Quina, K., Wingard, J.A. and Bates, H.G. (1987) 'Language style and gender stereotypes in person perception', *Psychology of Women Quarterly*, 11 (1): 111–22.

Rape Crisis Scotland (2007) *Survey on Attitudes to Rape Victims*. Retrieved 10 December 2007 from: http://www.rapecrisisscotland.org.uk.

Regan, P. and Baker, S. (1998) 'The impact of child witness demeanour on perceived credibility and trial outcome in sexual abuse cases', *Journal of Family Violence*, 13: 187–95.

Richardson, D. and May, H. (1999) 'Deserving victim? Sexual status and the social construction of violence', *Sociological Review*, pp. 308–31.

Robinson, K., Obler, L., Boone, R.T., Shane, H., Adamjee, R. and Anderson, J. (1998) 'Gender and truthfulness in daily life', *Sex Roles*, 38: 821–31.

Rogers, P. and Davies, M. (2007) 'Perceptions of victims and perpetrators in a depicted child sexual abuse case: gender and age factors', *Journal of Interpersonal Violence*, 22: 566–80.

Ross, D.F., Jurden, F.H., Lindsay, R.C. and Keeney, J.M. (2003) 'Replications and limitations of a two factor model of child witness credibility', *Journal of Applied Social Psychology*, 33: 418–31.

Schneider, L.J., Ee, J.S. and Aronson H. (1994) 'Effects of victim gender and physical vs. psychological trauma/injury on observers' perceptions of sexual assault and its after effects', *Sex Roles*, 30: 11–12.

Schuller, R. and Hastings, P. (2002) 'Complainant sexual history evidence: its impact on mock jurors' decisions', *Psychology of Women Quarterly*, 26: 252–61.

Schuller, R. and Wall, A.M. (1998) 'The effect of defendant and complainant intoxication on mock jurors' judgments of sexual assault', *Psychology of Women Quarterly*, 22: 555–72.

Shaver, K.G. (1970) 'Defensive attributions: effects of severity and relevance on the responsibility assigned for the accidents', *Journal of Personality and Social Psychology*, 14: 101–13.

Smirles, K.E. (2004) 'Attributions of responsibility in cases of sexual harassment: the person and the situation', *Journal of Applied Social Psychology*, 34: 342–65.

Stewart, A. and Maddren, K. (1997) 'Police officers' judgements of blame in family violence: the impact of gender and alcohol', *Sex Roles*, 37: 921–33.

Szymanski, L.A., Devlin, A.S., Chrisler, J.C. and Vyse, S.A. (1993) 'Gender role and attitudes toward rape in male and female college students', *Sex Roles*, 29: 37–57.

Tanford, S. and Penrod, S. (1984) 'Social processes in juror judgments of multi-offense trials', *Journal of Personality and Social Psychology*, 47 (4): 749–65.

Tetrault, P. (2006) 'Rape myth acceptance: a case for providing educational expert testimony in rape trials', *Behavioral Sciences and the Law*, 7: 243–57.

Thornton, B. and Ryckman, R.M. (1983) 'The influence of a rape victim's physical attractiveness on observers' attributions of responsibility', *Human Relations*, 36: 549–62.

Viki, G.T. and Abrams, D. (2002) 'But she was unfaithful: benevolent sexism and reactions to rape victims who violate traditional gender role expectations', *Sex Roles*, 47: 289–93.

Ward, C. (1988) 'The attitudes towards rape victims scale', *Psychology of Women Quarterly*, 12: 127–46.

Weiner, B., Frieze, I., Kukla, A., Reed, L., Rest, S. and Rosenbaum, R.M. (1971) 'Perceiving the causes of success and failure', in E.E. Jones, D.E. Kanouse, H.H. Kelley, R.E. Nisbett, S. Valins and B. Weiner (eds), *Attribution: Perceiving the Causes of Behavior*. Morristown, NJ: General Learning Press, pp. 95–120.

Wenger, A. and Bornstein, B. (2006) 'The effects of victim's substance use and relationship closeness on mock jurors' judgements in an acquaintance rape case', *Sex Roles*, 54: 547–55.

Wessell, E., Drevland, G., Eilertsen, D. and Magnussen, S. (2006) 'Credibility of the emotional witness: a study of ratings by court judges', *Law and Human Behavior*, 30 (2): 221–30.

Willis, C.E. (1992) 'The effect of sex role stereotype, victim, and defendant race, and prior relationship on race culpability attributions', *Sex Roles*, 26: 213–26.

Woolf LCJ (2001) *Weekly Law Reports*, 2038 26, pp. 213–26.

Chapter 8

Public attitudes towards offending, offenders and reintegration

Natalie Reynolds, Leam A. Craig and Douglas P. Boer

Introduction

Crime and criminals are popular subjects in the psychological research literature, in the media and in everyday public discussions. There has been much research into the effect offending has on an ex-offender's life and how a criminal record can be a hindrance for many years after the individual actually offended. The criminal justice system in many countries relies on the participation of the public (see also Wood, this volume), therefore it is worthwhile to examine how the general public feels about offenders and prisoners. In this chapter, we draw on research from the United States and United Kingdom to examine the attitudes of the public and psycho-social factors that could mediate attitudes. All of these factors are involved in a complex manner with regard to the reintegration of ex-offenders into the community and may be facilitative or have a negative effect in terms of reintegration.

Public perspectives on rehabilitation and incarceration

Perceptions of incarceration and attitudes towards offenders

There is a variety of different crimes that a criminal can commit. When an offender appears in the legal system, the public and often government workers rate these crimes in terms of their severity and sentences are based on such ratings. A US study by McCorkle (1993) measured public attitudes and sentiments to six common crimes, including: robbery, rape, molestation, burglary, drug sale and drug possession. Telephone surveys were conducted with 397 adults and participants were asked to indicate whether their orientation was towards punishment or rehabilitation across types of crime. The results of the study revealed that across the six crimes, the public were quite strongly orientated towards a punishment perspective on crime even though, somewhat paradoxically, there was strong support for rehabilitative programmes. The sample indicated that the implementation of rehabilitation programmes was especially supported when there were poor, young or minority group offenders involved. With regard to the dissonance that existed between the public's opinions of rehabilitation and punishment, McCorkle declared:

> The public clearly holds a strong punishment orientation. At the same time, however, Americans appear to recognize the limits of a purely punitive response to the crime problem. Beyond punishment, studies show most believe some understanding, energy and resources should be devoted towards addressing the genesis of offending behaviour. (McCorkle 1993: 241)

A common prejudice in many countries is the public perception that justice systems are not tough enough on crime. A study by Sprott (1999) challenged the view that public punitiveness was a one-dimensional concept that could be assessed by a simple measure examining whether the severity of sentences should be increased. Sprott examined whether there were gender differences between people in the public who would like tougher sentencing by looking at discrepancies between responses to broad questions, e.g. whether the person supported the increasing punitiveness of sentences in general compared to increasing punitiveness of a sentence in a particular case. This study found that women were more punitive than men and only tended to be less punitive when they were focusing on young offenders (Sprott 1999). Other research by Cullen et al. (1990) has supported the idea that members of the public are more lenient in their attitudes towards young offenders. In response to concern that United States citizens manifest little support for correctional treatment, Cullen et al. (1990) collected survey data in two major Ohio metropolitan areas: Cincinnati (Hamilton County) and Columbus (Franklin County). Three hundred adults in each area were surveyed.

Cullen *et al.* found that rehabilitation received considerable support, although this was not pronounced for certain types of offenders and treatment modalities. They found that respondents were more optimistic about rehabilitation for young and non-violent offenders.

Over the past decade, however, the campaign to get tough on crime has grown in strength. In this context, Sundt *et al.* (1998) questioned whether support for rehabilitation had diminished or maintained its hold on public thinking. They surveyed a random sample of 400 residents in Hamilton County (Cincinnati) and received 237 responses. They compared the results with the Cullen *et al.* (1990) survey and found that citizens' support for rehabilitation had declined meaningfully. However, they also found that the public continues to view treatment as a legitimate correctional objective, especially for juvenile and non-violent offenders.

Related attitudinal research by Schwartz *et al.* (1993) and Skovron *et al.* (1989) demonstrate that US men are more likely than women to support the death penalty and want youth offenders to be tried in court with adults and sent to adult prisons. Women in contrast to men have been found to believe that crime is on the increase and reported higher levels of fear of crime, which was consistent with research by Smith and Tortensson (1997) and Sprott and Doob (1997). However, when it came to reintegration, it appeared that women were more likely than men to think that offenders should be reintegrated into the community with 83.3 per cent of women, as opposed to 72.1 per cent of men, thinking that adults should be fully reintegrated back into the community after they had served time in prison (Sprott 1999).

When considering public attitudes towards offenders, it is important to also consider public attitudes to different crimes (Cullen *et al.* 1990). The distinction is often made by researchers in this field between street crime and white-collar crime like fraud. Early research suggested that white-collar crimes were not viewed as serious matters or were shown an indifference by the public (Rossi *et al.* 1974), especially in comparison to crimes committed against a person or the public (Geis 1973; Sutherland 1949; Wheeler *et al.* 1988). This perception is consistent with more recent research by Evans *et al.* (1993) and Schoepfer *et al.* (2007). Schoepfer *et al.* (2007) reported the results from single telephone interviews with US citizens aged over 18 which examined whether the perceived sanction and severity was different for street crime than it was for white-collar crime. In this research, fraud and robbery were used as two exemplars of white-collar crime vs. street crime, respectively. The findings of the research indicated that while the public perceived that street criminals were more likely to be caught and sentenced to severe sanctions than those who committed white-collar crime, it appeared that respondents believed that both robbery and fraud should be 'equally punished' and were 'on a par'. Eighty-two per cent of respondents in this study appeared to believe that robbery would result in more severe sentencing, whereas only 15 per cent thought that fraud would result in a more severe sentence. Thirty-one per cent of the respondents indicated that they believed that robbery and fraud should receive an equal level of punishment whereas 38 per cent believed that all crimes should be punished equally (Schoepfer *et al.* 2007).

Perceptions of rehabilitation and attitudes towards offenders

Research into the public perception of rehabilitation is an integral part of examining public perceptions related to offender issues, particularly sentencing and effective reintegration. There have been various studies into the concept of rehabilitation as crime rates rise. A study by Cullen *et al.* (1988) researched the public attitude to the principles and applications of rehabilitation via questionnaire research. The study indicated that the support for punitive justifications was widespread although rehabilitation continued to retain legitimacy also. It was interesting to note that even though there was a strong sentiment for punitive measures to be used with offenders, nearly seventy per cent (of the respondents) expressed confidence that giving prisoners vocational and educational training is the best way to rehabilitate them. The findings suggest that there is a 'duality to the public's sanctioning ideology – although citizens clearly want offenders punished, they continue to believe that offenders should be rehabilitated' (Cullen *et al.* 1988: 305). It is an interesting concept that the community still supported punishment to a certain extent and were prepared to toughen up on crime. However, the respondents in this sample felt that punishment should be accompanied by rehabilitation, that treatment can work and that prison inmates should be given the opportunity to reform themselves. This two-pronged finding – support for the 'just deserts' theory of punishment along with the 'need for rehabilitation', suggests that public attitudes towards crime are not one-dimensional. Instead, underlying the need for retribution is an element of optimism for the offenders to get well and become participating members of society.

When surveying public opinion towards offenders and punishment, youth justice is an important consideration. Allen (2002) argues that the basic orientation governing the concept of youth justice in the UK was established in the early 1990s when there were concerns about young offenders that gained prominence following the James Bulger murder. James Bulger, aged two, was senselessly and impulsively killed by two ten-year-old boys, Robert Thompson and Jon Venables, in Liverpool in 1993. Following the James Bulger case, it was documented that people in Britain held harsh attitudes towards offenders and the proportion of the population agreeing that offenders should be subject to harsher sentences appeared to rise from 67 per cent to 84 per cent in 1993 (Jowell *et al.* 1997). Nonetheless, in support of the principles of rehabilitation, it was reported that 'a majority (of those surveyed) supported the idea that if offenders were made more aware of the impact of their crime on the victim, they would be less likely to re-offend' (Home Office 2001: 9). Wood and Viki (2001) suggested that psychosocial factors mediate public attitudes towards crime and prejudice and that recidivist youth offenders are viewed less sympathetically by the public. Allen (2002) argued that youth justice needed to have increased understanding and that there needed to be an orientation in policy towards the treatment of youth offenders as a result of various research findings.

Although this chapter is primarily concerned with the discussion on attitudes towards general prisoners, a highly emotionally charged and often debated topic in the criminal justice system is the subject of sex offenders and possible punishment for sexual crimes. A study by Brown (1999) examined the attitudes and anticipated behaviour towards a sex offender treatment centre and the acceptance of sex offenders who had finished their sentences by using a survey of 500 UK community residents (see also Brown, this volume). From this research, it appeared that attitudes to sex offenders and their treatment in the community were positive; however, it appeared that the public also wanted some form of punishment to take place alongside the rehabilitation. People appeared to be less supportive of treatment taking place in the community and indicated that they would prefer sex offenders to be treated in prison rather than in the community.

In sum, this section shows that the public tends to have two parallel but somewhat paradoxical views regarding offenders: first, there is ample evidence of support for rehabilitation; second, there is a coincidental desire for punishment in keeping with the nature of the offence found elsewhere in this review (e.g. McCorkle 1993). Perhaps it is this quandary that poses one of the greatest obstacles to reintegration for offenders, particularly those convicted of a violent crime.

Psychosocial mediators of public attitudes

The way that the public view offenders is of paramount importance for the way that they are accepted into the community and their chances of successful reintegration. Religion, personal experience in law enforcement and political views can influence the way that people perceive ex-offenders and ex-prisoners. There are various factors that can influence the way that a person is perceived in the community and ex-offenders are often at a disadvantage as a result of their criminal records. Wood and Viki (2001) reported that psychosocial factors can mediate the attitudes of the public towards offenders. The psychosocial factors that are particularly notable are the public's emotional orientation, their prejudice (systemic obstacles to reintegration), fear of crime and criminal acts, criminal records, religion, public sector attitudes, gender and socio-economic factors (Allen 2002). We will now consider some of these areas in more detail.

Systemic obstacles to reintegration

In an examination of offenders and rehabilitation, it is necessary to examine the potential obstacles offenders face in the criminal justice system, both while incarcerated and upon release to the community. Many offenders face employment problems and difficulty finding a residence to live in as a result of their offending and their criminal acts. Many research studies have examined the various issues that arise for offenders once they are released into the community. For example, one common finding in the literature is that employment for ex-offenders is a very salient consideration for successful reintegration of offenders back into the community. However, whether ex-offenders will be rejected and refused employment on the basis of their criminal records is an open question. Gill (1997) examined the barriers that 'ex-offenders' faced in the UK when they tried to obtain employment. As part of this research, Gill conducted interviews with offenders in the last six months of their sentence, employers who had some experience in employing ex-offenders and other specialists including probation and employment officers. Gill noted:

> An important focus of the interviews was to find out more about inmates' attitudes to obtaining employment and their previous experiences. In all, four overlapping points emerged as explanations as to why ex-offenders did not get or keep jobs:

a lack of incentives, a failure to deal with the root causes of offending, difficulties in adjusting to civilian life, and a few commented on the lack of advice available. (Gill 1997: 341)

The results of Gill's research indicated that ex-offenders who were seeking work could not rely on help from the criminal justice system and it appeared that employers and ex-offenders were fairly ignorant about not only the risks of ex-offender employment, but also the opportunities that existed for them. The APEX Trust survey of employers and ex-offenders conducted in the UK in 1991 found that 15 per cent of private companies would not employ someone with a criminal record under any circumstances and 3 per cent of respondents in the public sector felt the same way. One in 20 employers (5 per cent), for example, reported that they did not recruit offenders and a further 38 per cent restricted their recruitment to certain posts. There was more concern about certain types of offending, such as sexual offences, property offences, violence, fraud/forgery and robbery. It was also found that some employers said they would not employ an ex-offender when there were other 'genuine' non-offender job seekers (p. 344). Overall, Gill concluded that there was little support for employment when ex-offenders were reintegrated into the community.

Female offenders have similar obstacles to effective reintegration to male offenders, but there are some factors that may be unique to women, including family separation and community isolation. A study by Dodge and Pogrebin (2001) examined the cost of imprisonment for women and the possible complications for integrating back into society. The data collected for this experiment was from unstructured interviews with 54 former inmates from the US and included discussions based around reflections and accounts of the costs that they have experienced as a result of imprisonment. The narratives that were obtained from the unstructured interviews detailed the difficulties that women felt in parenting and how their incarceration had affected their functioning in the community as a whole. It was reported by women that they were 'treated as outcasts, excluded from the job market and judged for their past criminal behaviours' (Dodge and Pogrebin 2001: 43). It was also reported that one of the most significant problems that women faced was finding some form of employment upon release from prison. Many women lacked job skills and therefore found low, dead-end jobs which contributed to their lowered self-esteem and lack of motivation to reach their potential.

Divorce and isolation were two other key factors reported by women in their release from prison. Divorce was reported to contribute to loneliness and separation, which is common for imprisoned women. However, one of the key factors which complicated reintegration back into the community was that women felt they had to constantly prove themselves as worthy citizens – again, an attitudinal issue. It was reported that 'once out of prison and on parole, women in this study reported the many difficulties they experienced in adjusting to living in the community. The one factor common to the experience of all the interviewees was the distrust community members communicated' (Dodge and Pogrebin 2001: 49).

The discussion of the isolation and the problems experienced by women who were incarcerated and the rehabilitation of offenders demonstrate many of the social attitudes towards incarceration that are conflated with seemingly non-attitudinal reintegration difficulties. For example, many members of the public do not want to reside with people who have been convicted of a crime punishable by imprisonment and, as a result, many ex-offenders find it difficult to find a stable abode. The Social Exclusion Unit (SEU 2002) reported that 'the government has expressed concern over the high rate of re-offending among former prisoners, particularly among young men and those who have served short sentences' (p. 137). As a result, it has been suggested that accommodation problems could 'increase the likelihood of re-offending by up to 20%' (p. 137). It is possible that the reason for this is because many former prisoners do not have the means or knowledge to purchase their own home or even to pay a deposit for a privately rented property. While the government in the United Kingdom has launched initiatives to aid ex-prisoners to find their own home, there still appears to be an issue with housing for those who have been incarcerated. A UK study by Harding and Harding (2006) examined the widespread housing difficulties that were experienced by former prisoners and also examined the failure of probation services to aid ex-offenders to find housing. This study also examined the tensions that underlie the government attempts to alleviate the housing situation faced by released inmates. Interviews with ex-prisoners who were known to have experienced some difficulty finding housing were conducted. Harding and Harding (2006) identified that the causes of widespread housing difficulties among former prisoners relate to a lack of appropriate advice in prisons and a failure to coordinate the work of the prison and probation services.

Criminal records and attitudes towards offenders

Criminal records are another source of attitudinal issues for the public's perception of offenders. Clearly accurate records are an important part of the criminal justice system. When an offender appears before the court, one of the key pieces of information that a judge is provided with is the criminal history of the individual. While there has been a fair amount of research into public perceptions of sentencing and the seriousness of crime, there has been limited research into the question of public support for the idea that a criminal record can aggravate the situation in the sentencing process (Roberts 1996). Roberts reports that the public appears to hold overly negative perceptions of the extent of the criminal history problem in the future as well as the past. In all likelihood the public overestimates both the likelihood and seriousness of reoffending (Roberts 1996). Thus, when a criminal has a record, the public are more likely to want a harsher sentence than when an offender has committed a crime for the first time. Roberts (1996) noted that the public were often guided by the 'just deserts theory' which is based on the principle of 'proportional punishment' (p. 496). As a result, the public appears to be unwilling to abandon the principle that low and moderate crimes should result in a punishment that is proportional to the gravity of the offending behaviour (Roberts 1996).

Similarly, employment is an issue for many people in the community. However, when a person has a criminal record, the attitude of the public towards that person changes dramatically and as a result serious issues with regard to employment may develop. A UK study by Brown *et al.* (2007) examined the process of reintegration of sex offenders after they were released from prison, with a particular focus on the barriers and opportunities to employment that these offenders encountered. Brown *et al.* identified three groups of research participants, including: sex offenders in custody, employers and service managers in probation. The research included telephone interviews, one-on-one interviews and postal questionnaires. The results of the research indicated that all respondents expressed the view that 'the nature of their offences would have an adverse impact on their chances of gaining employment. Most potential employers, they felt, would judge them and react negatively to their record, viewing them as unsuitable or undesirable' (Brown *et al.* 2007: 38). Most of the sex offenders expressed concern about the need to disclose their offences to potential employers and reported that they would feel shameful, nervous and embarrassed. It was stated that sex offenders experience more barriers or higher hurdles to gaining employment than the majority of offenders, which could possibly be a result of their lack of qualifications and work experience and employer reactions to the crime. This research also reported that half of the employers who were surveyed would not consider employing an individual who had been convicted of a sexual offence. However, only a small proportion of the employers surveyed cited moral reasons for not hiring a sex offender suggesting that social desirability may have been a factor in these results. Brown et al. (2007) concluded that the approach that the government had taken to address reintegrative needs actually reduced the opportunities available to sex offenders.

Previous research has supported Brown et al.'s (2007) claim that offences of a sexual nature significantly reduced the employment opportunities available for offenders. Metcalf et al. (2001) suggested that many factors contributed to the employment difficulties of sex offenders, including employer discrimination, lack of skills and experience, alcohol and drug involvements and lack of support from family and the community. Niven and Stewart (2005) reported that 70 per cent of prisoners leave prison without jobs and, compared to people in the general population, prisoners are 13 per cent more likely to be unemployed. The importance of employment for ex-prisoners and sex offenders is demonstrated in the results of research conducted by Hanson and Harris (1998). Hanson and Harris (1998) reported that sex offenders who committed further sexual offences were more likely to be unemployed and that employment reduced the chance of sex offenders reoffending. Thus stress about their employment situation may exacerbate high-risk situations for sex offenders, facilitating offending behaviour (Craig et al. 2005).

Religion and attitudes towards offenders

Religion provides many members of the public with strong and historical beliefs regarding the punishment of criminals. Studies, mainly in North America, have shown that highly religious people and those with a strong belief in a just world – the belief that good things will happen to good people and bad things will happen to bad people – held the most punitive attitudes towards offenders (Wood and Viki 2001). There is a growing body of international research that indicates that those with Christian beliefs are more punitive in response to the consequences of offending. One possible explanation for adherents to Christian beliefs to be more punitive in their responses to crime is that such beliefs promote the notion that offending behaviour results from the character of a person and not unjust or unfortunate environmental influences. This dispositional attribution style was the subject of Grasmick and McGill's (1994) research which examined the relationship between dispositional factors, conservative religious beliefs and punitiveness. The authors conclude that 'with a dispositional attribution style, crime is attributed to the offender's character; with a situational attribution, the offender's environment is viewed as the cause of crime' (p. 26).

Grasmick and McGill (1994) also investigated what kind of religious orientation was associated with higher punitive opinions. After controlling for gender, race, age and education, people who were 'affiliated with a "fundamentalist" denomination were found to be significantly more retributive in their punishment philosophy than liberal and moderate Protestants, Catholics and those with no religious affiliation' (Grasmick and McGill 1994: 24). It was also interesting to note that where people had a literal interpretation of the Bible, this led to greater punitiveness and a greater trend to attribute crime to dispositional factors, for both adult and juvenile offenders.

Public sector attitudes towards offenders

Non-religious prejudices are another set of important factors to consider in an examination of crime and punishment. People can often be biased in their opinions towards people as a result of their crimes and fictional stories that they may have heard with regard to certain crimes and the punishments that result. Employees in the public sector are not free from bias either and an examination of these potential biases is important. A study by Furnham and Alison (1994) investigated the theories of criminality, pre-trial juror bias, as well as the attitudes of the police ($n = 43$), members of the public ($n = 58$) and offenders ($n = 49$) towards to causes, treatments, punishments and biased judgments in response to criminal behaviour. The authors hypothesised that the police would be biased towards a prosecution mentality with a desire to have harsher sentences for criminal acts and that the police would view criminal acts as a deviation from a socially accepted 'norm'. It was also hypothesised that offenders would show a bias towards lenient sentencing and hold the belief that offenders were victims of their environment. Finally, it was expected that the general public would hold beliefs that were on neither of the extreme responses. Furnham and Alison (1994) administered a range of questionnaires to survey attitudes to answer the hypotheses: the Consensus-Conflict Attitudes and Beliefs Scale (C-CABS; see

Furnham and Alison 1994); (2) the Juror Bias Scale (JBS; Kassin and Wrightsman 1983); (3) Belson's Social Philosophy Questionnaire (BSPQ; Belson 1975); (4) the Attitudes to Punishment Scale (APS; Alison and Furnham 1992). They found that all of these hypotheses were supported. There was an almost perfect symmetry between the three groups: i.e. the police fell towards prosecution bias, the offenders to the defence bias, and the control group was intermediate between the two with the mean score averaging at neutral. It could be said that the offenders tend to put the blame on society while police officers put the blame on the individual. The authors suggest that one's role has some influence on the information that one attends to. In the case of the police, one might suspect that the number of cases on which individuals are not tried and convicted for crimes, where the officer involved is convinced the defendant was guilty, become more salient than those on which the individual is convicted.

The findings of Furnham and Alison (1994) are consistent with Ortet-Fabregat and Perez's (1992) findings, which suggested that police officers are more likely to be pro- rather than anti-punishment relative to other groups (in their study – social workers, individuals in the judicial system and students). It appears that attitudes are consistent with the role of the individual – in the case of police: detention, apprehension and interrogation. Furnham and Alison also argue that levels of risk are also likely to influence punishment beliefs – it may be that in the present study, police officers' attitudes to punishment are shaped by their increased risk of receiving aversive stimuli from offenders. These general findings also confirm Furnham and Henderson's (1983) findings that there are a number of different attitudes towards theories of crime. The general public did not express any extreme views on any of the dimensions relative to the other two groups and, as in Furnham and Henderson's (1983) study, there appears to be a concern for some educational, situational and social problems that people are, in part, responsible for criminal behaviour. Interestingly, the general public group had a marginal leaning to the conflict view of crime which is more consistent with the offender's beliefs than those of the police.

The effect of occupation on attitudes towards offenders has also been reported elsewhere. Melvin et al. (1985) developed a 36-item scale specifically designed to assess general attitudes towards prisoners (ATP). In developing the scale they demonstrated good test-retest reliability and internal consistency and the measure was found to be free of response distortions. They found significant differences in attitudes across six groups: reform/rehabilitation groups (n = 19), prisoners (n = 157), students (n = 90), community sample (n = 64), correctional officers (n = 56) and law enforcement officers (n = 23). Perhaps not surprisingly, the reform/ rehabilitation and prisoner groups expressed the most favourable attitudes towards prisoners, whereas the law enforcement and correctional officer groups showed the least favourable attitudes. Hogue (1993) replicated Melvin et al.'s study with similar results, but also adapted the ATP scale by replacing all references to 'prisoners' with a reference to 'sex offenders' to develop a measure to assess attitudes towards sex offenders (ATS; Hogue 1993; see also Brown, this volume). Like Melvin et al., Hogue found significant differences in attitudes held by correctional and law enforcement officers compared with treatment facilitators towards both prisoners and sex offenders. Police groups expressed the most negative attitudes to sex offenders whereas prison officers who acted as treatment facilitators held significantly more positive views towards sex offenders than those prison officers who had not received specialist training.

Gender and attitudes to offenders

It is important to consider the role that gender plays with regard to punitive attitudes and perceptions of crime. Research on fear of crime and being the victim of criminal acts has shown that more women compared to men were fearful of street crimes (Conklin 1998; Ferraro 1995; Haghighi and Lopez 1998; Haghighi and Sorensen 1996; Silverman and Kennedy 1985; Skogan and Maxfield 1981; Stinchcombe et al. 1980; Warr 1984; Warr and Stafford 1983). It has been argued that public perceptions of prisons and offenders can be linked to the concept of fear and that as the fear grows so does the public support for more punitive measures to deal with criminals (Flanagan and Caulfield 1984; Haghighi and Lopez 1998; Wright 1987). For example, Haghighi and Lopez (1998) conducted research into the differences in punitive attitudes of men and women, and the perceptions of prisons and prisoners by this sample group. The data for this research was gathered from the Survey Research Program at Sam Houston University and the Public Policy Research Institute of Texas A & M University (Haghighi and Lopez 1998). It was found that women were more in favour than men of punishing serious offenders and that women with a college education were more likely to oppose those offenders who had been paroled for serious offences than those women who did not have a higher education. Women respondents tended to oppose the notion of shorter sentences and paroling those people who had previously been on parole. Single men and women respondents were more optimistic about rehabilitating offenders with early intervention and requiring prisoners to learn skills prior to release than their married counterparts. However, Haghighi and Lopez (1998) report that this difference of opinion was more a function of respondents' race/ethnicity, income, education, marital status and the source of their crime news than gender itself.

While the research by Haghighi and Lopez (1998) identified that there were differences between men's and women's opinions, they also speculated as to why these differences exist. For example, it was argued the differences may have been due to the respondents' ethnicity, education, reported income, source of news and the crime they watched on television.

There are various ways that a person can receive information about the criminal justice system, for example newspapers, crime shows and news on television and radio. It appears that men and women may receive crime information differently and women who tend to rely on television to inform them about crime appear to be more punitive with regard to shortening sentences and allowing the Parole Board more jurisdiction over which prisoners they release. In short, 'white, wealthier, educated, single, women who relied on television as their main source of crime news appeared to be more punitive toward incarcerated felons than their male counterparts' (Haghighi and Lopez 1998: 463). However, women who indicated that they received their information about crime from the newspaper tended to show more of an opposition to prisoners being paroled more than once. With regard to rehabilitation, single men and women respondents were more optimistic about rehabilitating offenders (Haghighi and Lopez 1998). Women respondents tended to be more optimistic than men that early intervention could result in reformation of prisoners; however, men supported the idea that releasing prisoners early for good behaviour would be a good practice. Both men and women supported the notion that programmes to acquire skills before being released from prison would be a good practice.

Socio-economics and attitudes towards offenders

It has been well established in the research literature that people are fairly punitive in nature (but see also Cullen *et al.*, this volume). However, it needs to be established if people of different socio-economic classes have different standards in terms of punishing offenders. Payne *et al.* (2004) conducted research in an attempt to answer this question. A selection of Virginia residents were surveyed to determine what sanctions they would recommend regarding five different offences. Payne and colleagues used multivariate models to examine the relationships between demographic descriptors and punishment justifications. The results from the study suggested that justifications for why an offender should receive a certain sentence were strongly aligned with the punitive attitudes of the people sampled. Thus it appeared that there was a relationship in the data between punitive attitudes and the idea that punishment is a general deterrent across race and gender (Payne *et al.* 2004) regardless of socio-economic status.

However, the research by Schoepfer *et al.* (2007) indicated that there were differences of opinion between people with different socio-economic backgrounds. For example, the authors noted that people who reported a higher income bracket were less likely to believe that white-collar criminals would be caught, and if caught, would likely receive less serious sanctions. Similarly, Schanzenbach and Yeager (2003) reported variations with regard to the sentencing of offenders based on their education, income, age and the number of defendants. Schoepfer *et al.* (2007) also found that people who were politically conservative were 'less likely to believe that the white-collar crime should be punished more severely and more likely to believe that both crimes should be equally likely to receive harsh punishments' (p. 159). In terms of gender, females were also less likely to believe that street crime should be punished more severely and indicated that they believed the punishments should be equal for both offences. This finding is in contrast to that of Sprott (1999) who found that women were more punitive than men. This difference may be explained due to differences in socio-economic and political biases of the different samples.

The attribution of blame for crime and socially unacceptable behaviour is an important consideration in the formation of public attitudes towards crime. Furnham and Henderson (1983) reported that Conservative voters asserted that a lack of education, or poor education, resulted in delinquency; however, Labour voters tended to focus more on societal factors. Other work by Reuterman (1978) and Feather (1974) has shown that sex and age are also factors which can affect one's attributional style. It was reported that women were more inclined to blame a person's upbringing and parental factors, whereas older people were more inclined to blame the individual person for their acts (Furnham and Alison 1994). Wood and Viki (2001) reported that older people were more punitive than younger people in society.

They note that people who worked in manual-based jobs were more likely to be punitive than those who worked in positions that were not manual occupations.

Conclusion

The present chapter has found several themes in the literature regarding public attitudes towards crime, offenders and reintegration. A central finding was that the public largely believes in a 'just deserts' philosophy – if you do crime, you can expect to do time. However, a parallel finding was that these same people also believe in the value of rehabilitation prior to release. This is a less well-known and optimistic finding and one that gives a great deal of support to the current trends in justice system approaches to crime, i.e. effective reintegration is based on astute punishment with an aim to rehabilitation as a prerequisite for consideration for early release. Essentially, if you do the crime and are doing the time but want out early, you'll have to do the time in effective programming, not just watching the television or lifting weights. Offenders have to take responsibility not by serving time but by doing whatever they can to reduce their risk to the public, otherwise they can expect to spend the duration of their sentences behind bars.

Some of the literature related to this chapter indicates that many people believe that it is possible to alleviate societal stressors which contribute to crime and deviant acts. For example, Wood and Viki (2001) reported that in times of economic prosperity and optimism, attitudes of the public towards offenders tend to be more sympathetic. Likewise, in times of economic crisis or impending stressors on the economy, attitudes to offenders were less sympathetic. The authors also reported that people who were highly religious or who had a strong upbringing that involved a belief in a 'just world' where good things happen to good people and bad things will happen to bad people were more likely to be punitive in their attitudes towards offenders and offending behaviour.

With fear of crime and the general public perception that crime is on the rise, it is important to consider what may be done to alleviate public fears and reduce the risk of crime in the process. The field of restorative justice is an alternative to the more traditional approaches to crime and justice. Restorative justice approaches allow the victims to play a part in the justice process and aid the system to hold the offender accountable and repair the harm they have caused (Bonta *et al.* 2006). Indeed, this is consistent with research for the Halliday Review which supported the idea that if offenders were made more aware of the impact of their crime on the victim, they would be less likely to reoffend (Home Office 2001). In a restorative justice process, the victims meet the offenders and allow them to express the harm and hurt that they have felt as a result of the crime. A reparation plan is devised with the help of the victim and all parties have an equal say in the process. Bonta *et al.* (2006) note that on average, restorative justice programmes were associated with a 7 per cent reduction in recidivism. Therefore there is general hope in the justice system that alternative methods of treatment are available and have the desired results of reducing crime and improving the lives of those who have offended.

Finally, there is growing evidence that correctional programmes are effective (e.g. Andrews 1995; Palmer *et al.* 2007), and there is an increasing literature on the effectiveness of rehabilitative programmes for juvenile offenders (e.g. Dowden and Andrews 1999), violent offenders (e.g. Polaschek and Dixon 2001) and sexual offenders (e.g. Craig *et al.* 2003; Hall 1995; Hanson *et al.* 2002). A growing sense of optimism may be warranted, given the 'nothing works' sentiments of the 1970s, from the preponderance of effectiveness data in the late 1990s and early 2000s. Of course, attitudinal changes follow behavioural changes, so it is hoped that as offenders reoffend less as a result of effective programming the obstacles that currently impede reintegration will improve with time. There is a large amount of research needed to tease apart the component parts of the public's attitudes towards crime, criminals and the seemingly opposing attitudes towards reintegration and rehabilitation. It is hoped that this chapter may have contributed to this discussion.

References

Alison, L. and Furnham, A. (1992) 'Attitudes to Punishment Scale'. Unpublished instrument, University College London.

Allen, R. (2002) 'There must be some way of dealing with kids: young offenders, public attitudes and policy change', *Youth Justice*, 2 (3): 3–13.

Andrews, D.A. (1995) 'The psychology of criminal conduct and effective treatment', in J. McGuire (ed.), *What Works: Reducing Reoffending: Guidelines from Research and Practice*. Chichester: John Wiley, pp. 35–62.

Apex Trust (1991) *The Hidden Workforce*. Available from: Apex Trust, Wingate House, Fare Street, London EC2.

Belson, W.A. (1975) *The Public and the Police*. London: Harper & Row.

Bonta, J., Rugge, T.A., Cormier, R.B. and Jesseman, R. (2006) 'Restorative justice and recidivism: promises made, promises kept?', in D. Sullivan and L. Tifft (eds), *Handbook of Restorative Justice: A Global Perspective*. London and New York: Routledge, pp. 108–18.

Brown, K., Spencer, J. and Deakin, J. (2007) 'The reintegration of sex offenders: barriers and opportunities for employment', *Howard Journal of Criminal Justice*, 46 (1): 32–42.

Brown, S. (1999) 'Public attitudes toward the treatment of sex offenders', *Legal and Criminological Psychology*, 4 (2): 239–52.

Conklin, J.E. (1998) *Criminology*. Needham Heights, MA: Allyn & Bacon.

Craig, L.A., Browne, K.D. and Stringer, I. (2003) 'Treatment and sexual offence recidivism', *Trauma, Violence, and Abuse*, 4 (1): 70–89.

Craig, L.A., Browne, K.D., Stringer, I. and Beech, A. (2005) 'Sexual recidivism: a review of static, dynamic and actuarial predictors', *Journal of Sexual Aggression*, 1: 63–82.

Cullen, F.T., Cullen, J.B. and Wozniak, J.F. (1988) 'Is rehabilitation dead? The myth of the punitive public', *Journal of Criminal Justice*, 16: 303–17.

Cullen, F.T., Skovron, S.E., Scott, J.E. and Burton, V.S. Jr (1990) 'Public support for correctional treatment: the tenacity of rehabilitative ideology', *Criminal Justice and Behavior*, 17: 6–18.

Dodge, M. and Pogrebin, M.R. (2001) 'Collateral costs of imprisonment for women: complications of reintegration', *Prison Journal*, 81 (1): 42–54.

Dowden, C. and Andrews, D.A. (1999) 'What works in young offender treatment: a meta-analysis', *Forum on Corrections Research*, 11: 21–4.

Evans, T.D., Cullen, F.T. and Dubeck, P.J. (1993) 'Public perceptions of white collar crime', in M.B. Blankenship (ed.), *Understanding Corporate Criminality*. New York: Garland, pp. 85–114.

Feather, N. (1974) 'Explanations of poverty in Australia and American samples: the person, society and fate', *Australian Journal of Psychology*, 26: 199–226.

Ferraro, K.F. (1995) *Fear of Crime: Interpreting Victimization Risk*. Albany, NY: State University of New York Press.

Flanagan, T.J. and Caulfield, S. (1984) 'Public opinion and prison policy: a review', *Prison Journal*, 64 (2): 31–46.

Furnham, A. and Alison, L. (1994) 'Theories of crime, attitudes to punishment, and juror bias amongst police, offenders and the general public', *Personality and Individual Differences*, 17 (1): 35–48.

Furnham, A. and Henderson, M. (1983) 'Lay theories of delinquency', *European Journal of Social Psychology*, 13: 107–20.

Geis, G. (1973) 'Deterring corporate crime', in R. Nader and M.J. Greed (eds), *Corporate Power in America*. New York: Grossman, pp. 182–97.

Gill, M. (1997) 'Employing ex-offenders: a risk or an opportunity?', *Howard Journal*, 36 (40): 337–51.

Grasmick, H.G. and McGill, A.L. (1994) 'Religion, attribution style, and punitiveness towards juvenile offenders', *Criminology*, 32 (1): 23–46.

Haghighi, B. and Lopez, A. (1998) 'Gender and perception of prisons and prisoners', *Journal of Criminal Justice*, 26 (6): 453–64.

Haghighi, B. and Sorensen, J. (1996) 'America's fear of crime', in T.J. Flanagan and D.R. Longmire (eds), *Americans View Crime and Justice: A National Public Opinion Survey*. Thousand Oaks, CA: Sage, pp. 16–30.

Hall, N.G.C. (1995) 'Sexual offender recidivism revisited: a meta-analysis of recent treatment studies', *Journal of Consulting and Clinical Psychology*, 63: 802–9.

Hanson, R.K. and Harris, A.J.R. (1998) *Dynamic Predictors of Sexual Recidivism*, User Report 1998-01. Ottawa: Solicitor General of Canada.

Hanson, R.K., Gordon, A., Harris, A.J.R., Marques, J.K., Murphy, W., Quinsey, V.L. and Seto, M.C. (2002) 'First report of the collaborative outcome data project on the effectiveness of psychological treatment for sex offenders', *Sexual Abuse: A Journal of Research and Treatment*, 14: 169–94.

Harding, A. and Harding, J. (2006) 'Inclusion and exclusion in the re-housing of former prisoners', *Journal of Community and Criminal Justice*, 53 (2): 137–53.

Hogue, T.E. (1993) 'Attitudes towards prisoners and sex offenders', in N.C. Clark and G. Stephenson (eds), *DCLP Occasional Papers: Sexual Offenders*. Leicester: British Psychological Society.

Home Office (2001) *Making Punishments Work*. London: Stationery Office.

Jowell, R., Curtice, J., Park, A., Brook, C., Thomson, K. and Brough, C. (1997) *British Social Attitudes: The 4th Report*. Ashgate: Aldershot.

Kassin, S.M. and Wrightsman, L.S. (1983) 'The construction and validation of a juror bias scale', *Journal of Research in Personality*, 17 (4): 423–42.

McCorkle, R. (1993) 'Research note: punish and rehabilitate? Public attitudes towards six common crimes', *Crime and Delinquency*, 39 (2): 240–52.

Melvin, K.B., Gramling, L.K. and Gardner, W.M. (1985) 'A scale to measure attitudes towards prisoners', *Criminal Justice and Behavior*, 12: 241–53.

Metcalf, H., Anderson, T. and Rolfe, H. (2001) *Barriers to Employment for Offenders and Ex-Offenders*, DWP Research Report No. 155. Leeds: Corporate Document Services.

Niven, S. and Stewart, D. (2005) *Resettlement Outcomes from Release from Prison 2003*, Home Office Findings No. 248. London: Home Office.

Ortet-Fabregat, G. and Perez, J. (1992) 'An assessment of the attitudes towards crime among professionals in the criminal justice system', *British Journal of Criminology*, 32: 193–207.

Palmer, E.J., McGuire, J., Housome, J.C., Hatcher, R.M., Bibly, C.A.L. and Hollin, C.R. (2007) 'Offending behaviour programmes in the community: the effects on reconviction of three programmes with adult male offenders', *Legal and Criminological Psychology*, 12 (2): 215–64.

Payne, B.K., Gainey, R.R., Triplett, R.A. and Danner, M.J. (2004) 'What drives punitive beliefs? Demographic characteristics and justifications for sentencing', *Journal of Criminal Justice*, 32: 195–206.

Polaschek, D.L. and Dixon, B.G. (2001) 'The Violence Prevention Project: the development and evaluation of a treatment programme for violent offenders', *Psychology, Crime and Law*, 7: 1–23.

Reuterman, N. (1978) 'The public's view of delinquency causation: a consideration in comprehensive juvenile justice planning', *Juvenile and Family Court Journal*, 29: 39–47.

Roberts, J. (1996) 'Public opinion, criminal record and the sentencing process', *American Behavioural Scientist*, 39 (4): 488–99.

Rossi, P.H., Waite, E., Bose, C.E. and Berk, R.E. (1974) 'The seriousness of crimes: normative structure and individual differences', *American Sociological Review*, 39: 224–37.

Schanzenbach, M. and Yeager, M.L. (2003) 'Prison time and fines: explaining racial disparities in sentencing for white-collar criminals', *Federal Sentencing Reporter*, 15: 194.

Schoepfer, A., Carmichael, S. and Leeper-Piquero, N. (2007) 'Do perceptions of punishment vary between white-collar and street crimes?', *Journal of Criminal Justice*, 35: 151–63.

Schwartz, I.M., Guo, S. and Kerbs, J.J. (1993) 'The impact of demographic variables on public opinion regarding juvenile justice: implications for public policy', *Crime and Delinquency*, 39 (1): 5–28.

Silverman, R. and Kennedy, L. (1985) 'Loneliness, satisfaction and fear of crime', *Canadian Journal of Criminology*, 27: 1–13.

Skogan, W. and Maxfield, M. (1981) *Coping with Crime: Individual and Neighborhood Reactions*. Beverly Hills, CA: Sage.

Skovron, S.E., Scott, J.E. and Cullen, F.T. (1989) 'The death penalty for juveniles: an assessment of public support', *Crime and Delinquency*, 35 (4): 546–61.

Smith, W.R. and Tortensson, M. (1997) 'Gender differences in risk perception and neutralizing fear of crime: toward resolving the paradoxes', *British Journal of Criminology*, 37 (4): 608–34.

Social Exclusion Unit (2002) *Reducing Re-Offending by Ex-Prisoners: Summary of the Social Exclusion Unit Report*. London: Social Exclusion Unit.

Sprott, J.B. (1999) 'Are members of the public tough on crime? The dimensions of public "punitiveness"', *Journal of Criminal Justice*, 27 (5): 467–74.

Sprott, J.B. and Doob, A.N. (1997) 'Fear, victimization, and attitudes to sentencing, the courts and the police', *Canadian Journal of Criminology*, 39: 275–91.

Stinchcombe, A.L., Adams, R., Heimer, C.A., Scheppele, K.L., Smith, T.W. and Taylor, D.G. (1980) *Crime and Punishment: Changing Attitudes in America*. San Francisco: Jossey-Bass.

Sundt, J.L., Cullen, F.T., Applegate, B.K. and Turner, M.G. (1998) 'The tenacity of the rehabilitative ideal revisited: have attitudes toward offender treatment changed?', *Criminal Justice and Behavior*, 25 (4): 426–42.

Sutherland, E.H. (1949) *White-Collar Crime*. New York: Dryden Press.

Warr, M. (1984) 'Fear of victimization: why are women and elderly more afraid?', *Social Science Quarterly*, 65: 681–702.

Warr, M. and Stafford, M. (1983) 'Fear of victimization: a look at the proximate cause', *Social Forces*, 61: 1033–43.

Wheeler, S., Mann, K. and Sarat, A. (1988) *Sitting in Judgment: The Sentencing of White-Collar Offenders*. New Haven, CT: Yale University Press.

Wood, J. and Viki, G.T. (2001) *Public Attitudes to Crime and Punishment. Report for the Esmée Fairbairn Foundation*. London: Esmée Fairbairn Foundation.

Wright, K.N. (1987) *The Great American Crime Myth*. New York: Praeger.

Chapter 9

Attitudes towards sexual offenders and their rehabilitation: a special case?

Sarah Brown

> The quest for effective social responses to sex offenders is typically sparked by a sexually motivated murder of a child or a woman. The precipitating events have a chilling similarity: someone is reported missing, days pass, the body is found, the identified perpetrator is discovered to be someone with a criminal record of other sex offences. (Lieb 2000: 423)

The link, although by no means straightforward, between such cases and social policy responses can be most clearly observed in the relatively recent naming (both official and unofficial) of legislation after the victims of such murders. In the USA, the federal legislation requiring state registries of sex offenders was named the Jacob Wetterling Crimes Against Children and Sexual Violent Offender Registration Act 1994 in honour of Jacob Wetterling who was abducted from his home town in Minnesota in 1989, aged 11 (neither he nor his abductor have been located). Much more commonly and widely known is 'Megan's Law', which is the unofficial name for US legislation requiring public notification of information (the type of information and the means of notification vary from state to state) contained in state registries. Lieb (2000: 428) observes that 'Megan's Law' is so widely known that it was defined as 'any of various laws aimed at people convicted of sex-related crimes, requiring community notification of the release of offenders, establishment of a registry of offenders, etcetera' when it was included in the new words section of Webster's College Dictionary in 1996. 'Megan', seven-year-old Megan Kanka, was raped and killed by her neighbour who had two previous convictions for child sexual abuse and who lived with two other sex offenders. Those campaigning for 'Megan's Law' argued that Megan's murder would have been prevented had Megan's parents been given information about the sex offenders living in their community.

Yet more stringent approaches designed to protect communities from sex offenders were introduced in the USA in 2005. The Jessica Lunsford Act is the proposed federal legislation that would mandate stricter, electronic/GPS tracking of sex offenders, modelled on 'Jessica's Law' which was enacted in Florida in 2005 and subsequently replicated in most other states. Nine-year-old Jessica Lunsford was abducted from her home, raped and murdered by a paroled sex offender who had completed (mostly served on parole) a ten-year sentence for a sexual offence. The Florida provision introduced mandatory minimum sentences of 25 years imprisonment and lifetime electronic monitoring of adults convicted of sexual battery of a minor under 13 years of age, presumably using the argument that Jessica would not have been murdered if the offender had served a longer period of imprisonment and/or was more effectively monitored in the community.

This naming of legislation after victims is not confined to the US. In the UK, following the abduction and murder of eight year old Sarah Payne in the summer of 2000 by an offender who had been imprisoned and released for the abduction and sexual assault of another eight-year-old girl, many campaigned for the introduction of 'Sarah's Law', i.e. a UK version of 'Megan's Law'. 'Natalie's Law' was enacted in Germany following the rape and murder of seven-year-old Natalie by a paroled sex offender (Albrecht 1997, cited in Lieb 2000) and more recently (2006) there were calls for Germany to enact a sex offender register following the rape and murder of a 39-year-old nurse. The alleged offender had been convicted of rape, kidnapping and extortionate robbery five years earlier and released in September 2006, despite being sentenced to eight years in prison (DW-World.De 2006).

Public response to community notification

Although the naming of legislation after victims is a relatively new phenomenon, the public outcry and subsequent policy responses following this type of case is not new. Lieb (2000) discusses the work of Sutherland who in 1950 observed that sexually motivated murders of children commonly preceded the introduction of state sexual psychopathy laws. He felt that it was the incomprehensibility of the crimes that fuelled the public's fears, particularly when a manhunt for a child killer had taken place. Sutherland noted that following the murder, 'agitated activity' took place in the community, which made a political response essential. In identifying this response all possible remedies were examined and the most recent, most popular innovation would be implemented as a solution (Lieb 2000). Such a pattern of policy enactment can be clearly seen in the policies discussed above; 'Megan's Law', for example, was enacted by most US states before it was required by federal law and requests for the introduction of similar legislation have been seen in other countries such as Germany and the UK following high-profile murders.

There is no doubt that government registries and in particular community notification of the details of these registries has strong public support. Mori polls of 1,004 (Mori 2000, *Naming and Shaming Poll*) and 614 (Mori 2001, *News of the World – Crimes Against Children Poll*) adults commissioned by the *News of the World* (a UK tabloid newspaper that campaigned extensively for the introduction of 'Sarah's Law' in 2000 following the murder of Sarah Payne: see Ashenden 2002, for a more detailed discussion of this action) revealed that 58 per cent of 1,004 adults agreed with the statement that 'convicted paedophiles should be publicly named', 76 per cent agreed that 'local people should know if there is a convicted paedophile in their neighbourhood' and 52 per cent 'strongly supported' and a further 30 per cent 'tended to support' the introduction of 'Sarah's Law'. The *News of the World* focused on the latter finding that 82 per cent supported the introduction of the law (Ashenden 2002), though there was much less mention of the fact that 51 per cent said that the 'naming and shaming' policy that had been adopted by the paper was 'wrong'. Similar responses were obtained by the 2001 survey, although it is unclear which question (or perhaps combination of questions) provided support for the newspaper's heading (described by Ashenden 2002: 210): '88% say name and shame'.

Comparable levels of support have been found in the USA. Lieb (2000) cites the following examples of adults polled in 1997: 82 per cent support was observed in Washington State for community notification in a public opinion survey (Phillips and Troyano 1998); and 79 per cent agreed with the statement that 'the public has a right to know of a convicted sex offender's past, and that right is more important than the sex offender's privacy rights' in a state-wide newspaper poll of Georgia (Hansen 1997: D11).

Clearly this type of legislation has intuitive appeal but it is not entirely clear how community notification increases public safety (see Matson and Lieb 1996, for a discussion of the arguments for and against registration). A question of what would be done with information about sex offenders living in the community was actually raised by some, though only by a tiny minority, of those contributing to the on-line discussion following calls for the introduction of 'Sarah's Law' (BBC News 2006). Joe from Leeds said: 'All this will do is exacerbate the climate of irrational fear that is already so prevalent. What are the parents going to do if they find out a paedophile is in the area? Lock the children in their bedroom? Move to the Shetlands? Ridiculous.' And 'Real Polar Bear', St Albans, said:

> I'm confused. Even if I know that 'Bill Bloggs of 42 Acacia Avenue' is a sex offender what am I supposed to do with the information? Scare him away? Try to get a good look at him so I'd know him again if he turned up at the playground? Or am I supposed to keep my children as safe as possible and teach them about the dangers of talking to strangers … as normal?

Community notification efficacy

While it is perhaps possible that those closest in geographical terms to the named sex offenders are afforded some protection from their knowledge of the offenders living near them, those outside the notification area are not afforded the same protection and it is easy for offenders to travel to different localities to offend. In 2000, the Iowa Department of Human Rights compared recidivism in 233 offenders required to register following the establishment of the State's sex offender registry with 201 who would have had to register had the register been in place when they were released. A slight (3.5 per cent compared to 3 per cent over a 4.3 year follow-up period) decrease, which was not statistically significant, in sexual recidivism was found once registration had been implemented; however, nearly 21 per cent of new offences and 38 per cent of new sexual offences in the registered group occurred out of state, compared to 16 per cent and 0 per cent respectively of new offences in the unregistered group.

There is also concern that public notification encourages offenders to go 'underground' and some have argued that it makes the killing of victims more likely as offenders seek more drastic measures to avoid detection (for example, see West 2000). There is a great deal of evidence (see Nieto and Jung 2006, for example) that many offenders fail to register or register inaccurate details, or that registers quickly become out of date. Seventy-five per cent of addresses in an investigation of 81 addresses provided by sex offenders in Chicago (Tribune Staff 2006, cited in Nieto and Jung 2006) were abandoned buildings or places where the offenders did not reside. 'According to the Illinois Prison Review Board, these findings raise questions about how many sex offenders are going underground to avoid monitoring, and/or the difficulty they have in finding housing' (Nieto and Jung 2006: 9). Furthermore, it is not clear what the police and other agencies are supposed to do with the registers to prevent new sexual offences from occurring, particularly given their often limited resources.

Vigilante action against named sex offenders has also been reported; for example, in the UK in 1997 neighbours burned down the house of an alleged paedophile. A child in the house, unbeknown to the neighbours, died as a result of the fire. A number of attacks of alleged paedophiles took place during the *News of the World* campaign, including a now notorious attack on a paediatrician. However, in the US far fewer vigilante cases have occurred than might have been expected (Lieb *et al.* 1998, cited in Lieb 2000), though this may be a result of extensive efforts by the police to inform communities in a 'safe' manner with education about the risks and consequences of vigilantism. Whether there is a cultural difference between the US and UK that makes people in the UK more likely to engage in vigilante action is difficult to determine: Lieb (2000) points out that football hooliganism, which is a significant concern in Europe, is unknown in the US; hence, it cannot be assumed that the US response to notification would be replicated in other countries.

This type of legislation is also premised on the assumption that children and adults are most at risk from strangers, while all the evidence suggests that we are most at risk of being sexually violated and/or murdered by those we know and trust. Stop It Now! (2003) found that eight in ten child sex abuse victims knew their abuser and Myhill and Allen (2002) found that only 8 per cent of the rapes of women that were reported to the British Crime Survey were committed by strangers. Forty-five per cent were committed by current partners, 11 per cent by ex-partners, 10 per cent by other intimates, 11 per cent by dates and 16 per cent by acquaintances. Each year, in the USA there are 60,000 to 70,000 arrests for child sexual assault (US Justice Department, cited in Nieto and Jung 2006) of which only about 115 are abductions by strangers. Furthermore, about seven in ten female rape or sexual assault victims state that the offender was an intimate, other relative, a friend or an acquaintance.

There appears to be a mismatch, then, between what the public apparently want to protect themselves from sexual abuse (and presumably think will be effective) and the less than convincing evidence for the efficacy of these 'wanted' policies. This mismatch may be attributed to, at least partially, the inaccurate assumptions on which these 'wanted' policies are based. Public attitudes to crime research shows that the public lack knowledge about crime and criminal justice responses to it (see Wood, this volume). Allen (2003: 5, cited in Green 2006: 132) argued that ignorance pervades the interplay between crime, politics and public opinion: '[c]lose analysis would suggest that there is something of a "comedy of errors" in which policy and practice is not based on a proper understanding of public opinion and that the same opinion is not based on a proper understanding of policy and practice.' Such ignorance can be found in many of the common assumptions about sex offenders.

Lieb (2000: 429) observed that, in signing the Jacob Wetterling Act, President Clinton claimed: 'We have taken steps to help families protect their children, especially from sex offenders, people who, according to study after study, are likely to commit their crime again and again …' Similarly, the New York Governor, George Pataki, said: '… studies have shown that sex offenders are more likely to repeat their crime than any other crime' (reported by Zgoba et al. 2003: 135). These statements are actually completely inaccurate: most sex offenders are never convicted of another sexual crime (Hanson and Bussière 1996). Although average rates of recidivism mask a great deal of variation between offenders, average rates of sexual recidivism for untreated sex offenders is approximately 15 per cent over a five-year follow-up period and 20 per cent over a ten-year follow-up period (Hanson and Bussière 1998; Hanson and Thornton 2000). Even when researchers thoroughly search for re-offences and employ long follow-up periods, recidivism rates in excess of 40 per cent are rarely observed (Hanson and Bussière 1996).

Furthermore, the risk of reoffence for sex offenders is not higher than other groups of offenders. The average reconviction rate for adult male prisoners in England and Wales released in 1998 and followed-up for two years was 55 per cent (Home Office 2001). The highest recidivism rates were found for the offences of burglary (75 per cent) and theft and handling (74 per cent) and medium rates for violent offences (43 per cent). In contrast, one of the lowest rates of recidivism (18 per cent), and a rate well below the average rate, was exhibited by sex offenders.

Closely related to misperceptions about rates of recidivism is the view that sex offenders are untreatable and that rehabilitation attempts are unlikely to have an impact. Evaluating offender treatment programmes is a difficult task and the constraints and realities of the criminal justice system mean that conclusive results are unlikely; however, there is now more published evidence to suggest that treated sex offenders have lower recidivism rates than untreated offenders than research that suggests that treatment programmes have no or a detrimental impact (see Brown 2005, and Hanson *et al.* 2002). There is still a great deal of debate about the efficacy of treatment programmes but it seems likely that some offenders can be rehabilitated by these interventions. When combined with the relatively low recidivism rates of many offenders (as mentioned previously, recorded sexual recidivism rates in Iowa were 3 to 3.5 per cent), the positive treatment efficacy research findings contradict the pervasive view that sex offenders are incurable predators who prey on ever increasing numbers of victims.

Stereotyping sexual offenders

A consequence of the media image of sexual offending that focuses on the most violent and shocking cases is that we tend to imagine the most serious crimes when we think of this issue. However, sexual offending encompasses a wide range of behaviours from exposure to penetration, enacted using force that varies from subtle coercion through to overt physical violence. In addition, as West (2000) points out, in many instances the long-term impact of the minor offences (perhaps the majority of incidents) is minor, despite the fact that we tend to assume that 'abuse' is likely to induce severe long-term consequences (which it can do in *some* cases). West argues that the use of the term 'abuse' is not helpful as it covers such a broad range of behaviours and people tend to think the worst when this is often not warranted.

Perceptions of sex offenders tend to follow a number of stereotypes that do not reflect the true nature of offenders. For example, most are shocked to discover that arrest statistics and victim surveys indicate that approximately 30 per cent to 50 per cent of incidents of child sexual abuse and 20 per cent of all rapes are carried out by adolescents (Brown *et al.* 1984, and Deisher *et al.* 1982, cited in Davis and Leitenberg 1987). Most also assume that sex offenders are readily identifiable, abnormal and different to the rest of the population; yet 'the available research suggests greater similarities than differences between sexual offenders and other people' (Marshall 1996: 322), which means that it is difficult to identify offenders aside from the identification of their offending behaviour.

Attitudes towards sex offenders

As well as following high publicity cases, new legislation is campaigned for and introduced on the basis that it is what the public wants. Given this, and the severity of the restrictions that have been imposed on sex offenders by recent legislative changes, it is perhaps surprising to note that we actually know relatively little about public attitudes towards sex offenders. At the time of writing, my own study focused on attitudes towards sex offenders (Brown 1999) and research completed by Clarke *et al.* (2002) investigating attitudes towards rape (specifically date and relationship rape) for the Sentencing Advisory Panel (an independent body originally providing advice to the Sentencing Guidelines Council, which issues sentencing guidelines to all courts in England and Wales) are the only detailed published studies focusing on the views of the *public*. Since the focus of these studies is on responses (i.e. punishment and rehabilitation) to sex offenders, they will be discussed in more detail later in the chapter.

Empirical research investigating professionals' attitudes towards sexual offenders

There have been more studies comparing the attitudes of different groups of professionals, and in some instances students, in their attitudes towards sex offenders. Most of these studies have used Hogue's (1993) Attitudes Towards Sex Offenders Scale (ATS). This scale was adapted (by replacing all references to 'prisoners' with references to 'sexual offenders') from Melvin *et al.*'s (1985) 36-item scale that assesses general attitudes towards prisoners (ATP), which had shown good reliability and validity (Hogue 1993). Respondents indicate whether they 'strongly disagree', 'disagree', are 'undecided', 'agree' or 'strongly agree' to 36 statements such as 'sex offenders are different from most people', 'only a few sex offenders are really dangerous' and 'sex offenders have feelings like the rest of us'. The answers to these questions are used to calculate a score that ranges from 0 to 144,[1] with higher scores indicating more positive attitudes towards sex offenders (or prisoners in the original ATP). This type of scale does not provide a great deal of description or detail about the views expressed by those who complete it, but the standardised nature of the scale enables comparisons to be made across different groups of people.

In order to validate the ATS, Hogue (1993) compared responses on both the ATP and ATS across British groups of police officers ($n = 33$), prison officers with no treatment experience ($n = 21$), prison officers with treatment experience ($n = 50$), probation officers/psychologists ($n = 32$) and sexual offenders ($n = 28$). All groups expressed more favourable attitudes to prisoners than to sexual offenders apart from the sex offenders who displayed not only the most positive views towards both groups, but also held very similar attitudes to both offender groups (mean score of 98.4 for prisoners compared to 99.1 for sex offenders). Of the professional groups, the probation/psychologist group showed the statistically significantly most favourable attitudes (98.5 for prisoners and 90.7 for sex offenders). Prison officers with treatment experience had more favourable views (84.3 and 80.0) than the prison officers without treatment experience (80.0 and 71.5) and as Hogue had predicted the police officers held the least positive views of both offender groups (71.1 and 62.6). In order to place these responses into some type of context, it might be helpful to note that someone with very neutral views would score around the mid-point (72) while someone who broadly 'agreed' to positive statements and 'disagreed' to negative statements would score in the region of 108.

Hogue and Peebles (1997) found that British police officers had significantly less favourable attitudes towards sex offenders (ATS score of 72.5) compared to other British professionals, including mental health workers, social workers, probation or parole officers (whose average score was 81.2), who had registered and were stand-bys for a two-day symposium on working with sex offenders. Radley (2001) supported previous findings revealing that a group of 20 non-discipline prison staff (i.e. probation officers and psychologists) had significantly more favourable attitudes towards sex offenders than a group of 20 discipline staff (prison officers). Ferguson and Ireland (2006) compared the attitudes of 49 non-psychology undergraduate students and an opportunity sample of 90 staff working in forensic settings including psychologists, prison officers, prison governors, counsellors and administrative assistants. Forensic staff demonstrated more positive attitudes towards sex offenders than students did.

Four-hundred and thirty-seven counsellors who were members of the American Mental Health Counselors Association (AMHCA) or the International Association of Addictions and Offender Counselors (IAAOC) completed the ATS in Nelson, Herlihy and Oescher's (2002) postal survey. Nelson *et al.* used an unusual scoring method which makes it difficult to compare their findings to the other ATS studies, though they claimed that their finding revealed that counsellors had more positive attitudes towards sex offenders than the groups in Hogue's (1993) study. They also observed that as there was a statistically significant difference (calculated with a one-sample t-test) between the counsellors' mean total ATS score (3.34 using their scoring method) and the scale's neutral value (3.0, i.e. the midpoint of the 5-point Likert scale used in the ATS) that counsellors had, on average, positive attitudes to sex offenders. Nelson *et al.* found that experience of counselling sex offenders was positively correlated with attitudes towards sex offenders (i.e. the more experience, the more positive the attitudes). Similarly, attitudes were more positive with a greater caseload of sex offenders.

Sanghara and Wilson (2006) compared 71 teachers from greater south London, with 60 members of the National Organisation for the Treatment of Abusers (NOTA), which is a UK-based multi-disciplinary organisation of professionals working to prevent sexual abuse. Teachers responded to a series of rape vignettes in a more stereotypical way than NOTA members did. Attributions of guilt were higher in teachers when sex offenders were described in stereotypical ways; however, there were no differences in guilt attributions when sex offenders were described inconsistently from stereotypes, i.e. NOTA members did not consistently give lower guilt attributions. The NOTA members had significantly more positive attitudes towards sex offenders and more knowledge about child abuse (measured by a scale developed specifically for this study) than the teachers did. Endorsement of stereotypes was negatively correlated with attitudes towards sex offenders (i.e. more positive attitudes were linked to decreased endorsement of stereotypes) and knowledge of child sexual abuse. As knowledge of child sexual abuse increased, positive attitudes towards sex offenders also increased.

Using a qualitative methodology, Lea *et al.* (1999) interviewed 23 professionals and paraprofessionals whose work involved contact with sex offenders and demonstrated that both positive and negative views towards sex offenders could be held simultaneously. Previous quantitative findings were confirmed, however, as the most stereotypical views were held by police officers, especially those with least experience of working with sex offenders or who had no specialist training in this work.

Taken together these studies show that the type of contact professionals have with sex offenders is related to their attitudes towards them: those working in a rehabilitative way with offenders have, on average, more positive views of their clients than do professionals who come into contact with those with an investigative/apprehension (police) or incapacitative/punitive (prison officers) role. Care needs to be taken in interpreting these findings, however, as it could be that people with positive attitudes are more likely to take on these roles rather than it being the roles/occupations themselves that generate the range of attitudes.

A small number of studies using diverse methodologies have examined the differences in attitudes to different sex offender groups. Lea *et al.* (1999) found that during interviews, respondents discussed and compared different types of sex offenders, which reveals a complexity of attitudes that is often hidden in studies using quantitative methods. The most common distinction, however, was made between rapists and 'paedophiles'. Rapists were seen to be more violent and aggressive than 'paedophiles' were, and to be driven by needs of domination and control. 'Paedophiles' were described as having low-self esteem, being sexually deviant and driven by a need for company and affection. Some support for the differing attitudes towards these two groups of offenders was offered by Weekes *et al.* (1995) who used a 19-item perception scale (a modified version of a scale used by Kropp *et al.* 1989) to assess the attitudes of 82 correctional officers in two Canadian federal institutions towards three different offender groups: sex offenders against women, sex offenders against children and non-sex offenders.

> Sex offenders were perceived to be more dangerous, harmful, violent, tense, bad, unpredictable, mysterious, unchangeable, aggressive, weak, irrational, and afraid compared with non-sex offenders. Sex offenders against children were rated as significantly more immoral and mentally ill than sex offenders against women, who, in turn, were judged to be more immoral and mentally ill than non-sex offenders.
>
> (Weekes *et al.* 1995: 59).

In contrast, however, Ferguson and Ireland (2006) found no statistically significant differences in ATS scores completed with reference to different groups of sex offenders.

A number of other characteristics such as gender and victimisation have also been investigated in these studies. Hogue and Peebles

(1997) and Nelson *et al.* (2002) found that attitudes did not vary according to gender, in contrast however, Radley (2001) found that 20 female prison officers and non-discipline prison staff had significantly more positive attitudes than the 20 men in her sample. Similarly, Ferguson and Ireland (2006) found that women in their study were more positive in their attitudes and displayed similar attitudes to all groups of offenders compared to men in the study who viewed offenders who had sexually abused children more negatively than those who had raped unknown women (stranger rapists). Weekes *et al.* (1995), who employed a predominantly male sample, also found that offenders who had committed offences against children were perceived to be more 'immoral' and mentally disordered than those who had committed offences against adult women. Ferguson and Ireland (2006) suggested that there may be a two-way relationship between gender and offender type, which has important implications for staffing, though given the small sample sizes in both studies, these findings would have to be replicated and investigated further before any firm conclusions can be drawn or changes in practice implemented.

Another issue that has been investigated is that of victimisation, with a common assumption being that those with a history of victimisation would have more negative attitudes towards sex offenders: in fact the research does not support this assumption. Hogue and Peebles (1997) found that attitudes (measured via the ATS) did not vary significantly according to prior sexual offence victimisation. In my study (Brown 1999) those who had been victims of abuse, or who were close to someone who had been a victim, did not generally respond differently to the majority of the sample who had no such experience of victimisation. However, Ferguson and Ireland (2006) and Nelson *et al.* (2002) found that people who had experienced themselves, or were close to someone who had experienced, sexual abuse had more positive attitudes to sex offenders than the non-'victim' sample. This is an interesting counter-intuitive finding though more research is needed to explore this issue more fully. Nelson *et al.* argued that since people are more likely to be abused by people they know, survivors' attitudes could be based on personal experience and a greater understanding of the complexity of the issues surrounding these offences rather than stereotypes and inaccurate perceptions. If this was to be the case, then providing people with more 'experience' of sex offenders through education and media portrayals that do not always focus on the most extreme cases etc. may be a way to engender more positive attitudes, though much more research is needed to investigate this more thoroughly.

In terms of the link between attitudes and preferred criminal justice responses, Hogue and Peebles (1997) found a strong relationship between low ATS scores and recommendations for jail (versus probation); in fact ATS scores were more able to predict sentencing choices (jail versus probation) in a mock scenario than the experimental manipulations of the mock offender's intent and remorse. ATS scores predicted responses 65 per cent of the time. Similarly Proeve and Howells (2006) found that a recommended sentence other than imprisonment (similar to scenarios used by Hogue and Peebles 1997) was associated with a higher ATS score; however, the effect was less strong than in the Hogue and Peebles study. No relationship was found to the length of sentence or the length of non-custodial sentence recommendations.

Empirical research investigating the public's attitudes towards sexual offenders

As briefly mentioned above, much less is known about public attitudes towards sex offenders despite the fact that the media and politicians often claim or imply that they have a good understanding of public opinion on this issue. Many studies, including the more limited opinion poll method of data collection (see Viki and Bohner, this volume), suggest that while the public do wish to see sex offenders punished, and often severely punished, they will also endorse rehabilitative approaches if questions directly focus on rehabilitation or treatment.

In 1995, Stop It Now! conducted a random-digit dialled telephone survey of households in Vermont conducting a total of 200 interviews (Tabachnick et al. 1997). Although nearly all respondents had heard about child sexual abuse, just over half (53 per cent) were unable to define it, or repeated the term in the definition (e.g. 'child sexual abuse is the sexual abuse of children'). Seventy-nine per cent reported that they thought treatment programmes can help stop child sexual abuse and 87 per cent thought that persons who sexually abuse children should get help in prison; however, only 31 per cent believed that adults who sexually abuse can stop if motivated to do so. There seems to be some contradiction in these responses: treatment programmes train offenders to control their behaviour yet four-fifths of the sample thought treatment programmes could help stop offending while only one-third thought offenders could control their behaviour. This contradiction may be due to the limited understanding of what 'treatment' refers to or includes, which is highly likely given the number who could not define sexual abuse and the misleading nature of the term in this context.

These findings are similar to those found by Vallient et al. (1994) who investigated the opinions of Canadian first- ($n = 30$) and third-year ($n = 43$) female undergraduate psychology students. There was unanimous agreement among these students (100 per cent) that sex offenders should be incarcerated for at least two years and that they should receive treatment; however, 67 per cent of the first-years and 63 per cent of the third-years thought that treatment should be received indefinitely because of the gravity of their crime.

A very detailed study showing how a qualitative approach can yield more interesting data that is more able to explore the complexities and variations in attitudes than a quantitative approach was conducted by Clarke et al. (2002). Two methods of data collection were employed: 28 discussion groups were held and 62 interviews with individuals were conducted. Discussion groups were chosen to reflect age, gender, social class, sexual orientation and geographical location, while interviews were selected to reflect different ages and experiences of rape issues. The majority of respondents felt that a prison sentence should be mandatory for rape, with five years of actual imprisonment being seen by many to be the minimum period of incarceration. In addition, though, almost all felt that prison should serve as both punishment and an opportunity for rehabilitation, confirming findings from the quantitative studies discussed here. However, there was widespread support for the view that serial rapists could not be 'cured' highlighting the complexity of people's views when different categories of offenders are taken into account. Some, including some survivors of rape, felt that imprisonment was not appropriate as it did little in the long term and did not do anything to 'undo' the harm caused, which clearly illustrates the variety and divergence of views that can be found on these issues. Generally there was little confidence in the justice system, particularly from the point of view of the poor treatment most felt that survivors of rape received.

In my (Brown 1999) postal survey of residents in Cardiff, South Wales (UK), 312 members of the public (from the original 500 selected from the electoral register) completed and returned a 58-item questionnaire investigating stereotypes of sex offenders, attitudes towards the punishment and rehabilitation of sex offenders and attitudes towards a treatment facility being located in the local community. Sixty per cent had not known about treatment of sex offenders prior to completing the questionnaire, though it is likely that this will have changed since then as treatment is now an integral part of the criminal justice system in the UK compared to when this study was conducted. Nevertheless this should be borne in mind as two-thirds responding to the 'idea' or 'concept' of treatment had little knowledge about what it might involve.

Ninety-five per cent of respondents felt that offenders serving determinate prison sentences (i.e. those who would definitely be released into the community at the end of their sentence, or more commonly at some point in the sentence) should receive treatment; however, 45 per cent thought that treatment should only be provided in prison and 51 per cent thought that it should be provided in both prison and community settings. Despite the support for treatment, few felt that it would be a huge success: 60 per cent thought it could 'sometimes' work with a quarter believing that it would 'never' be effective and only 38 per cent thought that a sex offender could learn to control their behaviour to avoid reoffending. Thirty-four per cent were undecided on this issue and 28 per cent believed offenders could not control their behaviour in this way.

When it came to the realities of the rehabilitative approach – that sex offenders would have to be treated and later live and work in the community – respondents were less supportive. Two-thirds stated that they would not support a treatment facility being located in their community and two-fifths stated that such a centre would stop them moving into an area. A quarter of those opposed to such a facility said that they would start a campaign to oppose the centre, one-third would join a campaign and four-fifths would sign a petition against it. Those in favour of a facility were much less prepared to take action to demonstrate this support, suggesting that the views of those opposed to residential centres are likely to be heard 'loudest', which is indeed what has happened. Local campaigns against proposed residential treatment facilities in the UK have meant that it has been impossible to identify an appropriate site and many sex offenders, particularly on release from prison, struggle to find appropriate accommodation.

NIMBYism: the 'not in my back yard' phenomenon

This 'not in my back yard' phenomenon, more commonly referred to as 'NIMBY' or 'NIMBYism', is not confined to sex offender or criminal justice interventions (for examples, see Piat 2000: housing for deinstitutionalised people; Zippay 2007: psychiatric residences;

Tempalski 2007: syringe exchange programmes); however, it has important consequences for the rehabilitative ideal. Three-quarters of the survey respondents (Brown 1999) said that they would not rent accommodation to a known sex offender who had completed his or her sentence and only 30 per cent said that they would employ such an individual. If sex offenders are to be rehabilitated they need to be able to live full and active lives in the community (for example, see the Good Lives Model: Ward 2002; Ward and Stewart 2003): many believe that ostracism from the local community, stress, loneliness, lack of social supports, etc. would be more likely to 'encourage' a sex offender underground and/or back to their offending behaviour (Prentky 1996).

Recent residency restriction legislation that has been introduced in many states in the USA is a more extreme version of 'NIMBYism'. In the spring of 2005, following many high-profile cases similar to the cases discussed at the start of this chapter, hundreds of jurisdictions in the US introduced housing restrictions with increasingly large buffer zones, often 1,000 or 2,500 feet (see Levenson 2005, and Nieto and Jung 2006, for more detailed information). These restrictions are centred around schools, school bus stops, parks, daycare centres and other places where children are 'located' and effectively have meant that sex offenders are no longer able to live in some cities.

These restrictions are yet another example of seemingly intuitive policies that are designed to protect children: if sex offenders do not live near children then children will be protected from them. Yet this assumes that offenders only abuse children in their local neighbourhood and, furthermore, that they have limited mobility away from their homes. Not surprisingly, then, there is no evidence to show that housing restrictions protect children from sex offenders and there is some evidence to suggest that residency restrictions actually decrease children's safety, as sex offenders are forced or encouraged 'underground'. For example, Nieto and Jung (2006: 24) report an account from Sheriff Don Zeller of Linn County, Iowa. In 2002 when the state residency restriction law first came into effect, the county had 435 sex offenders registered. Of those, 114 moved, 74 were charged with violating the restrictions and others just disappeared when the residency restrictions were implemented: 'We went from knowing where about 90 percent of them were. We're lucky if we know where 50 to 55 percent of them are now ... the law created an atmosphere that these individuals can't find a place to live.'

Those in favour of such restrictions believe that these laws reduce the likelihood that sex offenders will come into contact with potential victims. Nieto and Jung (2006) and Levenson (2005) report a number of findings, however, that suggest these views are unfounded. In Colorado for example (Colorado Department of Public Safety 2004), sex offenders who reoffended while under supervision did not appear to live closer than those who did not reoffend to schools or childcare centres. More importantly it was found that residency restrictions did not control recidivism or deter sex offenders from reoffending and sex offenders who had positive support systems had lower recidivism and fewer rule violations than offenders without such support. The Minnesota Department of Corrections (2003) found that recidivism was not related to sex offenders' proximity to schools or parks yet sex offenders were forced into rural areas where they lacked social support, employment opportunities, etc. Furthermore, the restrictions led to homelessness and 'transience' which limited tracking, monitoring and supervision opportunities. Although Walker *et al.* (2001) found that sex offenders in Arkansas who abused children seemed to live closer to schools, daycare centres or parks than rapists of adults did, Nieto and Jung and Levenson report that the authors could not establish an empirical relationship between sex offender housing and recidivism.

These residency restrictions are also based on the erroneous beliefs discussed previously: that offenders are more likely to attack 'stranger' victims, that recidivism rates are high and that treatment and/or rehabilitation is not possible. There also seems to be an assumption that offenders would not offend outside their local neighbourhoods should there be a 'lack of opportunity' in the local community. As reported previously many reoffences by Iowan sex offenders took place out of state.

Clearly these negative attitudes and inaccurate perceptions about sex offenders help 'promote' the introduction and spread of legislation that places increasingly tighter restrictions on sex offenders. This has human rights implications for these offenders, though the current rhetoric (in the UK and US at least) places the emphasis firmly on the protection of the public, which is seen to be paramount and overrides any human rights concerns in relation to offenders who may jeopardise the safety of the public. (For more information on human rights approach to treating sex offenders, see Ward *et al.* 2007.) In addition to this, there are also a number of other harmful consequences of these negative attitudes towards sex offenders (see West 2000, for discussion of a wide range of consequences).

Improving attitudes towards sexual offenders

Known sex offenders are treated poorly by all communities; for example, Ireland and Archer (1996) observed that sex offenders were identified by 46 per cent of male adult offenders as being likely to be bullied in prison. While many people will probably have little sympathy for sex offenders in this respect, as mentioned previously, it is likely that this type of response is more rather than less likely to lead to future reoffending. These attitudes also have an impact on the relatives of these offenders who have done no wrong. Negative stereotypes and inaccurate perceptions about the reliability of sexual abuse can also have a detrimental effect on victims. This is particularly noteworthy when the victims are relatives of the offender, who may get caught up in the community's negative response and ostracism of the offender. Furthermore, some rape survivors who participated in Clarke et al.'s (2002) study felt that stereotypes of rape being perpetrated by strangers had undermined their experiences, which they felt had had a significant effect on the court cases they had been involved with.

Negative attitudes surrounding sex offenders can also have a detrimental impact on staff who work to try to increase public protection. Lea et al. (1999) highlighted that professionals have to display tolerance and understanding of sex offenders in an attitudinal context that is at odds with the intolerant, negative attitudes of society and even of their colleagues. Furthermore, they risk attracting a courtesy stigma because others may perceive them to have sympathy for sex offenders. A quarter of Lea et al.'s sample reported that negative stereotypes had a negative impact on their practice. Ellerby (1997, cited in Shelby et al. 2001) found that treatment providers received little or no support from the community, correctional system or colleagues who do not treat sex offenders. Ninety per cent of respondents reported negative responses to their work and only 47 per cent reported positive reactions. Furthermore, 71 per cent felt that they had to justify their work.

In addition, these fears encourage parents (Kidscape 1993, cited in Gallagher et al. 2002) and women to place restrictions on their own lives and the lives of their children in order to avoid victimisation, though most of these strategies are aimed towards the prevention of a stranger attack, which as discussed above is not the most common form of sexual abuse. Hillman (1993) reported that fear of 'molestation' featured significantly in parents' reasons for restricting children in coming home from school alone (just over 20 per cent cited this fear, though the same percentage also mentioned that their child was 'unreliable' and the greatest fear, noted by over 40 per cent, was 'traffic danger') and was the predominant reason parents gave for not letting their children out alone after dark. Isolated reports in the media suggest that these restrictions render children at greater risk because they are not 'streetwise' or that they negatively impact on children's social and psychological development. West (2000), for example, argues that social learning is affected if children are not allowed to play with their friends out of sight of their parents. It might also be the case that these 'protective' measures increase children's risk from other harmful events, such as being injured as a passenger in a road traffic accident.

Sanghara and Wilson (2006) outline a number of other problems with negative attitudes and in particular the limited knowledge and stereotype endorsement in relation to sex offenders: this is particularly noteworthy in their study where the group with limited knowledge and who endorsed stereotypes was teachers who are a potentially crucial element in the protection of children. The researchers felt that inaccurate perceptions could lead to 'unstereotypical' offenders being less likely to be reported and investigated and, if identified, less likely to be prosecuted and convicted. Parents and teachers who seek safety in wrong places may have a false sense of security and give children unhelpful advice (e.g. don't talk to strangers).

Given these detrimental effects, it might be helpful to consider strategies that could help change public attitudes, although the current climate and rhetoric around sex offenders would not lead one to assume that there would be a great deal of motivation from politicians, the media or the public to pursue such a course of action, particularly if effort and resources (money) were required. Organisations such as Stop It Now![2] and many researchers and experts in the area (for example, see Laws 2000) have suggested that a public health approach to the prevention of sexual abuse would be preferable to the current approach that only deals with offenders who have been identified usually after they have a history of offending (tertiary level of prevention), and which omits crucial primary prevention (preventing deviant behaviour before it begins) and secondary prevention (targeted at those who are most at risk of offending, or who have recently started offending) strategies.

Given current attitudes, primary prevention would have to involve educating the public. Social marketing techniques have often been employed in such situations, for example 'No Means No' campaigns. For this to work, however, huge resources would have to be invested and Green (2006) does not hold much hope that it would have a huge impact: these 'attempts are not especially promising in the long term because most do not foster opportunities for the public to work towards formulating durable and informed preferences' (p. 131). He argues that these approaches overlook the importance of deliberation in the generation of durable and informed opinions: social market and education programmes 'rely instead on flawed, one-way exchanges between the expert and the public, insufficient to make a lasting impact on public knowledge and attitudes' (Green 2006: 132). Green instead promotes use of the 'deliberative poll' as this provides opportunities for deliberation and, he argues, lasting changes in attitudes and knowledge; however, since deliberative polls take an awful lot of effort, not to mention resources, to organise, it seems unlikely that they would be used systematically by governments who currently do not seem to be motivated to change public opinion in relation to sex offenders: it would, after all, take a brave or foolish politician in the current climate to suggest a less punitive, more 'understanding' approach to sex offenders.

In some instances, for example professionals who work with sex offenders, there may be more support for work to improve attitudes towards sex offenders, particularly if it could be linked to public protection. There is some support for the suggestion that professionals who have positive attitudes of offenders (and sex offenders) are more effective in working with them, particularly in a rehabilitative way. For example, Marshall et al. (2002) found that treatment providers of the England and Wales sex offender treatment programme who showed warmth and empathy were more likely to induce treatment change in their clients.

Lea et al. (1999) found that professionals who had received no training differed in their attitudes to those who had training and those who worked more closely with sex offenders. Although most in the sample slipped into using stereotypes of offenders from time to time, it was those who had not received training who were more prone to do this. Hogue and Peebles (1997) found that attitudes did not vary significantly according to training. Interestingly, Nelson et al. (2002) found that there was no relationship between the training that had been received by the counsellors in their study; however, there was a positive relationship between the counsellors' attitudes to sex offenders and their views of how well the training they had received prepared them for working with sex offenders. This would suggest that it is the impact of the training rather than just receiving it that make the most difference. Weekes et al. (1995) found that just over two-thirds of the correctional officers they studied wanted more training in working with sex offenders, suggesting a demand for training.

A small number of studies have been conducted to investigate the impact of training programmes on professionals who work with sex offenders. Taylor *et al.* (2003) found that a 2.5-day training programme designed to raise awareness, provide information and introduce participants to a range of issues involved in working with sex offenders with learning difficulties significantly improved participants' (66 care staff, i.e. nurses and social workers) overall attitudes towards and knowledge of sex offenders. Furthermore, most (95 per cent) of the trainees believed that they had a better understanding of sex offenders when they had completed the training and three-quarters (76 per cent) felt more confident in working with this group of offenders.

Hogue (1995) found that the training programme designed to train staff to deliver the new sex offender treatment programme in English and Welsh prisons significantly improved (from an average ATS score of 82.0 to 89.1) attitudes towards sex offenders in multi-disciplinary staff groups (n = 81) that included prison and probation officers, psychologists and education staff. This effect was observed immediately after training and maintained six months later. Scores significantly shifted in a positive direction on the following items: 'sex offenders are different than most people'; 'sex offenders never change'; 'bad prison conditions just make a sex offender more bitter'; 'trying to rehabilitate sex offenders is a waste of time and money'; 'sex offenders only think about themselves'; 'sex offenders will listen to reason'; 'sex offenders should be under strict harsh discipline'; 'I would like associating with some sex offenders'; and 'sex offenders respond only to brute force'.

Craig (2005) conducted a similar study with 63 residential hostel workers and 11 probation officers who responded to an advert to complete a two-day training workshop in working with sex offenders and who had not received any prior training in this area, despite the fact that they all supervised sex offenders living in the community on a daily basis. After the completion of training there was no overall significant change in ATS responses. Craig discussed a number of reasons why the training in his study may not have had a positive influence on attitudes as did the training in Hogue's (1995) study. The pre-training attitudes of the two groups differed, with more negative attitudes being displayed by Craig's professionals. Furthermore, the staff in Hogue's study had volunteered and been selected to work on a treatment programme. In addition the type of training and the aims of the training were different, with the training in Craig's study being more focused on increasing knowledge, which does not necessarily lead to attitude change, compared to the training in Hogue's study which was in how to deliver a treatment programme. Given Nelson et al.'s (2002) finding that it was the impact of the training in preparing professionals to work with sex offenders that was linked to attitudes rather than the completion of training per se, it may have been the case that the training in Hogue's study performed a similar function, while the training in Craig's study may have had the impact of making trainees feel less confident in working with offenders. The limited number of studies, the small sample sizes and the range of professionals and training programmes means that much more research is needed in this area to fully explore the impact of training and to identify the most effective method of improving attitudes towards sex offenders in those who work with them.

Conclusions

Legislative developments in criminal justice responses to sex offenders, then, have become 'trapped', so that it has become extremely difficult for leaders, politicians, etc. to suggest and introduce anything other than increasingly punitive responses to this group of offenders. The public appear to have high levels of fear that they or their children/ loved ones will become the victims of sexual abuse and are prepared to curtail their own and others' freedoms to reduce this 'probability'. This is despite the fact that all research shows that children and adults are most often sexually offended against by those they know, love and trust and that by restricting their own movements, people are only potentially avoiding the attacks of strangers. At the same time, however, when asked the sorts of questions that will reveal the complexities of their opinions, the public endorse both rehabilitative and punitive attitudes concurrently and have complex opinions, though NIMBYism seems to ensure that the positive attitudes to rehabilitative measures are likely to have a limited impact on actual behaviour.

It is extremely difficult to see how public attitudes to sex offenders can be modified, though it must be remembered that, despite claims from the media and politicians to the contrary, we actually know very little about these attitudes. It could be that improving knowledge about the 'true' characteristics of sex offenders, sexual offences, etc. would help improve attitudes, reduce fear and better enable people to protect themselves and their loved ones; however, given that huge resources would be required to introduce measures that would be likely to have a long-term impact on opinions, it is unlikely that this will happen in the current climate. Given the lack of research, it is also not clear if improving knowledge in this way would have an impact on attitudes and/or behaviour towards this group of offenders. More research is needed in this area, not least because there is evidence to suggest that the attitudes of professionals working with offenders is linked to the effectiveness of their work; currently, however, there is no clear understanding of what work or training is required to improve the attitudes of such professionals. As this work is underpinned by a desire to protect the public through improved efficacy in practice that aims to successfully rehabilitate and manage offenders in the community, it is possible that resources can be found to investigate this issue further, though it is unlikely to be an easy task.

Notes

1 Note that some researchers have not calculated the scores in exactly the same way as Hogue, failing to subtract 36 which anchors the scale at 0. In this instant the scores range from 36 to 180. Comparisons cannot be made across studies that have employed different scoring methods. Average scores have only been reported here when the study has clearly used Hogue's original scoring method.
2 See: http://www.stopitnow.org/ and http://www.stopitnow.org.uk/about.htm.

References

Albrecht, H.J. (1997) 'Dangerous criminal offenders in the German criminal justice system', *Federal Sentencing Reporter*, 10 (2): 69–73.
Allen, R. (2003) ' "There must be some way of dealing with kids": young offenders, public attitudes and policy change', *Youth Justice*, 2: 3–13.
Ashenden, S. (2002) 'Policing perversion: the contemporary governance of paedophilia', *Cultural Values*, 6 (1 & 2): 197–222.
BBC News (2006) *Sex Offenders Near Schools: Your Views*, 'Have Your Say On-Line Debate', BBC News On-Line, 18 June.
Brown, E.J., Flanagan, T.J. and McLeod, M. (eds) (1984) *Sourcebook of Criminal Justice – 1983*. Washington, DC: Bureau of Justice Statistics.

Brown, S.J. (1999) 'Public attitudes towards the treatment of sex offenders', *Legal and Criminological Psychology*, 4: 239–52.

Brown, S.J. (2005) *Treating Sex Offenders: An Introduction to Cognitive-Behavioural Sex Offender Treatment Programmes*. Cullompton: Willan.

Clarke, A., Moran-Ellis, J. and Sleney, J. (2002) *Attitudes to Date Rape and Relationship Rape: A Qualitative Study, Sentencing Advisory Panel Research Report 2, May 2002*. Sentencing Advisory Panel. Retrieved 26 January 2008 from: http://www.sentencing-guidelines.gov.uk/docs/research.pdf.

Colorado Department of Public Safety, Sex Offender Management Board (2004) *Report on Safety Issues Raised by Living Arrangements for and Location of Sex Offenders in the Community*. Denver, CO: The Board, 15 March.

Craig, L.A. (2005) 'The impact of training on attitudes towards sex offenders', *Journal of Sexual Aggression*, 11: 197–207.

Davis, G.E. and Leitenberg, H. (1987) 'Adolescent sex offenders', *Psychological Bulletin*, 101: 417–27.

Deisher, R.W., Wenet, G.A., Paperny, D.M., Clark, T.F. and Fehrenbach, P.A. (1982) 'Adolescent sexual offense behavior: the role of the physician', *Journal of Adolescent Health Care*, 2: 279–86.

DW-World.De (2006) *German Politicians Propose Internet Registry for Sex Offenders*. Retrieved 30 January 2008 from: http://www.dwworld.de/dw/article/0,,2203141,00.html?maca=en-rss-en-ger-1023-rdf.

Ellerby, L. (1997) 'Impact on clinicians: stressors and providers of sex offender treatment', in S.B. Edmunds (ed.), *Impact: Working with Sexual Abusers*. Brandon, VT: Safer Society Press, pp. 51–60.

Ferguson, K. and Ireland, C.A. (2006) 'Attitudes towards sex offenders and the influence of offence type: a comparison of staff working in a forensic setting and students', *British Journal of Forensic Practice*, 8: 10–19.

Gallagher, B., Bradford, M. and Pease, K. (2002) 'The sexual abuse of children by strangers: its extent, nature and victims' characteristics', *Children and Society*, 16: 346–59.

Green, D.A. (2006) 'Public opinion versus public judgment about crime: correcting the "comedy of errors"', *British Journal of Criminology*, 46: 131–54.

Hansen, J.O. (1997) 'Sexual predators: why Megan's Law is not enough', *Atlanta Journal Constitution*, 10 June, p. D11.

Hanson, R.K. and Bussière, M.T. (1996) 'Sex offender risk predictors: a summary of research results', *Forum of Correction Research* [on-line], 8 (2). Retrieved 16 July 2004 from: http://198.103.98.138/text/pblct/forum/e082/082c_e.pdf.

Hanson, R.K. and Bussière, M.T. (1998) 'Predicting relapse: a meta-analysis of sexual offender recidivism studies', *Journal of Consulting and Clinical Psychology*, 66: 348–62.

Hanson, R.K. and Thornton, D. (2000) 'Improving risk assessments for sex offenders: a comparison of three actuarial scales', *Law and Human Behavior*, 24: 119–36.

Hanson, R.K., Gordon, A., Harris, A.J.R., Marques, J.K., Murphy, W., Quinsey, V.L. *et al.* (2002) 'First report of the collaborative outcome data project on the effectiveness of psychological treatment for sex offenders', *Sexual Abuse: A Journal of Research and Treatment*, 14: 169–94.

Hillman, M. (1993) 'One false move ... an overview of the findings and issues they raise', in M. Hillman (ed.), *Children, Transport and the Quality of Life*. London: Policy Studies Institute, pp. 7–18. Retrieved 9 February 2008 from: http://www.psi.org.uk/mayerhillman/Children%20Transport%20Quality%20of%20Life.pdf.

Hogue, T.E. (1993) 'Attitudes towards prisoners and sexual offenders', in N.C. Clarke and G. Stephenson (eds), *DCLP Occaisonal Papers: Sexual Offenders*. Leicester: British Psychological Society, pp. 27–32.

Hogue, T.E. (1995) 'Training multi-disciplinary teams to work with sex offenders: effects on staff attitudes', *Psychology, Crime and Law*, 1: 227–35.

Hogue, T.E. and Peebles, J. (1997) 'The influence of remorse, intent and attitudes toward sex offenders on judgements of a rapist', *Psychology, Crime and Law*, 3: 249–59.

Home Office (2001) *Prison Statistics England and Wales, 2001*. London: HMSO.

Iowa Department of Human Rights, Division of Criminal and Juvenile Justice Planning, and Statistical Analysis Center (2000) *The Iowa Sex Offender Registry and Recidivism Study*. Des Moines, IO: The Department, December. Retrieved 8 February 2008 from: http://www.iowaccess.org/dhr/cjjp/images/pdf/01_pub/SexOffenderReport.pdf.

Ireland, J.L. and Archer, J. (1996) 'Descriptive analysis of bullying in male and female adult prisoners', *Journal of Community and Applied Social Psychology*, 6: 35–47.

Kidscape (1993) *How Safe Are Our Children?* London: Kidscape.

Kropp, P.R., Cox, D.N., Roesch, R. and Eaves, D. (1989) 'The perceptions of correctional officers toward mentally disordered offenders', *International Journal of Law and Psychiatry*, 12: 181–8.

Laws, D.R. (2000) 'Sexual offending as a public health problem: a North American perspective', *Journal of Sexual Aggression*, 5: 30–44.

Lea, S., Auburn, T. and Kibblewhite, K. (1999) 'Working with sex offenders: the perceptions and experiences of professional and paraprofessionals', *International Journal of Offender Therapy and Comparative Criminology*, 43: 103–19.

Levenson, J.S. (2005) *Sex Offender Residence Restrictions. Sex Offender Law Report*. Civil Research Institute. Retrieved 30 January 2008 from: http://theparson.net/so/Levenson.pdf.

Lieb, R. (2000) 'Social policy and sexual offenders: contrasting United States' and European policies', *European Journal on Criminal Policy and Research*, 8: 423–40.

Lieb, R., Quinsey, V. and Berliner, L. (1998) 'Sexual predators and social policy', in M. Tonry (ed.), *Crime and Justice: A Review of Research*, Vol. 23. Chicago: University of Chicago Press, pp. 43–114.

Marshall, W.L. (1996) 'The sexual offender: monster, victim, or everyman?', *Sexual Abuse: A Journal of Research and Treatment*, 8: 317–35.

Marshall, W.L., Serran, G., Moulden, H., Mulloy, R., Fernandez, Y.M., Mann, R.E. and Thornton, D. (2002) 'Therapist features in sexual offender treatment: their reliable identification and influence on behaviour change', *Clinical Psychology and Psychotherapy*, 9: 395–405.

Matson, S. and Lieb, R. (1996) *Sex Offender Registration: A Review of State Laws*. Olympia, WA: Washington State Institute for Public Policy, Evergreen College. Retrieved 8 February 2008 from: http://www.wsipp.wa.gov/rptfiles/regsrtn.pdf.

Melvin, K.B., Gramling, L.K. and Gardner, W.M. (1985) 'A scale to measure attitudes towards prisoners', *Criminal Justice and Behavior*, 12: 241–52.

Minnesota Department of Corrections (2003) *Level Three Sex Offenders Residential Placement Issues*, 2003 Report to the Legislature. St Paul, MN: The Department.

Mori (2000) *Naming and Shaming Poll*. Retrieved 27 January 2008 from: http://www.ipsos-mori.com/polls/2000/notw000818.shtml.

Mori (2001) *News of the World – Crimes Against Children Poll*. Retrieved 27 January 2008 from: http://www.ipsos-mori.com/polls/2001/notw-011214.shtml.

Myhill, A. and Allen, J. (2002) *Rape and Sexual Assault of Women: Findings from the British Crime Survey*, Research Findings No. 159. London: Home Office Research, Development and Statistics Directorate.

Nelson, M., Herlihy, B. and Oescher, J. (2002) 'A survey of counsellor attitudes towards sex offenders', *Journal of Mental Health Counselling*, 24: 51–67.

Nieto, M. and Jung, D. (2006) *The Impact of Residency Restrictions on Sex Offenders and Correctional Management Practices: A Literature Review*. Sacramento, CA: California Research Bureau, California State Library. Retrieved 26 January 2008 from: http://www.library.ca.gov/crb/06/08/06-008.pdf.

Phillips, D.M. and Troyano, R. (1998) *Community Notification as Viewed by Washington's Citizens*. Olympia, WA: Washington State Institute for Public Policy.

Piat, M. (2000) 'The NIMBY phenomenon: community residents' concerns about housing for deinstitutionalized people', *Health and Social Work*, 25: 127–38.

Prentky, R.A. (1996) 'Community notification and constructive risk reduction', *Journal of Interpersonal Violence*, 11: 295–8.

Proeve, M.J. and Howells, K. (2006) 'Effects of remorse and shame and criminal justice experience on judgements about a sex offender', *Psychology, Crime and Law*, 12: 145–61.

Radley, L. (2001) 'Attitudes towards sex offenders', *Forensic Update*, 66: 5–9.

Sanghara, K.K. and Wilson, J.C. (2006) 'Stereotypes and attitudes about child sexual abusers: a comparison of experienced and inexperienced professionals in sex offender treatment', *Legal and Criminological Psychology*, 11: 229–44.

Shelby, R.A., Stoddart, R.M. and Taylor, K.T. (2001) 'Factors contributing to levels of burnout among sex offender treatment providers', *Journal of Interpersonal Violence*, 16: 1205–17.

Stop It Now! (2003) *What We All Need to Know to Protect our Children*. Retrieved 17 December 2003 from: http://www.stopitnow.org.uk/Stop%2002.pdf.

Tabachnick, J., Henry, F. and Denny, L. (1997) 'Perceptions of child sexual abuse as a public health problem – Vermont, September 1995', *Morbidity and Mortality Weekly Report*, 29 August, 46 (34), Atlanta, GA. Retrieved 27 Janaury 2008 from: http://www.cdc.gov/mmwR/preview/mmwrhtml/00049151.htm.

Taylor, J.L., Keddie, T. and Lee, S. (2003) 'Working with sex offenders with intellectual disability: evaluation of an introductory workshop for direct care staff', *Journal of Intellectual Disability Research*, 47: 203–9.

Tempalski, B. (2007) 'Placing the dynamics of syringe exchange programs in the United States', *Heath and Place*, 13: 417–31.

Tribune Staff (2006) 'Sweep of addresses shows many sex offenders have gone underground', *Chicago Tribune*, 31 March.

US Department of Justice, Office of Justice Programs, Bureau of Justice Statistics (2004) *Crime Characteristics: Victim/Offender Relationship*. Washington, DC: Department of Justice.

Vallient, P.M., Furac, C.J. and Antonowicz, D.H. (1994) 'Attitudes toward sex offenders by female undergraduate university students enrolled in a psychology program', *Social Behaviour and Personality*, 22: 105–10.

Walker, J.T., Golden, J.W. and VanHouten, A.C. (2001) 'The geographic link between sex offenders and potential victims: a routine activities approach', *Justice Research and Policy*, 3: 15–33.

Ward, T. (2002) 'Good lives and the rehabilitation of offenders: promises and problems', *Aggression and Violent Behavior*, 7: 513–52.

Ward, T. and Stewart, C.A. (2003) 'The treatment of sex offenders: risk management and good lives', *Professional Psychology: Research and Practice*, 34: 353–60.

Ward, T., Gannon, T.A. and Birgden, A. (2007) 'Human rights and the treatment of sex offenders', *Sexual Abuse: A Journal of Research and Treatment*, 19: 195–21.

Weekes, J.R., Pelletier, G. and Beaudette, D. (1995) 'Correctional officers: how do they perceive sex offenders?', *International Journal of Offender Therapy and Comparative Criminology*, 39: 55–61.

West, D. (2000) 'Paedophila: plague or panic?', *Journal of Forensic Psychiatry*, 11: 511–31.

Zgoba, K.M., Sager, W.R. and Witt, P.H. (2003) 'Evaluation of New Jersey's Sex Offender Treatment Program at the Adult Diagnostic and Treatment Center: preliminary results', *Journal of Psychiatry and Law*, 31: 133–64.

Zippay, A.L. (2007) 'Psychiatric residences: notification, NIMBY, and neighborhood relations', *Psychiatric Services*, 58: 109–13.

Chapter 10

Stigma and offenders with mental illness

Patrick W. Corrigan and Jessica L. Walton

Introduction

The life goals of offenders with mental illness are affected by both exigencies of the criminal justice system (CJS) and disabilities related to specific psychiatric disorders. A third set of factors also influence outcome: public attitudes about offenders with mental illness. Namely, the way in which the general population stigmatises offenders with mental illness will influence their opportunities and the quality of life that corresponds with achieving personal aspirations. Our focus in this chapter is on mental illness attitudes as they interact with the CJS within the United States. We begin this chapter with consideration of the fairly extensive literature on stigma and mental illness. Mental illness, here, refers to serious psychiatric disorders such as schizophrenia, major depression, bipolar disorder and anxiety. We then seek to make sense of the extent of the problem; we attempt to describe stigma effects on forensic issues. Insights from this body of knowledge can be used to inform models about the person with mental illness who is also an offender. Still, review of existing data and theory requires careful and critical analysis. We attempt this recommendation in consideration of epidemiology and violence for people with serious mental illness. We end the chapter with discussion of ways to challenge these stigmatising attitudes.

The size of the problem

Offenders with mental illness are a significant and burgeoning problem for service providers in criminal justice and mental health systems. One way to get hold of these numbers is by examining the rate of diagnoses in prison systems. Specific rates depend on prison governance; i.e. state prisons, federal prisons or local jails. About 56 per cent of inmates in state systems report concurrent mental illness (James and Glaze 2006). Similar numbers are found for federal prisons (45 per cent) and local jails (64 per cent). These findings come from analyses of 2005 data from the Bureau of Justice Statistics in the US Department of Justice. These rates seem a bit higher than the frequency of involvement with criminal justice found in another sample of 6,624 people with mental illness (Cuellar *et al.* 2007). Twenty-four per cent of that sample had at least one arrest in a ten-year period. The difference in rates might be understood in terms of the dramatic increase of inmates with mental illness. This is evident when comparing the 2005 survey conducted by the Bureau of Justice Statistics (James and Glaze 2006) with a similar survey completed in 1998 (Ditton 1999). Depending on governance, the percentage of inmates with mental illness varied from 7.4 to 16.3 per cent in 1998. This corresponds to a separate literature review reported in 1998 that showed 6 to 15 per cent of people in jail and 10 to 15 per cent of those in state prisons have been diagnosed with mental illness (Lamb and Weinberger 1998). That suggests the American prison system experienced a three- to six-fold increase in prisoners with mental health problems. Another research review showed changes in the number of offenders with mental illness represented a 154 per cent increase in the proportion of persons with mental illness in jail between 1980 and 1992 (Travis 1997).

Some evidence suggests that the large and disproportionate numbers of individuals with mental illness in our jails and prisons is attributable to the criminalisation of mental illness (Lamb and Weinberger 1998; Teplin 1984). Criminalisation refers to the movement of persons who would have been treated previously in mental health programmes into the criminal justice system for reasons other than increased criminality (Lamb and Grant 1982; Teplin 1984). This assertion is supported by research that suggests people exhibiting symptoms and signs of serious mental illness are more likely than others to be arrested by police (Teplin 1984), and, if taken to jail, spend more time in jail than people without serious mental illnesses (Steadman *et al.* 1989). A number of causes for the increase in arrest rates have been cited. Changes in mental health laws have made civil commitment criteria more stringent and have strengthened the right to refuse treatment, making mandated treatment more difficult to impose (Lamb and Weinberger 1998). Hence, many individuals who previously would have been hospitalised and treated against their wishes may now choose to remain untreated in the community and thereby come to the attention of the police.

At the same time, the number of available public hospital beds has been dramatically reduced and access to services in the community is limited (Belcher 1988; Cuellar *et al.* 2007; Jemelka *et al.* 1989; Lamb *et al.* 1999; Steadman *et al.* 1995). Thus even individuals who would prefer treatment have difficulty accessing services. Added to the shortage of services is the increasing public fear of individuals with mental illness (Martin *et al.* 2000) and the growing intolerance of offenders that has led to harsher laws and has hampered effective treatment planning for offenders with mental illness (Cuellar *et al.* 2007; Jemelka *et al.* 1989; Lamb and Weinberger 1998). As is evident here, the question of mental illness, violence and crime is complex and varies depending on the perspective. We make this point because we return to these questions later in the chapter in order to make more sense about mental illness stigma.

The stigma of mental illness

Mental illness stigma is a multifaceted construct that consists of three concepts: stereotypes, prejudice and discrimination. Stereotypes are the knowledge structures that represent generalisations about a group of individuals ('People with mental illness are dangerous!') and results in a label assigned to all members of the group regardless of diversity among members (Aronson *et al.* 2002). Stereotypes serve as an effortless method for efficiently categorising information about social groups and are considered 'social' because they collectively represent agreed upon notions of groups. Stereotypes are most often a result of 'cues' or 'marks'. Obvious marks, such as psychotic behaviour, inappropriate appearance or social interactions can all lead to stereotypes. In addition, being labelled mentally ill can generate stereotypes (Link and Phelan 2001).

Prejudice is the endorsement and emotional reaction to a stereotype. An individual may be aware of existing stereotypes but may choose not to support them (Jussim *et al.* 1995). However, if the individual endorses existing stereotypes, and therefore yields negative emotional reactions and/or attitudes towards another group, then prejudice results ('All individuals with mental illness *are* dangerous and they all scare me!'). Prejudice may present in a variety of forms including anger, fear and blame towards individuals with mental illness (Corrigan

2000). Discrimination is the behavioural component of prejudice and is the act of withholding opportunities from members of a prejudiced group based solely on their association with that particular group. Discrimination towards individuals with mental illness is commonly expressed in the areas of housing and employment (Corrigan and Kleinlein, 2005). For example, an employer who believes that all individuals with mental illness are 'dangerous' (stereotype) may decide not to hire individuals with similar conditions because he/she is afraid that these individuals may cause harm to him/her or other employees (prejudice).

Public stigma, self-stigma and label avoidance

Mental illness stigma may appear in one of three forms: public stigma, self-stigma and label avoidance (Corrigan 2005). Public stigma refers to the negative reactions towards individuals with mental illness as displayed by the general population. Three kinds of stereotypes are common: (1) individuals with mental illness are dangerous and unpredictable which leads to perceptions of violence; (2) individuals with mental illness lack personal integrity and therefore are responsible for their mental illness; (3) individuals with mental illness are incompetent and unable to be successful in most areas of independent functioning. These stereotypes lead to prejudice and discrimination and, ultimately, deprive individuals of important life opportunities including gainful employment, safe and comfortable housing, relationships, community functions and educational opportunities (Corrigan and Kleinlein 2005; Farina and Felner 1973; Farina *et al.* 1974; Page 1995). Of specific interest here is the impact which prejudice has on the attitudes and behaviours of police officers and other members of the criminal justice system. This effect is discussed more fully later in this chapter.

Self-stigma

Some individuals internalise public stigma, resulting in harm to themselves in both a cognitive and behavioural sense (Corrigan and Watson 2002; Link 1987). This is *self-stigma* and comprises four factors. (1) Awareness – is the individual aware of the relationship between marks of mental illness and the corresponding stereotype? (2) Agreement – if the individual is aware of the stereotype, does he or she endorse it? (3) Apply – are the recognised and endorsed stereotypes applied to oneself? (4) Finally, does endorsing and applying the stereotype to oneself diminish self-esteem and self-efficacy? In addition to decrements in self-esteem and self-efficacy, the discrimination of self-stigma may lead to what is known as the 'why-try' effect which occurs when one's confidence is undermined due to the deterioration of self-efficacy (Corrigan *et al.*, in review), ultimately leading to diminished efforts in pursuing and accomplishing life goals such as getting a job, living independently and developing meaningful relationships. 'Why should I try to get work? Someone like me is not able to handle a job!'

Label avoidance
Mental illness stigma is capable of causing harm to a third group: those individuals who do not have a previous history of mental illness and who avoid mental health care in an effort to escape being marked or labelled as mentally ill. Called *label avoidance*, this process differs from the experiences found in public or self-stigma. Public stigma is what the population does to individuals with mental illness through the endorsement and implementation of stereotypes, prejudice and discrimination. Self-stigma is what individuals with mental illness do to themselves. Those individuals who avoid the label are aware of the stereotypes associated with mental illness and may even agree with them. However, they are adamant about escaping the stigma and seek to avoid any group which will lead to this mark. One way to obtain group identity is by associating with the group; individuals who are known to be receiving mental healthcare may be labelled as 'crazy' or 'weak.' Therefore those who avoid treatment escape mental illness prejudice and discrimination. This is a significant number. Epidemiological research suggests that one half to two-thirds of people who might benefit from mental health services never seek them out (Corrigan and Penn 1999).

The public stigma of offenders with mental illness

Much of the work on mental illness stigma and criminal justice has examined public stigma, the prejudice and discrimination applied by the general population to offenders with mental illness. There is little in research on self-stigma and how it may be related to attitudes of offenders. Similarly, research on label avoidance and inmates with mental illness are also absent from the professional literature. Hence, this section is limited to the relatively substantial literature on public attitudes and behaviours towards offenders with mental illness.

Offenders are frequently viewed as being dangerous and unpredictable. Dangerousness is also believed to be characteristic of mental illness, especially the serious mental illnesses (Harris and Lurigio 2007). One might assume that people with mental illness are more dangerous and committing more frequent crimes because of their propensity for violence. The research, however, is not clear about the frequency of dangerousness in serious mental illness. Instead, there is some concern that opinions about dangerousness and corresponding crimes represent stigmatising attitudes. Hence we begin this section examining epidemiological research on mental illness and dangerousness. This review addresses whether violence about mental illness is a stigma or based on fact. We then segue into research that links perceptions of dangerousness and stigmatising attitudes.

Given the breadth of public attitudes about mental illness and dangerousness, how does the criminal justice system respond to people with mental illness? Typically, police officers are gatekeepers to the criminal justice system. Hence it is important to consider attitudes they endorse and how it affects relationships with people known to have mental illness. The second half of this section addresses this issue.

Stigma and violence

Regardless of where someone stands on the issue of mental illness and dangerousness, advocates of all kinds agree that it is a major source of prejudice and discrimination against people with mental illness. Results of a nationwide probability survey showed that as much as 75 per cent of the public view people with mental illness as dangerous (Link et al. 1999; Pescosolido et al. 1999). Another analysis of these data found that twice as many Americans view people with mental illness as dangerous as they did 40 years ago (Phelan et al. 2000). Why do so many members of the general public think mental illness is strongly linked to a potential for violence, and why is this perception on the rise?

Those who believe that mental illness is strongly associated with dangerousness view rising public concern in this area as an accurate reflection of increased violence by people with mental illness that is a result of diminished care (Torrey 1994). Others argue that titillating media portrayals of people with mental illness as violent, especially in the entertainment industry, contribute to the widespread misperception that mental illness and dangerousness go hand in hand (Wahl 1995). Advocates for the two contrary perspectives on mental illness and dangerousness interpret a large amount of research examining violence in people with mental illness to support each of their claims. We consider here the two perspectives on danger and mental illness.

The stigma is based on fact: mental illness is strongly related to dangerousness

Researchers cite a body of studies to support this assertion. People with mental illness seem to be over-represented in the CJS. In a 1979 review of research on case records examining arrest ratios, it was found that offences of people with mental illness in comparison to other community residents, varied from 1.16 to as high as 15 (Rabkin 1979). Rabkin's summary was mirrored by subsequent studies in which people with mental illness were consistently more likely to be arrested for violent crimes compared to non-psychiatric samples (Harry and Steadman 1988; Holcolmb and Ahr 1988; McFarland *et al.* 1989). A body of practice-based evidence also seems to provide empirical support for the perception of a strong link between mental illness and dangerousness. Reviews of admission records for inpatient units have found that between 18 and 41 per cent of people with mental illness had been violent prior to admission (Humphreys *et al.* 1992; Johnstone *et al.* 1986; Lagos *et al.* 1977). This research reflects the *clinical* practice perspective that many mental health providers come to adopt because of their direct experience (Wessely 1997). Proponents of the clinical perspective believe that the news media's focus on the dangerousness of people with mental illness reflects reality. They argue that news stories will shift focus away from dangerousness only when the actual level of violence by people with mental illness diminishes (Torrey 1994, 2002).

Probability samples of dangerousness and mental illness

Making sense of dangerousness values is a difficult task indeed (Lidz *et al.* 2007). In order to more authoritatively address the question of dangerousness – fact or fiction – studies have been completed using probability samples; that is, groups of people with mental illness were randomly selected from geographic areas in stratified formats so key demographics relevant to crime and violence are appropriately distributed. Comparison groups were also drawn from the general population and were representative of all key variables. This line of research has produced two important findings. First, evidence suggests that people with mental illness are more likely to commit violent crimes than are comparable samples of people without mental illness in the general population. Research completed in the United States shows a two- to sixfold increase in the rate of violence in samples of people with mental illness compared to samples of people without mental illness drawn from the general population (Corrigan and Watson 2005; Link *et al.* 1992; Steadman *et al.* 1998; Stueve and Link 1997; Swanson *et al.* 1990). Note that the rate of crime in people with mental illness increases dramatically when that person has a co-morbid history of substance abuse; in fact, analysis from one study suggested higher violence rates due to mental illness may actually be attributable to co-morbid substance abuse (Steadman *et al.* 1998).

We need to put these findings in perspective, however, by transferring these ratios into percentages of the population. We seek to change the question from 'Is there a causal relationship between mental illness and dangerousness?' (the answer seems to be yes) to 'How strong is this relationship?' Or more to the point, 'How much of an association is needed to justify stereotypic attitudes (e.g. "People with mental illness are potentially violent!") and discriminatory behaviours (e.g. "People with mental illness should be avoided")?' Swanson and colleagues (1990) took a major step in answering this question by analysing data from the Epidemiologic Catchment Area (ECA) Study (see Table 10.1). As a baseline, Swanson and others (1990) found that only 2.05 per cent of people in the study with no psychiatric disorders reported violent behaviour in the past year. That compared to almost 5 per cent of people diagnosed with phobias and about 11 to 13 per cent for each of the following disorders: obsessive compulsive disorder, panic disorder, major depression, bipolar disorder and the schizophrenias. This suggests that violence is about six times greater in these various mental disorders compared to the non-disordered population. But this ratio does not clearly suggest the *size* of the problem because it ignores the base rates of the various groups. One way to appreciate the size of the relationship is to use the ECA data to conduct the following thought experiment. The task in this exercise is to protect an American community of one million by identifying those among the community who are potentially dangerous using various existing predictors. How does mental illness compare to demographics that have been shown to also be significantly related to violence and crime?

The second column of Table 10.1 lists the point prevalence rates for the various diagnoses also gleaned from the ECA data (Regier and Burke 1995). The third column represents the number of people in the community of one million who would be identified as potentially

Table 10.1 Rates of violent behaviour in diagnostic groups and two key demographics

	% violent in ECA data	% of general population	Correct identifications	False positives
Phobia	4.97	6.2[1]	3,038	58,962
OCD	10.66	1.3	1,378	11,622
Panic Disorder	11.56	0.05	580	4,420
Major Depression	11.68	2.2	2,574	19,426
Bipolar Disorder	11.02	0.04	440	3,560
Schizophrenias	12.69	0.07	889	6,111
Subtotal			8,899	104,101
Age (18–29)	7.34	13.9[2]	10,203	
Male	5.29	49.1	25,974	

[1]Diagnoses represent one month point prevalence rates from the ECA.
[2]Demographic data determined from the 2000 US Census.

violent based on their diagnosis (determined as the product of the per cent violent rate, the per cent of general population and the total community population (N = 1,000,000)). The sum of correct identifications across the six groups is 8,899, though this number is slightly inflated because some ECA respondents met criteria for more than one disorder thereby increasing the index representing the total per cent of those classified as violent. This number suggests 0.9 per cent of one million would be potentially violent because of mental illness.

How does this finding compare to numbers of potentially dangerous people identified by other key demographics, e.g. gender and age? Let's consider the ECA findings once again (Swanson *et al.* 1990); analyses suggest that the violence rate for young adults (aged 18 to 29) was 7.34 per cent, lower than most of the psychiatric diagnostic groups. However, the 2000 US Census shows that this age group makes up 13.9 per cent of the American population. Using these ratios, 10,203 young adults would be correctly identified as violent. This sample would be 115 per cent larger than the group identified through psychiatric diagnoses. The ECA data also showed that 5.29 per cent of males reported violent behaviour in the past year. With US Census data showing the population to be 49.1 per cent male, gender would lead to the identification of 25,974 individuals in the million as violent, a sample that is 292 per cent larger than the mental illness criterion. Clearly, if the goal is to identify potentially violent people, age is a slightly better predictor than diagnosis and gender can increase the net of potentially dangerous people almost threefold.

The last column of Table 10.1 lists the false positive rates: people who might potentially be identified as violent because of mental illness but are not. Note that 104,101 people would fall into this category, more than 10 per cent of the million person community! Hence, not only are there better predictors of violence than mental illness, psychiatric diagnosis will inaccurately identify vast numbers of potentially violent people. These analyses suggest the size of the problem is indeed small and that stressing the violence angle to mental illness represents stigma and not fact.

Very similar results were found for another nationwide epidemiological study, the National Comorbidity Study (NCS) (Corrigan and Watson 2005). How do these findings compare to the numbers of dangerous people identified by key demographics? In another hypothetical community of a million, between 2,000 and 7,300 people with mental illness would be identified as dangerous depending on the population. Fourteen thousand five hundred and twenty-three (14,523) young adults would be correctly identified, nearly twice the number identified by a single psychiatric disorder. Twenty-eight thousand four hundred and seventy-eight (28,478) males would be correctly identified, almost four times more than the sum of all the people identified by psychiatric diagnoses. The epidemiological research described above provides compelling evidence for a link between mental illness and dangerousness. However, it also muddies comprehension of the facts. In recognition of this body of evidence, the National Stigma Clearinghouse partnered with the MacArthur Research Network on Mental Health and the Law to develop a consensus statement that reflects the empirical research findings and seeks to contextualise them socially and politically (Monahan and Arnold 1996). The 41 researchers, service providers, and consumer advocates who signed the consensus statement agreed on three points.

1 The results of several large-scale studies suggest that mental illness is *weakly* associated with violence.
2 In spite of these findings, the public perceives a *strong* link to exist between mental illness and dangerousness; as a result, individuals with mental illness and their families experience high levels of stigma.

3 Resolving this injustice requires eliminating the stigma and discrimination as well as providing quality treatments to individuals with mental illness.

Effects of perceptions of mental illness and dangerousness

In some ways, the argument over what the facts say about people with mental illness and dangerousness are irrelevant to the issue of stigma. According to Link *et al.* (1999), the very act of *perceiving* people with mental illness as dangerous translates to *fact*, regardless of contrary epidemiological data, because situations that are defined as real are real in their consequences regardless of what evidence might say about them. If this is the case, then it is important to consider the issue of mental illness and dangerousness in a different light. What is the impact of public beliefs that many individuals with mental illness are dangerous? What effect does this belief have on the life opportunities of people with mental illness and on the mental health system that provides these people with services?

Highlighting dangerousness may increase resources for the mental health system. Some advocates believe that highlighting the relationship between violence and mental illness may be a significant wake-up call for state legislators who have traditionally ignored sufficient and equitable funding for mental health programmes (Torrey 2002). Jaffe (1999) succinctly made this point:

Laws change for a single reason, in reaction to highly publicised incidences of violence. People care about public safety. I am not saying it is right. I am saying this is the reality ... So if you're changing your laws in your state, you have to understand that ... It means that you have to take the debate out of the mental health arena and put it in the criminal justice/public safety arena.

Concerns about developing treatment programmes to deal with the problem of dangerousness among people with mental illness has led to a call for more mandated service programmes that range in coerciveness from relatively benign advanced directives to more intrusive measures like conditional release. Advocates of involuntary treatment programmes believe that a comprehensive mental health system that includes mandated care will reduce mental illness stigma by actually reducing the level of violence committed by individuals with mental illness (Torrey and Zdanowicz 2001).

Public perceptions of dangerousness may rob people of life opportunities
Despite hypothesised benefits, highlighting the dangerousness of people with mental illness will likely exacerbate prejudice and discrimination toward people with mental illness. Research by our group has shown that people who endorse beliefs that individuals with mental illness are dangerous are more likely to report fear and avoidance of them, i.e. not wanting to work with or live near people with mental illness (Corrigan *et al.* 2002). In addition, perceptions of dangerousness and fear make people less willing to help those with mental illness and more likely to endorse segregation and coercive treatment (Corrigan *et al.* 2003). Raising awareness of the link between mental illness and violence will likely increase stigma, social isolation and loss of opportunities for people with mental illness.

A separate body of research directly tests this hypothesis by means of a public education paradigm (Corrigan *et al.* 2004). In the study, members of the general public are randomly assigned to one of three education programmes. The first perspective is based on information provided by an advocacy group called the Treatment Advocacy Center (TAC) which highlights the violence of people with mental illness and the need for treatment programmes to address that violence. The second is based on prior anti-stigma research and contrasts common myths about mental illness with corresponding facts (Corrigan *et al.* 2001). The third was a control group. Analyses showed that participation in the TAC programme led to significantly greater endorsement of attitudes that people with mental illness are dangerous, should be feared and must be segregated compared to the control group (Corrigan *et al.* 2004). Stigmatising attitudes of people in the education group actually diminished compared to the control during this trial.

In addition to measuring changes in attitudes about mental illness, our study examined how education programmes might influence government spending for various mental health programmes. Research participants were asked to allocate a hypothetical state human services budget for programmes that address HIV/AIDS, women and children, and mental health. The relative amount of money budgeted for mental health services provides an index of the effect that the education programme had on public policy spending decisions. The study also asks research participants to divide the amount they budgeted for mental health programmes between mandated treatments (mental health courts, outpatient commitment and conditional release) and evidence-based practices that support community reintegration (e.g. supported employment and assertive community treatment). Research participants involved in the 'education-about-violence' group were significantly more likely to endorse mental health services consistent with coercion and segregation. They showed higher scores on a measure of social avoidance and reluctance to provide help to people with mental illness.

Police officers and stigma

The impact of mental illness stigma is especially poignant when people in certain powerful roles vis-à-vis people with psychiatric illness react to them based on prejudice. Police officers may assume this function for people with mental illness, often being the entry point for the person's first receipt of mental health services or for becoming involved in the CJS. Given this role, attitudes about violence and dangerousness may be especially meaningful to officers. Recent studies of law enforcement indicate that 2.7 per cent to 5.9 per cent of individuals considered suspects by police have a serious mental illness (Engel and Silver 2001; Teplin and Pruett 1992). Including contacts with persons with mental illness in other roles, medium and large police departments estimate that 7 per cent of their contacts with the public involve persons with mental illness (Borum et al. 1998; Deane et al. 1999). This kind of experience may yield negative attitudes about individuals with mental illness. One study in particular examined police attitudes about offenders with mental illness (Cooper et al. 2004). Officers were found to be frustrated with perpetrators with mental illness and with the lack of coordination between police and mental health services.

When officers encounter persons with mental illness, they have discretion regarding the appropriate disposition of the contact. They may choose formal actions such as arrest or transportation to a hospital for psychiatric evaluation, or informal action such as a verbal warning or referral for services. Police officer perceptions and actions have important implications in terms of whether individuals receive treatment, remain in their current situation or face the problems inherent in a criminal justice system ill-prepared to meet their needs (Engel and Silver 2001; Lamb and Weinberger 2002; Teplin and Pruett 1992; Wachholz and Mullaly 1993). Therefore it is crucial that we understand how police officers' attitudes and beliefs shape these decisions. Social psychological research on prejudice and discrimination provides a useful lens for examining these issues.

One recent study (Bolton 2000) examined officers' perceptions of the dangerousness, credibility and self-sufficiency of an individual presenting with symptoms of schizophrenia. Officer age, race and training were related to perceptions of dangerousness, with younger, white officers and officers with less training related to mental illness perceiving more danger. Previous contact with individuals with mental illness was related to increased perceptions of credibility, and departmental focus on community policing was related to increased perceptions of self-sufficiency. Another study of police officers in the Midwest found that officers perceived subjects with a mental illness label as more dangerous, less credible and less responsible for their situation than an identical subject without such a label (Watson *et al.* 2004a, 2004b).

How does mental illness stigma influence police decision-making?
Based on what is known about mental illness stigma and the existing research on police interactions with individuals with mental illness, we can make some hypotheses about the role that this kind of stigma may play in police decision-making. Officers that endorse the dangerousness stigma may overestimate the risk of violence associated with mental illness and respond to situations with undue force. Ruiz (1993) suggests that dangerousness is the most prevalent misconception held by police officers about persons with mental illness. He posits that the heightened sense of alert triggered by dispatch codes for mental illness can become a self-fulfilling prophecy. Officers approaching a person with mental illness can inadvertently escalate the situation through threatening body language and speech. Ruiz indicates that a fear of personal injury and a lack of understanding and empathy on behalf of police officers, combined with the person with mental illness's difficulty or reluctance to comply with instructions, are the leading causes of violent confrontations between the two. Such violent confrontations risk injury to the officer, subject and bystanders.

Research on helping behaviour suggests that officers who believe that individuals are responsible for their illness may be less willing to provide appropriate assistance (Weiner 1995). Our research on mental illness stigma supports this relationship between responsibility and helping intentions and behaviours (Corrigan *et al.* 2001; Corrigan *et al.* 2002; Corrigan *et al.*, in press). In terms of police contact with persons with mental illness, this may occur in situations in which an individual needs assistance accessing or referral for mental health or other social services (Watson *et al.* 2005; Watson *et al.* 2004a). If an offence has occurred, officers that blame the individual for his/her illness may be more inclined to arrest, even if deferring to mental health services would be more appropriate. Officers may also be less willing to assist individuals with mental illness who are victims of crime, or fulfil their requests to control another citizen (Mastrofski *et al.* 2000; Watson *et al.* 2004a).

An additional stereotype about mental illness that is relevant to police work relates to credibility. People with mental illness are often viewed as untrustworthy and lacking integrity (Stone and Colella 1996). They also may be viewed as incompetent and unable (as opposed to unwilling) to provide reliable information (Harr and Hess 1998). Several studies have found that the perceived credibility of persons with mental illness affects police decisions to arrest or refer to mental health services in domestic violence situations (Finn and Stalans 1995; Stalans and Finn 1995). This is particularly important because persons with mental illness are more vulnerable to victimisation than members of the general population; however, the crimes committed against them often go unreported (Hiday *et al.* 1999; Marley and Buila 1999). Unfortunately, when they do report their crimes, they frequently are viewed as unreliable witnesses and little is done on their behalf.

The police actually have a complex relationship with people with mental illness. This is not limited to situations where the person is perpetrator. Research has examined how police officer attitudes vary by role – a person in need of assistance, a victim, a witness and a suspect (Watson *et al.* 2004b) – and the results were interesting. Being labelled mentally ill had no measurable effect on judgments of the person with mental illness as a suspect or witness. People with mental illness who were in need of assistance were viewed as more credible. Alternatively, people with mental illness that are victims of crime were perceived as less credible. The last finding is especially of concern given our earlier discussion that people with mental illness are vulnerable (Marley and Buila 1999). If they do seek assistance from the police, they may not be taken seriously. Continuing research is needed on police attitudes in terms of roles such as the four above and others.

Challenging the impact of public stigma

Research has identified three general categories of strategies for changing public stigma: protest, education and contact (Corrigan and Penn 1999). In *protest*, advocates appeal to a moral authority after reviewing the disrespectful ways in which mental illness is subject to banter. As a result, people who are objects of protest are asked to stop these beliefs. Unfortunately, protest seems to lead to rebound effects; people who are asked to suppress disrespectful endorsements may actually demonstrate worse attitudes (MacRae *et al.* 1994; Penn and Corrigan 2002). Keeping something out of mind is an active effort such that suppression of ideas actually maintains the idea in the fore of current thoughts. These effects might also result because of the 'don't tell me what to think' phenomenon. The rebound effect represents cognitive stubbornness.

If the goal is to change employer's minds about hiring people with mental illness, protesting against current beliefs will make attitudes worse. Although troublesome for attitude change, protest is likely to influence behaviour, especially when the target of this change is the media (Wahl 1995). Consider the effects of organised protest on an ABC-TV programme called *Wonderland*. Originally aired in the spring of 2000, the first episode portrayed a person with mental illness shooting at several police officers and stabbing a pregnant psychiatrist in the belly with a hypodermic needle. Advocacy groups came together to inform ABC sponsors that they would boycott the network and their products unless the tone of the show was amended. ABC realised people with mental illness and their families are an economic force to be reckoned with. As a result, *Wonderland* was pulled from the network; ABC was willing to take a loss to their evening line-up rather than risk a boycott. Anecdotes like these suggest the behavioural effects of protest. More careful research on protest needs to be conducted to support stories like these with corresponding evidence.

During *education*, myths about mental illness are contrasted with facts (National Mental Health Awareness Campaign 2002; Pinfold *et al.* 2003). Consider the incompetence myth, the belief that people with mental illness are incapable of living independently or holding down a real job. The myth is diminished when contrasted against long-term follow-up research (Harrison *et al.* 2001) which shows that most people with mental illness are able to live on their own and hold down a job. Research suggests that education yields small effects on attitudes (Holmes *et al.* 1999; Keane 1991; Penn *et al.* 1999; Penn *et al.* 1994); unfortunately, this attitude change is not maintained over time (Corrigan *et al.* 2001, 2002). Nevertheless, education is widely endorsed for influencing prejudice and discrimination. One reason is because education processes are believed to be fundamental to human behaviour. If only the person had the correct knowledge or effective problem-solving skills he or she would be able to give up public stigma and deal with associated concerns more directly. A second reason why education is touted for social change is exportability. The development of an anti-stigma manual is relatively easy and matter-of-fact. A group of authors can come to a consensus about an anti-stigma programme and outline it in a straightforward manner quickly. These manuals can then be disseminated relatively easily using regular mail or the Internet. As these kinds of efforts progress, evaluators of individual programmes need to collect data to show their effects. At this point, process and outcome research is mostly limited in this arena.

Contact seems to yield the most robust and positive findings with regard to public stigma change (Pettigrew and Tropp 2000). Public stigma is challenged when people from the stigmatised group interact with the targeted populations. Interaction may be formal in nature, like a speaker's bureau that provides individuals who are willing and able to talk about their mental illness (Wood and Wahl 2006). Alternatively, it may be casual as when a person learns that his co-worker has depression. This kind of real-world connection has perhaps the greatest effect on changing stigma.

Contact effects are enhanced when the person providing contact and the public group are perceived to be on the same social level (Allport 1954/1979; Gaertner *et al.* 1996). The contact should not be viewed with pity. Nor should he or she be seen as aloof from the situation. Contact and public groups have the most impact when they share a common goal. This might include working together on a community project or solving a neighborhood problem. Contact can also be augmented by including empathy into its programme (Batson *et al.* 1997). That is to say, participants of a contact programme who are instructed to 'walk in the other's shoes – try to imagine yourself as a person with mental illness' show greater benefits than the person who is encouraged to 'remain aloof and experience the situation as a scientist might'.

Although changing public stigma in the whole population is a worthy goal, stigma change is more successful when limited in scope. Challenging public stigma is most effective when it targets social interactions of primary interest to people with mental illness – landlords, employers, police officers, healthcare providers and legislators. Targets also outline relevant behaviours by social role – landlords who may decide whether the person lives independently, employers who may hire the person, police officers who might engage with people with mental illness in an emergency, healthcare providers who yield the breadth of services, and legislators who determine available resources for mental health. Anti-stigma programmes are more effective when individual groups of people are sought within regularly existing meetings, e.g. Rotary International for employers, and to a lesser extent landlords, or the morning roll-call for police officers.

Conclusion

The stigma of mental illness interferes with many of the life opportunities of people with corresponding disorders. Double trouble results when people have mental illness and are involved with the criminal justice system. In this chapter, we reviewed the nature of stigma and its corresponding stereotypes, prejudice and discrimination. We focused on public stigma and its impact on people with mental illness in general, as well as offenders with psychiatric disorders. We considered specific stereotypes, most notably dangerousness, and its effects on discrimination. We discussed strategies for addressing and diminishing the stigma of offenders with mental illness. In the process, we laid out a platform that directs public advocates in their efforts to address stigma as well as guide researchers in their goal of better explaining stigma and stigma change.

As suggested early in this chapter, we illuminated only a part of the stigma picture for offenders with mental illness. Relevant concepts like self-stigma and label avoidance were not discussed because there is little or no research on these issues in terms of offenders with mental illness. Nevertheless, they proffer avenues for the development of future information. Self-stigma is the internalisation of stereotypes resulting in diminished self-esteem and limited self-efficacy (Corrigan and Watson 2002). Group identification seems to be a candidate for diminishing the impact of self-stigma, that is people who recognise their mental illness and affiliate with others also with mental illness will experience less self-stigma (Frable et al. 1997). Instead, people who identify with their group show more personal empowerment (Rappaport 1987). Consumer-operated services are one group with which people might identify (Davidson et al. 1999). These include self-help groups, drop in centres and advocacy training programmes (Clay 2005).

Even less is known about label avoidance. At this point of knowledge development, we would expect anti-stigma strategies for the public to have positive effects on individuals who may be risking the label by participating in treatment. Hence, contact with people with mental illness may influence a person's decision about the pursuit of treatment. Education may also challenge myths about mental illness which may interfere with care-seeking or participation. Clearly, label avoidance describes phenomena that need to be at the centre of future research on stigma change. In fact, the chapter is replete with directions for future research as well as advocacy studies. This kind of agenda will provide a better understanding of the stigma of offenders with mental illness and ways to challenge it.

References

Allport, G. (1954/1979) *The Nature of Prejudice*. Reading, MA: Addison-Wesley.

Aronson, E., Wilson, T. and Akert, R. (eds) (2002) *Social Psychology*, 4th edn. New York: Prentice Hall.

Batson, C., Sager, K., Garst, E., Kang, M., Rubchinsky, K. and Dawson, K. (1997) 'Is empathy-induced helping due to self-other merging?', *Journal of Personality and Social Psychology*, 73 (3): 495–509.

Belcher, J. (1988) 'Are jails replacing the mental health system for the homeless mentally ill', *Community Mental Health Journal*, 24: 185–95.

Bolton, M. (2000) *The Influence of Individual Characteristics of Police Officers and Police Organizations on Perceptions of Persons with Mental Illness*. Dissertation, Virginia Commonwealth University, Richmond, VA.

Borum, R., Deane, M., Steadman, H. and Morrisey, J. (1998) 'Police perspectives on responding to mentally ill people in crisis: perceptions of program effectiveness', *Behavioral Sciences and the Law*, 16 (4): 393–405.

Clay, S. (2005) *On Our Own Together: Peer Programs for People with Mental Illness*. Nashville, TN: Vanderbilt University Press.

Cooper, V., McLearen, A. and Zapf, P. (2004) 'Dispositional decisions with the mentally ill: police perceptions and characteristics', *Police Quarterly*, 7 (3): 295–310.

Corrigan, P. (2000) 'Mental health stigma as social attribution: implications for research methods and attitude change', *Clinical Psychology: Science and Practice*, 7: 48–67.

Corrigan, P. (ed.) (2005) *On the Stigma of Mental Illness: Practical Strategies for Research and Social Change*. Washington, DC: American Psychological Association.

Corrigan, P. and Kleinlein, P. (2005) 'The impact of mental illness stigma', in P.W. Corrigan (ed.), *On the Stigma of Mental Illness*. Washington, DC: American Psychological Association, pp. 11–44.

Corrigan, P. and Penn, D. (1999) 'Lessons from social psychology on discrediting psychiatric stigma', *American Psychologist*, 54 (9): 765–76.

Corrigan, P. and Watson, A. (2002) 'The paradox of self-stigma and mental illness', *Clinical Psychology: Science and Practice*, 9 (1): 35–53.

Corrigan, P. and Watson, A. (2005) 'Findings from the National Comorbidity Survey on the frequency of violent behavior in individuals with psychiatric disorders', *Psychiatry Research*, 136 (2–3): 153–62.

Corrigan, P., Larson, E. and Kuwabara, S. (under review) 'Social psychology of stigma for mental illness: public stigma and self-stigma', in J.E. Maddux and J.P. Tangley (eds), *Social Psychological Foundations of Clinical Psychology*.

Corrigan, P., Markowitz, F. and Watson, A. (in press) 'Structural levels of mental illness stigma and discrimination', *Schizophrenia Bulletin*.

Corrigan, P., Markowitz, F., Watson, A., Rowan, D. and Kubiak, M. (2003) 'An attribution model of public discrimination towards persons with mental illness', *Journal of Health and Social Behavior*, 44: 162–79.

Corrigan, P., River, L., Lundin, R., Penn, D., Wasowski, K., Campion, J., Mathisen, J., Gagnon, C., Bergman, M., Goldstein, H. and Kubiak, M. (2001) 'Three strategies for changing attributions about severe mental illness', *Schizophrenia Bulletin*, 27: 187–96.

Corrigan, P., Rowan, D., Green, A., Lundin, R., River, P., Uphoff-Wasowski, K., White, K. and Kubiak, M. (2002) 'Challenging two mental illness stigmas: personal responsibility and dangerousness', *Schizophrenia Bulletin*, 28: 293–310.

Corrigan, P., Watson, A., Warpinski, A. and Gracia, G. (2004) 'Stigmatizing attitudes about mental illness and allocation of resources to mental health services', *Community Mental Health Journal*, 40 (4): 297–307.

Cuellar, A., Snowden, L. and Ewing, T. (2007) 'Criminal records of persons served in the public mental health system', *Psychiatric Services*, 58 (1): 114–20.

Davidson, L., Chinman, M., Kloos, B., Weingarten, R., Stayner, D. and Tebes, J. (1999) 'Peer support among individuals with severe mental illness: a review of the evidence', *Clinical Psychology: Science and Practice*, 6: 165–87.

Deane, M., Steadman, H., Borum, R., Veysey, B. and Morrisey, J. (1999) 'Emerging partnerships among mental health and law enforcement', *Psychiatric Services*, 50: 99–101.

Ditton, P. (1999) *Mental Health and Treatment of Inmates and Probationers*. Washington, DC: US Department of Justice, Office of Justice Programs, Bureau of Justice Statistics.

Engel, R. and Silver, E. (2001) 'Policing mentally disordered suspects: a reexamination of the criminalization hypothesis', *Criminology*, 39: 225–52.

Farina, A. and Felner, R. (1973) 'Employment interviewer reactions to former mental patients', *Journal of Abnormal Psychology*, 82: 268–72.

Farina, A., Thaw, J., Lovern, J. and Mangone, D. (1974) 'People's reactions to a former mental patient moving to their neighborhood', *Journal of Community Psychology*, 2: 108–12.

Finn, M. and Stalans, L. (1995) 'Police referrals to shelters and mental health treatment: examining their decisions in domestic assault cases', *Crime Delinquency*, 41: 467–80.

Frable, D., Wortman, C. and Joseph, J. (1997) 'Predicting self-esteem, well-being, and distress in a cohort of gay men: the importance of cultural stigma, personal visibility, community networks, and positive identity', *Journal of Personality*, 65: 599–624.

Gaertner, S., Dovidio, J. and Bachman, B. (1996) 'Revisiting the contact hypothesis: the induction of a common group identity', *International Journal of Intercultural Relations*, 20: 271–90.

Harr, J. and Hess, K. (1998) *Constitutional Law for Criminal Justice Professionals*. Belmont, CA: West/Wadsworth.

Harris, A. and Lurigio, A. (2007) 'Mental illness and violence: a brief review of research and assessment strategies', *Crime Classification and Offender Typologies*, 12 (5): 542–51.

Harrison, G., Hopper, K., Craig, T., Laska, E., Siegel, C. and Wanderling, J. (2001) 'Recovery from psychotic illness: a 15- and 25-year international follow-up study', *British Journal of Psychiatry*, 178: 506–17.

Harry, B. and Steadman, H. (1988) 'Arrest rates of patients treated at a community mental health center', *Hospital and Community Psychiatry*, 39: 862–6.

Hiday, V., Swartz, M., Swanson, J., Borum, R. and Wagner, H. (1999) 'Criminal victimization of persons with severe mental illness', *Psychiatric Services*, 50: 62–8.

Holcolmb, W. and Ahr, P. (1988) 'Arrest rates among young adult psychiatric patients treated in inpatient and outpatient settings', *Hospital and Community Psychiatry*, 39: 52–7.

Holmes, E., Corrigan, P., Williams, P., Canar, J. and Kubiak, M. (1999) 'Changing public attitudes about schizophrenia', *Schizophrenia Bulletin*, 25: 447–56.

Humphreys, M., Johnstone, E., MacMillan, J. and Taylor, P. (1992) 'Dangerous behaviour preceding first admissions for schizophrenia', *British Journal of Psychiatry*, 161: 501–5.

Jaffe, D. (1999) *Assisted Outpatient Treatment*. Presented at the annual conference of the National Alliance for the Mentally Ill, Chicago, IL, 30 June – 3 July.

James, D. and Glaze, L. (2006) *Mental Health Problems of Prison and Jail Inmates*. Washington, DC: Bureau of Justice Statistics.

Jemelka, R., Trupin, E. and Chiles, J. (1989) 'The mentally ill in prisons: a review', *Hospital and Community Psychiatry*, 40: 481–91.

Johnstone, E., Crow, T., Johnson, A. and MacMillan, J. (1986) 'The Northwick Park Study of first episodes of schizophrenia. I. Presentation of the illness and problems relating to admission', *British Journal of Psychiatry*, 148: 115–20.

Jussim, L., Nelson, T., Manus, M. and Soffin, S. (1995) 'Prejudice, stereotypes, and labeling effects: sources of bias in person perception', *Journal of Personality and Social Psychology*, 68: 228–46.

Keane, M. (1991) 'Acceptance vs. rejection: nursing students' attitudes about mental illness', *Perspectives in Psychiatric Care*, 27: 13–18.

Lagos, J., Perlmutter, K. and Saexinger, H. (1977) 'Fear of the mentally ill: empirical support for the common man's response', *Journal of Psychiatry*, 134: 1134–7.

Lamb, H. and Grant, R. (1982) 'The mentally ill in an urban county jail', *Archives of General Psychiatry*, 39: 17–22.

Lamb, H. and Weinberger, L. (1998) 'Persons with severe mental illness in jails and prisons: a review', *Psychiatric Services*, 49: 483–92.

Lamb, H. and Weinberger, L. (2002) 'A call for more program evaluation of forensic outpatient clinics: the need to improve effectiveness', *Journal of the American Academy of Psychiatry Law*, 30: 548–52.

Lamb, H., Weinberger, L. and Gross, B. (1999) 'Community treatment of severely mentally ill offenders under the jurisdiction of the criminal justice system: a review', *Psychiatric Services*, 50: 907–13.

Lidz, C., Banks, S., Simon, L., Schubert, C. and Mulvey, E. (2007) 'Violence and mental illness: a new analytic approach', *Law and Human Behavior*, 31 (1): 23–31.

Link, B. (1987) 'Understanding labeling effects in the area of mental disorders: an assessment of the effects of expectations of rejection', *American Sociological Review*, 52: 96–112.

Link, B. and Phelan, J. (2001) 'Conceptualizing stigma', *Annual Review of Sociology*, 27: 363–85.

Link, B., Cullen, F., Mirotznik, J. and Struening, E. (1992) 'The consequences of stigma for persons with mental illness: evidence from the social sciences', in P. Fink and A. Tasman (eds), *Stigma and Mental Illness*. Washington, DC: American Psychiatric Press, pp. 87–96.

Link, B., Phelan, J., Bresnahan, M., Stueve, A. and Pescosolido, B. (1999) 'Public conceptions of mental illness: labels, causes, dangerousness, and social distance', *American Journal of Public Health*, 89: 1328–33.

McFarland, B., Falkner, L., Bloom, J., Hallaux, R. and Bray, J. (1989) 'Chronic mental illness and the criminal justice system', *Hospital and Community Psychiatry*, 40: 718–23.

MacRae, C., Bodenhausen, G., Milne, A. and Jetten, J. (1994) 'Out of mind but back in sight: stereotypes on the rebound', *Journal of Personality and Social Psychology*, 67: 808–17.

MacRae, C., Neil, B., Galen V., Milne, A. and Jetten, J. (1994) 'Out of mind but back in sight: stereotypes on the rebound', *Journal of Personality and Social Psychology*, 67 (5): 808–17.

Marley, J. and Buila, S. (1999) 'When violence happens to people with mental illness: disclosing victimization', *American Journal of Orthopsychiatry*, 69 (3): 398–402.

Martin, J., Pescosolido, B. and Tuch, S. (2000) 'Of fear and loathing: the role of "disturbing behavior," labels, and causal attributions in shaping public attitudes toward people with mental illness', *Journal of Health and Social Behavior*, 41: 208–23.

Mastrofski, S., Snipes, J. and Parks, R. (2000) 'The helping hand of the law: police control of citizens on request', *Criminology*, 38: 307–42.

Monahan, J. and Arnold, J. (1996) 'Violence by people with mental illness: a consensus statement by advocates and researchers', *Psychiatric Rehabilitation Journal*, 19: 67–70.

National Mental Health Awareness Campaign (2002) *Vol. 2002.* Retrieved 2002 from: http://www.nostigma.org.

Page, S. (1995) 'Effects of the mental illness label in 1993: acceptance and rejection in the community', *Journal of Health and Social Policy*, 7: 61–8.

Penn, D. and Corrigan, P. (2002) 'The effects of stereotype suppression on psychiatric stigma', *Schizophrenia Research*, 55: 269–76.

Penn, D., Corrigan, P., Martin, J., Ihnen, G., Racenstein, J., Nelson, D., Cassisi, J. and Hope, D. (1999) 'Social cognition and social skills in schizophrenia: the role of self-monitoring', *Journal of Nervous and Mental Disease*, 187 (3): 188–90.

Penn, D., Guynan, K., Daily, T. and Spaulding, W. (1994) 'Dispelling the stigma of schizophrenia: what sort of information is best?', *Schizophrenia Bulletin*, 20: 567–78.

Pescosolido, B., Monahan, J., Link, B., Stueve, A. and Kikuzawa, S. (1999) 'The public's view of the competence, dangerousness, and need for legal coercion of persons with mental health problems', *American Journal of Public Health*, 89 (9): 1339–45.

Pettigrew, T. and Tropp, L. (2000) 'Does intergroup contact reduce prejudice? Recent meta-analytic findings', in S. Oskamp (ed.), *Reducing Prejudice and Discrimination: Social Psychological Perspectives.* Mahwah, NJ: Erlbaum, pp. 93–114.

Phelan, J., Link, B., Stueve, A. and Pescosolido, B. (2000) 'Public conceptions of mental illness in 1950 and 1996: what is mental illness and is it to be feared?', *Journal of Health and Social Behavior*, 41: 188–207.

Pinfold, V., Toulmin, H., Thornicroft, G., Huxley, P., Farmer, P. and Graham, T. (2003) 'Reducing psychiatric stigma and discrimination: evaluation of educational interventions in UK secondary schools', *British Journal of Psychiatry*, 182: 342–46.

Rabkin, J. (1979) 'Criminal behavior of discharged mental patients: a critical appraisal of the research', *Psychological Bulletin*, 86 (1): 1–27.

Rappaport, J. (1987) 'Terms of empowerment/exemplars of prevention: toward a theory for community psychology', *American Journal of Community Psychology*, 15: 121–48.

Regier, D. and Burke, J. (1995) 'Epidemiological methods in psychiatry', in H. Kaplan and B. Sadock (eds), *Comprehensive Textbook of Psychiatry.* Baltimore, MD: Williams & Wilkins, pp. 378–97.

Ruiz, J. (1993) 'An interactive analysis between uniformed law enforcement officers and the mentally ill', *American Journal of Police*, 12: 149–77.

Stalans, L. and Finn, M. (1995) 'How novice and experienced officers interpret wife assaults: normative and efficiency frames', *Law and Society Review*, 29 (2): 287–322.

Steadman, H., McCarty, D. and Morrisey, J. (1989) *The Mentally Ill in Jail.* New York: Guilford Press.

Steadman, H., Morris, S. and Dennis, D. (1995) 'The diversion of mentally ill persons from jails to community-based services: a profile of programs', *American Journal of Public Health*, 85: 1630–5.

Steadman, H., Mulvey, E., Monahan, J., Robbins, P., Appelbaum, P., Grisso, T., Roth, L. and Silver, E. (1998) 'Violence by people discharged from acute psychiatric inpatient facilities and by others in the same neighborhoods', *Archives of General Psychiatry*, 55: 393–401.

Stone, D. and Colella, A. (1996) 'A model of factors affecting the treatment of disabled individuals in organizations', *Academy of Management Review*, 21: 352–401.

Stueve, A. and Link, B. (1997) 'Violence and psychiatric disorders: results from an epidemiological study of young adults in Israel', *Psychiatric Quarterly*, 68 (4): 327–42.

Swanson, J., Holzer, C., Ganju, V. and Tsutomu, R. (1990) 'Violence and psychiatric disorder in the community: evidence from the Epidemiologic Catchment Area Surveys', *Hospital and Community Psychiatry*, 41 (7): 761–70.

Teplin, L. (1984) 'Criminalizing mental disorder: the comparative arrest rate of the mentally ill', *American Psychologist*, 39: 794–803.

Teplin, L. and Pruett, N. (1992) 'Police as street-corner psychiatrist: managing the mentally ill', *International Journal of Law and Psychiatry*, 15: 139–56.

The Council of State Government: Criminal Justice/Mental Health Consensus Project. New York Council of State Governments, June 2002.

Torrey, E. (1994) 'Violent behavior by individuals with serious mental illness', *Hospital and Community Psychiatry*, 45 (7): 653–62.

Torrey, E. (2002) 'Stigma and violence', *Psychiatric Services*, 53: 1179.

Torrey, E. and Zdanowicz, M. (2001) 'Outpatient commitment: what, why, and for whom', *Psychiatric Services*, 52: 337–41.

Travis, J. (1997) *The Mentally Ill Offender: Viewing Crime and Justice through a Different Lens*. Speech to National Association of State Forensic Mental Health Directors, September.

Wachholz, S. and Mullaly, R. (1993) 'Policing the deinstitutionalized mentally ill: toward an understanding of its function', *Crime, Law, and Social Change*, 19: 281–300.

Wahl, O. (1995) *Media Madness: Public Images of Mental Illness*. New Brunswick, NJ: Rutgers University Press.

Watson, A., Corrigan, P. and Angell, B. (2005) 'What motivates public support for legally mandated mental health treatment?', *Social Work Research*, 29 (2): 87–95.

Watson, A., Corrigan, P. and Ottati, V. (2004a) 'Police officer attitudes and decisions regarding persons with mental illness', *Psychiatric Services*, 55: 49–53.

Watson, A., Corrigan, P. and Ottati, V. (2004b) 'Police responses to persons with mental illness: does the label matter?', *Journal of the American Academy of Psychiatry and the Law*, 32: 378–85.

Weiner, B. (1995) *Judgments of Responsibility: A Foundation for a Theory of Social Conduct*. New York City: Guilford Press.

Wessely, S. (1997) 'The epidemiology of crime, violence, and schizophrenia', *British Journal of Psychiatry Supplement*, 170 (32): 8–11.

Wood, A.L. and Wahl, O.W. (2006) 'Evaluating the effectiveness of a consumer-provided mental health recovery education presentation', *Psychiatric Rehabilitation Journal*, 30 (1): 46–53.

Index

Added to a page number 'f' denotes a figure and 't' denotes a table.